D0006214

SIGHTINGS™

SIGHTINGS™

SUSAN MICHAELS

A FIRESIDE BOOK
PUBLISHED BY SIMON & SCHUSTER

NEW YORK LONDON TORONTO SYDNEY TOKYO SINGAPORE

FIRESIDE
Rockefeller Center
1230 Avenue of the Americas
New York, NY 10020

© 1996 by Paramount Pictures. All Rights Reserved.
Foreword copyright © 1996 by Tim White
All rights reserved,
including the right of reproduction
in whole or in part in any form.

SIGHTINGS is a trademark of Paramount Pictures.

FIRESIDE and colophon are registered trademarks
of Simon & Schuster Inc.

Designed by Jeffrey L. Ward

Manufactured in the United States of America

10   9   8   7   6   5   4   3   2   1

Library of Congress Cataloging-in-Publication Data

Michaels, Susan (Susan H.)
    Sightings / Susan Michaels.
        p.   cm.
    1. Ghosts.   2. Unidentified flying objects—Sightings and
encounters.   3. Parapsychology.   I. Title.
BF1461.M47   1996
001.9′4—dc20   96-583
                                                        CIP

ISBN 0-684-82369-1

Acknowledgments

I am grateful to the people whose true stories appear in this book. Their names have not been changed; the words are their own. Many of the people *Sightings* has interviewed over the years came forward at great personal and professional risk. Without their kind permission and consent, this book would not have been possible.

I am indebted to *Sightings*'s executive producers Henry Winkler and Ann Daniel, to whom this book is dedicated. Words cannot express the gratitude and esteem I feel for them. Ten thousand thank yous. Co-executive producer Stephen Kroopnick has been instrumental in the writing of this book. His guidance, knowledge, and insight have been essential to the success of *Sightings* and to my career. Tim White, the host of *Sightings*, has been my inspiration more times than I can count. He keeps me honest. I also thank Paramount Television, and especially John Kohler, for continuing support and confidence in my work as a writer.

Many members of the *Sightings* television staff contributed to the research and preparation of this book. Special thanks to executive-in-charge-of-production, David Johnson; supervising producer, Michelle Davis; director of research, Jonathan Jerald; head of research development, Lesley Taylor; graphic designers, Debra Matlock and Brad Grossman; post-production supervisor,

8   *Acknowledgments*

Cole Metcalf; and the researchers, segment producers, and directors who originally found, developed, and made the stories in this book come to life, especially Rob Morhaim, Phil Davis, and Andy Rothstein.

This book could not have happened without the diligence of Kristi Dixon and Greg Fein, *Sightings*'s clip-clearance mavens. They are the best in the business. I am also grateful to attorneys Cynthia Teele and William P. Jacobson.

Two exceptional people have assisted me throughout the writing of this book. Richard Brandt performed above and beyond the call of duty, keeping me focused, organized, and well fed. Ariana Johns was the best writer's assistant I could have hoped for, poring over every word and organizing the photographs.

I also acknowledge my family; my mother, Lila Michaels, who knows this book is the fulfillment of a lifelong dream; my friend, Josephine Vandermey; my husband, Frank Hoppe, and my daughter, Sophie, who make everything in my life worthwhile.

And finally, my deepest gratitude to the eternal spirit of my father, Jay Michaels.

To Ann Daniel and Henry Winkler

Contents

The Unexplained

Foreword

I am standing in the middle of a dirt-floor hut, stripped to the waist, arms extended. A ring of candles illuminates the room, and I can just make out the features of the Ecuadorian villagers who line the walls. They gaze at me calmly as the rhythmic drumming continues and Don Estaban—said to be the most powerful shaman in this volcano-framed valley—begins to circle. The diagnostic and healing ability of this small man in a feather headdress has drawn the attention of visiting American doctors and nurses. Already he has rubbed me head to toe with a stone from an Inca temple, covered me with carnation petals, and sprayed a fine mist of sugarcane alcohol on my front and back. Now it is time for the climax of this purification ceremony: Don Estaban will blow fire on me from four directions. As the first fireball rolls from his lips and engulfs my left arm, I feel the hair being singed from the skin. I flash on how far removed this moment is from anchoring the news, interviewing politicians, or teaching graduate students. But I am not doing any of those things now; I am doing a story for *Sightings*.

In the summer of 1991, I was an anchorman at the Fox station in Washington, D.C., when Henry Winkler called and asked me to host a TV special on UFOs. "If you are looking for someone to chase around after little green men," I told him, "you've got the wrong guy." Henry, now one of Hollywood's most successful producers, has an enthusiasm and sincerity "The Fonz" could never approach. He assured me the idea was to do something quite different. Stories of the paranormal and the unexplained would be examined with an eye not toward sensationalism but toward evidence. What was known, what was not known? Who was willing to speak about their personal experience, and what alternative explanations might science offer?

The first *Sightings* special aired on the Fox network in November of 1991 and set a ratings record for the time period. Subsequent specials did even better, and by the following summer *Sightings* was a weekly network show. When Paramount television took the program into first-run syndication in 1994, *Sightings* had already set a new standard for broadcast investigations into the unexplained. It had also spawned a rash of imitators that specialized in playing up the sensationalist aspects of their stories.

Henry Winkler's partner, Ann Daniel, assembled a production staff of bright and inquiring people. The tone she set for *Sightings* allows the entire team to question, probe, explore, and imagine. The staff argues back and forth. Each story is examined, explained, and challenged before it reaches the air. Many stories have been intensely pursued, only to be dropped when it became clear that fraud or hoax might be involved. The final test is always whether it shows possibility and credibility.

I found my personal interest in the paranormal growing, but, for the most part, I remained a skeptic. Physical evidence is hard to come by, and a journalist's mindset is not easily moved. However convinced one person may be that they have seen a ghost or been abducted by aliens, the rest of us seek proof. Still, intriguing stories kept rolling in, posing deeply disturbing questions not easily answered by logic or science. There *are* crop circles that no hoaxers have been able to duplicate. There *are* psychic detectives who turn up uncanny clues to crimes that seem unsolvable. There *are* hours of videotape of objects moving through the sky that are unlike anything known to earthly science, and credible eyewitnesses who claim to have first-person contact. There *is* the Peri

Reis map of 1513, based on much older maps, showing the nearly perfect topography of an ice-free region of Antarctica that could only have existed thousands of years before modern man. Who drew the first maps? The pyramids, the Nasca lines of Peru, and the fractured timelines of prehistory all call into question our understanding of civilization's beginnings. Stories of ghosts, spirits, and gods abound in all cultures over time. And quantum mechanics now challenges us to altogether redefine time and the universe itself.

Indeed, the hoaxers and magicians are always with us. From Piltdown man to Harry Houdini to Oliver Stone, the manipulation of reality has been widely pursued for fun and profit. Man, it seems, has a predisposition to believe. This human frailty makes the work of the professional skeptics of great value. The Committee for the Scientific Investigation of Claims of the Paranormal (CSICOP), James Randi, and other highly vocal debunkers cast a healthy doubt on the flimsy and the fake. But disdain and dismissal of the paranormal in the name of science does little to address questions that lie beyond what science can prove. Two hundred years ago, the best medical minds of the time helped bleed people to death. In the mid-1800s, Louis Pasteur was suspected of sharing kinship with the devil. The discovery of DNA is a relatively recent event. Today, science has little to say about life and death beyond the mechanics of those processes. The subtle workings of the brain remain a largely uncharted land. Something as basic as sleep is shrouded in mystery. Humility, it seems, would well serve all sides of the paranormal debate.

In this book, you will find stories that challenge your basic notions of what is true and what is possible. *Sightings* researchers and producers have tracked down stories, witnesses, and evidence all over the world. For some, ghosts, UFOs, ESP, and lost civilizations will always be figments of overactive imaginations or delusional fantasy. For others, the stories in this book will suggest a reality far more complex and mysterious than we could imagine.

After nearly an hour, Don Estaban finishes the purification ritual. I am exhausted and profoundly calm. The fire the shaman blew on me slightly singed some body hair, but left no burns. Later, through an interpreter, Don Estaban assures me that my health is good but I must guard against destructive spirits. The villagers are gathered around, nodding in agreement. Whether or not I believe in Don Estaban's power, it is clear that they do—and so does he. Modern medicine is beginning to accept the value of meditative focus to stimulate the immune system. Could it be that this focus can be introduced from outside the individual? Perhaps through a shaman using a healing practice thousands of years old? At that moment I recall the motto we use on *Sightings:* "No mystery is closed to an open mind."

Tim White
Washington, D.C.

Hauntings

The Ghost Writer

All John Matkowsky wanted was a nice little house in a quiet neighborhood. And he thought he'd found it, until the Ghost Writer moved in.

Mt. Washington is a hillside neighborhood of tree-lined streets and turn-of-the-century homes just minutes from the steel towers and gridlock of downtown Los Angeles. In a city of tract housing and disposable strip malls, Mt. Washington is unique, and when John Matkowsky found a rustic cabin there he knew he was home. It was fitting, he thought, that the house was on Future Street.

John Matkowsky moved into his dream house in 1985. Almost from the beginning he remembers hearing strange sounds, but the house was old and John figured that the sounds were just the normal creaking and groaning of aging floorboards and lath walls. Sometimes, late at night, he would feel a strange tingling sensation along his arms and neck, but the house was drafty. It was easy to dismiss the feeling as part of the price you pay for living in a house built in 1906.

Then, in 1990, the sounds and sensations intensified. John began to feel a presence. He would catch the barest glimpse of a shadow out of the corner of his eye, but when he turned his head, the shadow would be gone. There were loud bangs coming from a back room, but when John went to investigate, there was never anything there. "I felt sort of a sunburn on my arms. It was tingly, like a sunburn. That's how I would know there was some kind of presence here," John recalls.

Friends felt the presence, too. The Mt. Washington cabin was a favorite spot for weekend barbecues, and on one lazy summer afternoon, the presence crashed the party. John felt the now-familiar sensation of a sunburn and then, for no apparent reason, a blue porcelain salad bowl exploded nearby. John contacted the bowl's manufacturer, but the company could offer no explanation for how the bowl could have shattered into a million pieces.

Soon after that barbecue, John Matkowsky rented out part of his house to his friend John Huckert. Almost immediately, Huckert began to hear the strange noises. He saw the free-floating shadows moving across the floor, his desk, and the living room wall. Then, he felt the presence reach out of its world and into his.

"I was reading something at the desk, and I felt someone come up and place a hand on my shoulder. Of course, I turned around to see who it was and nobody was there. I got a sort of jolt of adrenaline. It made me nervous. I wasn't exactly sure what it was, but when I tried to mask out all the possibilities for what could be causing it, there was nothing causing it."

The two Johns were at once frightened and intrigued. The presence didn't appear to be trying to hurt them, only to get their attention. The more open the two became to the possibility that there was a ghostly presence in their house, the more the ghost made its presence known. John Huckert was the first to see the ghost in its human form. "I've seen this older man standing over near the couch," he says. "I see him for hardly a tangible instant, and then when I blink, he's not there anymore."

These fleeting glances, strange sensations, and odd sounds were the only evidence of the ghost's presence until John Huckert received a Christmas present in 1991 that would change everything. His father gave him a Polaroid instant camera. That camera would produce some of the best evidence of a ghost ever photographed.

Huckert took a few pictures of his family around the Christmas tree in Maryland and returned to Los Angeles with half of a cartridge of film still in the camera. He shot a few pictures around the house to show Matkowsky how the camera worked. All the pictures were clear, focused, and completely unextraordinary. Then, in early March, Huckert got the familiar feeling on the back of his neck that told him the ghost was nearby.

"I suddenly felt a sense of anxiety," he remembers. "I'm not sure how to describe it, but I just felt this strange feeling and I got up and I took a picture of the room. Nothing happened, so I thought, that was really stupid. Then, the bathroom door opened by itself. I took a picture of the bathroom door and got this really strange-looking thing that was either scary or comical. John came home and he took one, then I took a couple more and we got four photos that day."

It seemed unlikely that the same camera that had taken pictures of the Huckert family's Christmas was now chronicling the appearance of a ghost. The two Johns suspected the film was defective. They bought a fresh cartridge of film and tried it, but the ghostly images continued to appear. It happened over and over, at all hours of the day and night, but only when the ghost wanted to appear.

"We had people over waiting for the ghost say, 'Is he here yet? Is he here yet?' and he was never there. I guess he didn't want to do parlor tricks. He wasn't here to perform for us, he was here to inspire us," says Huckert.

John Matkowsky showed several of the pictures to his friends at a professional photo lab in Los Angeles. They could not explain how the images had gotten on the film. They made negatives from the instant prints and examined them closely. It did not appear to be a malfunction within the camera. Still, many of the friends who visited the Mt. Washington house remained skeptical about the authenticity of the photographs.

When Ross Harpold came to the house for a party, he looked at the photos but remained unconvinced. Laughingly, Ross asked Huckert if the ghost was with them now. Huckert answered honestly that he did not know. Ross picked up the camera, asked

"Are you here?" and snapped a picture. As the picture developed, the faint outlines of a word began to appear in the photograph. The word was "*Yes.*"

John Matkowsky asked, "What is your name?" and snapped his own picture. Clearly and boldly across the face of the photograph the word "*Wright*" appeared. "He told us his name was Wright, but we still didn't believe it. We continued asking questions to the middle of the air in the living room. We asked him if he was a good ghost or a bad ghost, just really inane questions to begin with. Then he answered, '*Friend.*' "

In the months that followed, John Matkowsky and John Huckert took nearly a hundred photographs on which ghost writing appeared. Usually, the response was in English, sometimes it appeared in Latin, but it was always a direct answer to a direct question. In response to the question "Where do you go when you're not here?" the answer was "*Flux.*" When they asked who Wright was, he replied in Latin, "*Et alia corpus delicti,*" meaning "Among other things, a murder victim."

In September of 1992, John Matkowsky wrote *Sightings* a letter describing the bizarre photographs. He asked for help in determining what was causing the inexplicable phenomena. *Sightings* assembled an investigative team led by Kerry Gaynor, the noted UCLA parapsychologist, and Edson Williams, a photo analyst from the prestigious Brooks Institute in Santa Barbara, California. Both researchers examined the photographs, interviewed Matkowsky and Huckert, and determined that the best way to study the Ghost Writer was to conduct a series of controlled experiments inside the Mt. Washington house.

The *Sightings* team brought four Polaroid instant cameras and several sealed film cartridges shipped directly from Polaroid to the house. Each camera and each cartridge was logged and monitored to try to eliminate the possibility that someone was perpetrating a hoax. John Matkowsky was concerned that the Ghost Writer would not appear in this kind of crowded, expectant atmosphere.

Several test shots were taken and no writing appeared. Kerry

Gaynor was openly skeptical. After more than four hundred ghost investigations, Kerry was no stranger to wild-goose chases. "In my line of work we spend a great deal of time waiting and watching and wondering and hoping. We don't experience phenomena very often, but when something happens, it's exciting. It's a moment of connectedness with the unknown," says Gaynor.

That "moment of connectedness" came several hours into the investigation. Marty Elcan, a friend of John Matkowsky's who had had several successful communications with the Ghost Writer, posed a question. "Are most spirits good spirits or bad spirits?" Marty asked.

As the film developed in the presence of the entire *Sightings* team, a cryptic message appeared. "*There are numerous remedial lemurs.*" A lemur is a long-tailed monkey found mostly in Madagascar. Was the Ghost Writer playing a practical joke? John Huckert found the answer in a Latin dictionary. In Roman mythology lemurs are the night-walking spirits of the dead.

The excitement in the room was palpable. Nervous laughter masked the tension. Kerry Gaynor was impressed, but wanted further controls. "You have to establish a chain of evidence. You have to be able to observe the phenomenon from the beginning to the end. So, we have to load the film from a sealed pack, show that it's our camera. We have to fire it. We have to control the film as it comes out."

Following Kerry's suggestions, *Sightings* trained one of its video cameras on a new Polaroid brought to the house by photographic expert Edson Williams. A sealed film package was opened and a new cartridge was inserted directly into the Polaroid. A member of the *Sightings* team posed the question "Are you here for John or for the house?"

A picture was taken. It was placed on a table in full view. After thirty seconds, a message appeared. "*Genius loci.*" (See Photo 1.) Kerry Gaynor looked up the word in the Latin dictionary. The exact translation of *genius loci* is "the guardian spirit of a man or a place." More pictures were taken in the same manner. The messages alternated between English (*"Time travel,"* *"Anything is possible,"* *"John*[2] *relax and learn"*) and Latin (*"Ad litteram"*).

Edson Williams had never seen anything like it in his twenty years as a photo analyst. "I actually watched them eject out of the Polaroid. There was a moment where I thought, Oh, my God, and I was in one of the Polaroids, which made it even spookier. It made me feel that there could be something in the house."

Near the conclusion of the night-long investigation, Marty Elcan asked, "Wright, will you be with them for a long time?" The Ghost Writer replied, *"Sed haec prius fuere."* (See Photo 2.) Translated, the phrase means "All this is over now." It was the last message the Ghost Writer would send.

After the field investigation, Edson Williams brought many of the photographs back to the Brooks Institute for analysis. Using a digital scanner, he was able to move in on the ghost writing and noticed that there appeared to be individual fibers in the text. (See Photo 3.) He concluded that the writing might have been created using pulled strands of cotton. In his laboratory, Williams attempted to duplicate the ghost writing.

"The initial step was to shoot pulled cotton with a 4 × 5 camera using E-6 film. The next step was to preexpose the Polaroid film. I removed the cover sheet of the Polaroid pack, inserted the transparency, and exposed the Polaroid to the text. I then removed the transparency, reinserted the cover sheet, and loaded the film normally." (See Photo 4.) Using this method, Edson Williams was able to duplicate the ghost writing; however, his method took over an hour to complete and required manipulation of the film, which would have been impossible to hide.

Howard Worzel, a photographic analyst at Polaroid's corporate headquarters in Waltham, Massachusetts, was also at a loss to offer a scientific explanation for the ghost writing. "We have never encountered this phenomenon and we've been selling film for fifty years now to billions of customers," Worzel noted. Parapsychologist Kerry Gaynor concurred. "I personally have never come across anything like this in the twenty years that I've been doing research. I'm quite familiar with the literature, and I've never seen anything like this in the literature either."

While the scientific investigation continued, *Sightings* contacted world-renowned psychic Peter James and asked him to visit the house and give his psychic impressions of the site. Peter has a long history of exploring and documenting cases of hauntings that are not understood by science, but he also has been involved in cases he has exposed as obvious frauds. At first, Peter was also skeptical about the Ghost Writer.

"In all my years of delving into the paranormal world, I've never seen an entity present itself in this fashion, but I will say that all things are possible," Peter remarked before entering the house. Once inside, however, the feeling that he was not alone was instantaneous. His legs began to shake. He felt a vibration throughout his body that Peter claims to feel when he is in the presence of spirits. He also began to receive several names telepathically.

"I received the name of Gilbert. There is a Robert. Amelia is throughout. I am getting an essence of all three of those names vibrationally," Peter told the assembled group. The two Johns were awestruck. They had already researched the names of the home's previous owners. They had not showed this list to anyone, especially Peter James, and yet Peter had correctly named Gilbert, Robert, and Amelia—three of the names on the list. Peter did not think that any of these three people were the Ghost Writer.

As he walked around the house, Peter stopped in one spot he called a "spiritual vortex," a kind of doorway through which he felt spirits were entering the house. "I feel a very strong vibration. Something is definitely coming up from the floor," he reported. "I get a tingling sensation. It's also very cold here. My legs are trembling. It feels like something is coming from below and it's going through my entire body."

John Matkowsky snapped several pictures of Peter James standing in the vortex. Strange ghostly images appeared to surround him. Peter felt two distinct spirits at this time. One he described as the spirit of an Indian tribe that had once used the land surrounding the house as a kiva, or ceremonial center. The other spirit he described was that of man who had been murdered and could be buried under the house.

After Peter James's psychic reading, John Matkowsky and John Huckert decided to investigate Peter's theories. They began to dig small test holes through their hillside property. In one of these holes they made an amazing discovery—shards of pottery that appeared to be Native American in origin. An archaeologist from the nearby Southwest Museum examined the site and found the artifacts significant enough to warrant a larger dig on the site. It was proof to Matkowsky and Huckert that Peter James had been right about the kiva.

As for the body under the house, the men have no doubt that it is there, but digging for it would be impossible without moving the house. And perhaps it is for the best. Years of living with Wright have made the two Johns philosophical. They know that when the Ghost Writer feels the time is right, he will appear again.

Ghost photographs have a long and dubious history in the world of paranormal investigation. In the late 1800s understanding of camera technology was rudimentary, and something as simple as a double exposure could easily fool the general public. The first known "ghost" photograph is the famous Lincoln photograph, in which the shadowy form of Abraham Lincoln is apparently standing behind his widow, Mary Todd Lincoln. (See Photo 5.) It was ruled a hoax in the early 1900s. Today, with advanced technology and computer scanners, legitimate ghost photographs are extremely rare.

After the *Sightings* investigation, Michael Weber, one of the best close-up magicians in the world, claimed that he could duplicate the ghost-writing phenomenon. In a closed studio in the presence of *Sightings* host Tim White and a camera crew, Weber was able to produce a photo with the words "*We are here*" printed across the front. However, Weber was quick to point out that his ability to duplicate the ghost writing did not disprove that it could have been caused by supernatural forces. It only proved that the same phenomenon could be reproduced under similar conditions. Weber reviewed the videotapes shot inside the house and said he did not notice any of the trademark movements—called "tells"—that would have indicated that either Matkowsky or Huckert was a professional magician.

Voices of the Dead

Sara Estep believes that she has recorded the voices of the dead on audiotape. The process is deceptively simple. Sara unwraps a factory-sealed high-bias cassette, inserts it into her portable tape deck, and presses Record. She lets the tape run to the end and then plays it back. Through her headphones, she hears the hiss and buzz of background noise, her own breathing, a car honking in the distance. And sometimes she hears clear, cogent messages from unknown voices. (See Photo 6.)

"I'm recording voices from other dimensions. I started a little over fifteen years ago, and at first I was skeptical about the phenomenon, but I decided to try it. After seven days, I started picking up voices and I have continued ever since." Sara Estep is the founder of the American Association–Electronic Voice Phenomena and is part of a worldwide network of researchers who have successfully recorded anomalous sounds in the environment.

EVP recorders conform to exacting standards in an effort to eliminate the possibility that their machines are simply picking up ambient sound or radio signals. Only new, factory-sealed, commercially produced tape is used. The ghostly voices are never audible during the recording process; they are only discovered later when the tape is played back. In some cases, the voices are recorded on the reverse side of the tape, a phenomenon that cannot be reproduced mechanically.

"Most people can eventually get voices on their own using a tape recorder. You don't have to use expensive equipment. Almost any tape recorder is satisfactory," Sara advises. "But it takes great patience and persistence in order to do it. I try to tape early in the morning—that is when they most often come through. I have heard from friends and loved ones and also from those that I have never known."

Sara makes most of her EVP recordings at her home in Maryland, but she finds that her best recordings are made in the field at locations already known to be haunted. She often visits the Westminster Church and Burying Ground in Baltimore, which contains one of the oldest cemeteries in America, and Sara believes that many spirits here have communicated with her through her tape recorder.

Beneath the church, catacombs reach deep into the earth. Edgar Allan Poe is buried here alongside his young wife, Virginia. It was in the dank stillness of their subterranean tomb that Sara recorded the voice of a young woman.

"*We're down beside you*," the voice intoned. Then, after a pause, another voice, a man's voice, was heard on the tape. "*I will be there. I will be there.*"

After more than fifteen years of recording these mysterious voices, Sara believes that she is, in a sense, a modern medium through which the souls of the dead can communicate with the living. The messages she receives almost always describe some aspect of the afterlife. On a recent visit to Westminster Sara received a disturbing message.

"At one of the [crypts] where I stopped, a clear voice came through and said, '*We leave the soul right down here*.' Well, I don't agree with that philosophy. I would like to go back and try to help this person move on," Sara says.

Sightings contacted Sara Estep during an investigation of Point Lookout State Park in St. Mary's County, Maryland. The *Sightings* research team had interviewed several people who had experienced paranormal phenomena, including hearing detached voices, inside the park. Would Sara's tape recorder be able to capture these voices? She agreed to go to the park and make several recordings.

Point Lookout State Park is located on a windy, open promontory where the Potomac River meets the Chesapeake Bay. (See Photo 7.) Many instances of haunting activity have been reported in this desolate place, activity that reflects the area's tragic past. During the Civil War, more than fifty thousand confederate prisoners of war were held here. Forced to endure freezing cold, disease, and near starvation, more than four thousand prisoners died. They were buried in shallow graves near Point Lookout Light, the lighthouse at the end of the point.

"The water table there was high, and the graves flooded, so they had to move them to another location, then another, and another," explains former park manager Jerry Sword. "Finally, they paid people to dig up the bones and carry them off and drop them in a mass grave just outside the park. Today, it's just one big hole with four thousand skeletons under there."

Park ranger Donny Hammet has worked at Point Lookout for more than twenty years, and in that time he has seen and heard things he cannot explain. He vividly recalls the night he encountered an elderly woman standing alone in a grove of trees. "She was searching for something in the grass, and when I approached her to ask if she needed help, she said she was looking for some grave markers that should be there." At the time, Ranger Hammet did not know about the flooded tombstones that had once lined the area. "I told her I didn't know anything about it and I turned to leave. Then I noticed she wasn't there anymore, but there was no way that she could have left without my seeing her."

Ranger Hammet has also seen the figure of a young man in long pants and a gray coat cross a stretch of road near the mass grave. "When I was driving, I saw a man run across the road behind me," Hammet remembers. "I immediately returned to see what the gentleman was running from, or where he was going. When I got to where I'd seen him, there was no trail coming out of the woods on one side, nor a trail into the woods on the other side." Since his first encounter with this ghost, Hammet has seen this same apparition several more times, always running south to north, always at that same point in the road.

During his tenure at the park, Jerry Sword also had several inexplicable encounters. It was while he was living at Point Lookout Light that his most memorable sightings occurred. One night in particular, there was a terrible storm. Lightning cracked just feet from the house and the rain poured down in torrents. There was a knock at the door. A man stood on the screened-in porch and stared through Sword's front door window. "I wasn't alarmed," Sword says. "There were often people coming to the door for help or a problem of some kind. But what seemed odd about the whole thing was the kind of clothing he had on; a sack coat, a kind of military uniform from the late 1800s. And it wasn't wet, although there was a storm."

Sword remembers that the man looked to be twenty-four or twenty-five years old, had long black hair, and was clean shaven. Through the window, the two men made eye contact. Sword opened his front door, and as he did, the man seemed to float backward away from him. "He just floated out through the screened porch. Didn't dent the wire, didn't break the wire, just floated through the little holes. I ran outside, and there was no one there."

Several months later, Sword was doing research for an upcoming park exhibit. He learned about a fatal accident off Point Lookout in 1870. A steamboat express broke up just off the point during a sudden storm. The lighthouse keeper tried to get the boat into the harbor but was unsuccessful. Sword read an account of the accident in an old newspaper story. "There were twenty-two people on that boat—all drowned but nine," he read. "One of the bodies that washed up on shore was one of the officers from the boat. He was twenty-five years old, clean-shaven, with long black hair. He had on a sack coat." The description matched the man who had come to the lighthouse door and then disappeared so mysteriously.

Jerry Sword has also heard the voices. "Often there would be sounds like large crowds of people talking. You couldn't understand what they were saying, but they were talking," Sword recalls. He heard the sounds near the lighthouse and along the shore where the prisoner pens had once stood. Sword might have thought he was losing his mind, if others hadn't heard the voices too.

"One night, a man stopped me on my way home and said he heard people in a boat calling for help. Then people from the bay shore came over and said they heard people hollering for help," recalls Sword. Sword shined a warning beacon out into the bay and saw nothing. He flashed his light five times. A light coming from the bay flashed back five times. Sword flashed again. Again, the light from the bay responded.

"I went to the office and called the Coast Guard. They sent out a search party and searched for hours. There was nobody there," says Sword. Again, the park manager searched for a paranormal explanation and found one. During the time Point Lookout had been a prisoner-of-war camp, many prisoners tried to escape in makeshift boats built out of coffins. Only a few escapees ever made it across the bay to Virginia. Most were caught or drowned.

When Sara Estep arrived at Point Lookout, she was joined by paranormal investigators Lynda Martin and Ron and Nancy Stallings. Lynda believes she has made several contacts with ghosts in the park through her psychic ability. "This is one of the best places I've investigated. The whole area is just full of activity," Lynda says. It's not just localized to one building or one spot on the grounds. It includes the whole area. I've never come in contact with anything like that before."

Ron and Nancy Stallings have investigated more than one hundred haunted sites throughout the United States. They have made several trips to Point Lookout and believe, like Lynda, that the entire area is haunted. But they have enjoyed their greatest investigative success working in the lighthouse. It was there that the Stallings captured the only known photographic evidence of a ghost at Point Lookout. Standing next to Nancy is the faint image of a man in what appears to be a Civil War–era uniform. (See Photo 8.)

The Stallings urged Sara Estep to make several recordings in the basement of the lighthouse where the photograph had been taken. Sara agreed, and almost immediately, she was successful. Just minutes into the first side of the first tape, there was the voice of a young man. He said, "*Let's talk.*"

Because EVP is not audible until the tape is played back, Sara did not know immediately that she had made the ghostly recording. As soon as she heard the apparent invitation to communicate with this strange entity, she returned to the lighthouse basement. She let the tape run, silently, for several minutes. Then she began to ask questions, hoping that perhaps she would get the answer on tape.

"Are you there? Who are you?" When the tape was played back, there was no response. "Hello, who are you? Would you like to speak?" No response. Then Sara appeared to ask a question that drew a ghostly response. "Were you a soldier here?"

The strong clear voice of a young man came through on the tape. He said, "*I was seeing the war.*" Sara describes the voice as "Perhaps that of a young southern soldier who died at the camp during the war."

It was the first time that an EVP recording appeared to match not only the history of the place where it was recorded, but also the photograph of a ghostly presence in the same area. But Sara does not feel that her job at Point Lookout Light is done.

She says, "After the recording, I felt there were more entities trapped there, that they had not been able to find their way to move on. I went back, as did Nancy and Ron, to try to help them move on into the spirit world. But they are still there. You can feel that there are unhappy, unseen entities still staying on."

The American Association–Electronic Voice Phenomena was founded by Sara Estep in 1982. Currently, the AA-EVP has over three hundred members in thirty-nine states and eleven foreign countries.

Many EVP recordings are connected to traumatic events in history. In March 1977, Sara Estep recorded numerous voices pleading *"Help me. Please help me."* Unbeknownst to Sara, at the same time the recordings were being made, two 747s collided over the Canary Islands. Six hundred people died.

In January 1982, an Air Florida 737 en route to Tampa from National Airport crashed into the Potomac River. Mercedes Shepanek recorded several voices which AA-EVP members believed to be those of the passengers killed in the disaster. Shepanek, the former Virginia state coordinator of the AA-EVP, received the messages *"Reach down into the snow"* and *"Come with me now."*

The Haunted Castle
of Berry-Pomeroy

I t looks like a haunted castle straight out of a Hollywood movie. Crumbling limestone ramparts cling to a craggy hilltop; windowless towers stand sentry over the desolate moors of the valley below. It may look like a movie set, but Berry-Pomeroy castle near Totnes, England, is real, a ruin that has been uninhabited since 1688. No one has wanted to live there for the past three hundred years because Berry-Pomeroy is the most haunted castle in England. (See Photo 9.)

The castle is open to the public, but surprisingly few visitors stop to explore this paranormal landmark. There are no roadside billboards beckoning tourists to explore the ghosts of Berry-Pomeroy. There are no souvenir shops capitalizing on the phenomena here. You won't find ghoulish T-shirts or spooky pencil sharpeners. In fact, most of the people who come to Berry-Pomeroy stumble upon it quite by accident and have no idea that they are entering a fifteenth-century castle with a five-hundred-year history of haunting.

"We were down there on holiday and saw a little sign to the castle," remembers one tourist, Anne Benney. "As we had an hour or two to spare, my husband and I decided to find out what it was." As the Benneys climbed the long drive to the castle entrance, Anne suddenly had a strange feeling of evil. "I said to my husband, 'I don't really want to go and see this place.' It felt very heavy and depressive even though it was a nice, hot, sunny day."

Richard Benney convinced his wife that she was just imagining things. They parked their car and walked among the ruins. They were drawn to one particular tower and noticed a spiral staircase descending into a dungeon below. Anne did not want to go down the stairs, but when Richard bounded ahead, she followed.

Anne recounts what happened next. "When we first went down the stairs into the dungeon, it was dark and damp. I heard footsteps coming down the stairs and a skirt rustling, but even though I watched the stairs, no one appeared. We waited for a minute or two—the sound was getting louder—but no one appeared. The closer it got, the more panic-stricken I felt. I had an overpowering sense of evil. I felt as though I was being enveloped by a cloud of evil and I couldn't breathe. My husband had to help me out of there."

"I've seen people faint here. I've seen people carried out. I've seen people come to the courtyard and say, 'No, I don't want to go in this place,' " says Jack Hazzard, the castle's former master stonemason. During his twenty-year tenure at Berry-Pomeroy, Jack had to assist many terrified visitors out of the castle. The tower where Anne Benney experienced an unseen evil is a focus of much of the haunting activity.

It is known as Margaret's Tower. According to legend, Lady Pomeroy and Lady Margaret, two sisters who lived in the castle during the sixteenth century, were both in love with the same man. When their father, Lord Pomeroy, left the castle to go on a crusade, he put his eldest daughter in charge. According to historian Deryck Seymour, who has studied the castle's history for more than fifty years, "Lady Pomeroy saw her chance. She laid hands upon her sister and locked her in the deepest dungeon of the tower and there did starve her to death. The ghost of the unfortunate Lady Margaret is seen quite frequently down in the dungeon, at the top of the stairs, and along the rampart walk."

The first written account of a ghost sighting at Berry-Pomeroy was found in the two-hundred-year-old diary of Sir Walter

Faulker, a physician to King George IV. While attending to the steward's wife in the gatehouse, Sir Faulker saw a mysterious apparition bathed in blue light. Her eyes glowered with hatred, according to the diary. Sightings of this mysterious woman— distinct from Lady Margaret—continue to the present day.

"The story is that one of the Pomeroys fathered the daughter of one of his own daughters," Deryck Seymour explains. "This child of incest was strangled by the mother, who did not want it, of course. She's seen quite frequently and people don't like the sight of her at all. She's very evil."

Local resident Simon Day believes that this is the ghost that he and a large group of friends saw on a recent trip to the castle. Inside the castle's main tower, an apparition appeared. "What we saw was the figure of a woman swathed in blue. You could see directly through her. She was just staring at us, saying '*Beware the hour. Beware the hour.*' I looked at my watch and it was just a few minutes before eleven o'clock," says Simon.

At precisely eleven o'clock, the digital alarm on Simon's wristwatch went off. Then, in front of the assembled group, the figure in blue disappeared and all the windows in the tower went black. This was extremely unusual, since even at night there was always moonlight—or lights from the nearby town—providing some degree of illumination. But at that moment, the room became pitch black. The wooden gate at the tower entrance began to shake violently. "There was nothing there," Simon remembers. "When we could find nothing to explain what was happening, we ran out of there. It was a terrifying night."

In addition to sightings of the Blue Ghost of Pomeroy, the wails of her murdered infant have also been heard. "The child that she bore is heard to cry throughout the castle," says Deryck Seymour. "Not long ago, a young nurse told me that she had heard the crying of a child while she was at the castle. She searched and searched but found no crying child anywhere on the grounds. She was very disturbed, until I told her she was not the only one who had heard the poor creature."

Jack Hazzard has seen the Blue Ghost, Lady Margaret, and

many other apparitions at Berry-Pomeroy. In 1986, he also took important photographs of ghostly images on the castle grounds. (See Photo 10.) He describes the day he took the pictures with a disc camera: "One Sunday morning, I went to the arbor with a sketch pad and my camera to catalog some of the ruins. I started sketching, and the leaves on the trees started shaking and the wind started to blow. I felt that something unusual was happening, and I took four or five shots with my camera, very quick. On three of them, light shapes appeared. I have no idea what they are, but it was a most unusual Sunday morning."

As it turns out, it was in this very arbor that a tragic family feud came to a bitter conclusion in the early seventeenth century. "It is called the ghost walk of Berry-Pomeroy," explains Seymour. "There were two lovers here—one was a Pomeroy, and the other was from a neighboring family of Darting Hall. There was a great feud between the families, and these two lovers were discovered in the arbor. Someone picked up a dagger and stabbed them both. Their ghosts are said to haunt this area and beckon to each other across time and space."

It may sound like a fable borrowed from Shakespeare, but the number of witnesses who have experienced these ghosts firsthand is growing. Tim King is another visitor who had a frightening encounter in the arbor. "I heard screeching," Tim remembers, "and my first reaction was that it was a fox, or some other wild animal. But the screeching got louder and louder. I was with a friend, and he was pretty freaked out."

The pair returned to Totnes, had a cup of tea, and calmed down. They laughed about their fear and agreed to return to the castle to determine what kind of animal had made that horrifying sound. Again in the arbor, they realized this was no animal. "When we went back up there, the sound was very faint. We looked across a long field and felt that it had moved quite far away. Right then, there was a really amazing roar, then a horrifying screech right next to where we were standing. It was winter and there were no leaves on the trees, but still we couldn't see where that noise was coming from. To be honest, we panicked and left there straightaway."

Tony Cornell is a paranormal investigator from Cambridge University who believes that Berry-Pomeroy castle is a treasure house of ghosts, apparitions, EVP, and psychic phenomena. He has interviewed many eyewitnesses but has been prevented from doing a thorough scientific investigation by British Heritage, the trustees of the castle. They do not believe that Berry-Pomeroy is haunted and do not want to encourage any long-term parapsychological pursuits in the area. Tony Cornell is frustrated by this attitude.

"Too many sensible people have seen things, and the phenomena has been going on too long for this to be just imagination. There's no doubt whatever that this is the most haunted castle in England, and we must do a serious investigation over a long period of time," Cornell asserts. Only one other paranormal researcher has ever been allowed access to the castle. But after his last visit to Berry-Pomeroy, investigator Bob Daulby doesn't want to go back.

"I was conducting an investigation, expecting nothing at all," Daulby recounts. "I was just about to leave when, just by the rampart walls and the stairs leading down, I saw this huge black cloud and, to me, it was the hugest, deepest, blackest thing I've ever seen. It was an evil entity." Daulby claims the black cloud trailed him through the castle and followed him back to his house in nearby Paignton. That same night, he asked a group of friends to help him try and make contact with what he felt was an evil entity.

Daulby remembers the frightening hours that followed: "We placed an inverted crystal goblet on a Ouija board and asked 'Is anybody there?' and 'Who are you?' The glass moved erratically around the board and began to spell something out. I . . . S . . . A . . . B . . . E . . . L . . . , and when the glass came back to the L a second time suddenly she popped up, Isabelle." The figure of a young girl in Restoration period dress appeared to Daulby and the other people who had their hands on the Ouija board. "She struck us as a very evil little girl," says Daulby.

Through the Ouija board, Isabelle communicated that she was the bastard child of a disinherited Pomeroy. Once she had delivered her message, the child ghost disappeared, only to reappear a few hours later in the Daulbys' bedroom.

"I went to bed early and left the group downstairs experimenting with the Ouija board," says Ann Daulby, Bob's wife. "I had the sensation of somebody sitting on the back of my legs while I was lying in bed. Thinking it was Bob messing about, I told him to get off. But when I turned over, it was actually a little girl with a maniacal grin on her face."

The Daulbys reported their encounter to Deryck Seymour, to see if he had reports of other sightings of this little girl. Seymour remembers the couple's sincerity and their terror. "Well, they both came to see me the next afternoon, and they were terrified. They were frozen with shock, incoherent, and I could hardly understand what they were saying."

No one is certain who this little girl may be or why she followed Bob and Ann Daulby home. However, it is not the first time that an evil force from within Berry-Pomeroy has traveled outside the castle walls. Jack Hazzard remembers what happened after he gave one of the stones from the castle rampart to a visitor as a souvenir.

Jack says, "Three years went by, and then I got a parcel from the woman in Ireland. In the parcel was the stone. She wrote, 'Since you gave this to me things are happening in my home. I am terrified and you must take it back.' Well, I felt sorry that she was so disturbed, so I said a little prayer and put the stone back in the wall." Deryck Seymour also got a similar package from another visitor.

"There was a letter enclosed," Seymour tells, "and the writer of the letter said he had taken a loose stone from a castle wall and slipped it in his pocket. When he got back home suddenly that night he woke up in a sweat of fear with his hair standing on end. He didn't know what he was terrified of, only that he had to get rid of that stone. He wrote me the letter confessing what he had done and begging me to put it back just where he had got it from."

This unreasonable fear is the hallmark of the hauntings at Berry-Pomeroy. Some people see the Blue Ghost, some hear the screams and howls in the night, others experience apparitions of evil entities, but nearly everyone feels a spine-chilling aura. In the past fifty years, Deryck Seymour has met hundreds of people who swear they will never visit Berry-Pomeroy castle again:

"One man, very intelligent, a real skeptical sort, came to the castle with his wife and children. As soon as he got inside the gate, he felt as though he had to protect his daughters, that they were in danger. He wouldn't let go of them. Suddenly he felt that he was being taken over by another person but he didn't know by whom. He lost his sense of time, he didn't know if he was in the past, the present, or the future. There was a great weight of sorrow and horror on his shoulders. His wife said, 'Good Lord, you're as white as a sheet. Are you ill?' and led him out of the castle.

"As soon as he got outside he felt quite all right again. He didn't know what had happened to him, and he has vowed that nothing on earth will ever make him come to Berry-Pomeroy castle again."

Until 1939, the Borley Rectory was considered the most haunted place in England. Since 1863, a succession of residents had reported seeing ghosts, experiencing psychokinesis, and hearing unearthly noises. In 1929, famed psychical researcher Harry Price conducted an investigation and witnessed a vicious paranormal attack; bottles and bricks were hurtled through the air seemingly of their own volition. A medium told Price that the spirit responsible for the attack had given her an important message: the rectory would burn down on March 27, 1938, and after the fire, the spirit would be revealed. The date passed without incident, but exactly eleven months later, on February 27, 1939, a mysterious fire destroyed the Borley Rectory. During the cleanup, police found the ancient skeletal remains of a young woman buried under layers of smoldering ash.

Echoes in Time

There's an invisible energy that exists between magnet and metal. You can't see it or touch it, but you know it's there. There is growing evidence that people generate that same kind of magnetic energy and that this energy remains in the environment even after death. You can't see it or touch it, but you know it's there.

Ghost investigators call this energy residue haunting. The term is used to describe hauntings in which energy from the past is seen in the form of apparitions or heard as ghostly sounds. In a residue haunting, these spiritual energies do not interact with the living, instead they are echoes in time replaying over and over like an old movie.

Just as people have memories, so do places. They retain images of the past that can be called up in the present. No one knows why certain places seem to be residual haunting magnets, or what triggers the haunting activity. Investigators can only wait and watch and wonder. They do that a lot at the Whaley House.

Since it was built in 1856, the Whaley House has been a favorite destination for travelers to San Diego County in southern California. (See Photo 11.) At first it was an inn, a welcome haven for stagecoach passengers after a long day on dusty trails. At the turn of the century, a new building was added, and the Whaley House became the county courthouse. There was a new clientele: cattle rustlers, con artists, and killers. Since then, the Whaley House has been a church, a school, a post office, a general store, and the town social center. Through it all, the Whaley House has been the home of the Whaley family, and it has always been haunted.

In 1919, Sir Arthur Conan Doyle, the creator of Sherlock Holmes, made a special trip to the Whaley House from his home in England. Conan Doyle was not only a famous novelist, he was also one of the world's leading authorities on all things supernatural. He came to the Whaley House to try to make contact with spirits that had been seen in the house by family members and travelers. He wanted to see the little dog that ran down the hall and into thin air. He wanted to see the fellow in the frock coat who seemed to float above the landing on the main staircase. Arthur Conan Doyle did not see these famous apparitions during his visit in 1919, but June Redding sees them all the time.

June Redding has worked at the Whaley House since 1954. Today, she is its resident historian and chief tour guide. June isn't shy about telling visitors about the little dog, or the fellow in the frock coat, or the footsteps of the hanging man. "I often hear the unmistakable sound of a man walking the floor with a heavy tread, like he was wearing boots. You can hear his heels hit the floorboards," June says.

The footsteps are believed to be those of a man who was executed on the Whaley House property in 1852. The man had been convicted of stealing a boat in San Diego Harbor. He was sentenced to death by hanging and was taken to a makeshift gallows outside the Whaley House. Witnesses at the scene say the man did not believe the sentence would be carried out. He thought the sheriff was only trying to frighten him. June Redding recounts the story of the hapless thief:

"Until the time he was pulled off the wagon platform, he didn't think he was going to die. He was giving a farewell speech when they pulled the wagon out from under him. He never got to finish that speech. Unfortunately, he fell only a few feet, because the gallows wasn't high enough to inflict a good hanging. It took forty-five minutes for him to die."

The footsteps of this man are not the only ghostly sounds to be heard at the Whaley House. Anna Whaley, the original owner of the house, has not returned in spirit form since her death, but the sounds of her spirit fill the house with music to this day. "We think perhaps her spirit isn't strong enough to return, but we have music coming from the music room when no one's there," reports June Redding. "Piano and violin music and the sound of a music box."

These sounds are infrequent and unpredictable. Many visitors, like Arthur Conan Doyle, have left Whaley House disappointed. But there is one ghostly sound that can be heard at any time by anyone, because it is a sound recorded on audiotape. It is the sound of a billiard game being played. The recording was made in 1986. The billiard game hadn't been played since the 1920s.

The recording was made by Sandy Stokes, a newspaper reporter for the *Riverside Press–Enterprise*. A few weeks before Halloween, 1986, Sandy got a routine assignment. Find a haunted house for the October 31 edition of the paper. Sandy contacted local historian and ghost investigator Richard Senate for a lead. He suggested the Whaley House and also suggested she bring along a tape recorder to see if she could get any of the house's famous haunting sounds on audiotape. Sandy thought the idea was silly, but Richard Senate was adamant.

"I challenged her. I said, go ahead, go down to the Whaley House. Use a tape recorder with brand-new music-quality tape. Go from room to room and when you're done, play it back. Just see if there isn't something that shouldn't be there," Senate told her.

Sandy took Richard Senate's challenge, sort of. She was planning to bring a tape recorder along anyway to record her interview with June Redding and to record June's tour through the house. Instead of turning the recorder on and off as she normally would, however, Sandy left it on the entire time she was in the house. June gave her a tour, told her many ghost stories, and

Sandy returned to her office ready to write a typical Halloween story. Twenty minutes into the B side of the tape, she could tell the story wasn't typical anymore.

There was a long stretch of silence and then a strange clacking sound. It wasn't a sound Sandy remembered hearing when she was at the Whaley House. She called Richard Senate. "When I got the call from Sandy, she was a changed person. The bravado was gone, and she was very shaken by what she had heard on that tape. She heard strange sounds that shouldn't be there, like a pool game. She called back to the Whaley House only to discover that the room where she got those sounds had once been a billiard parlor."

Richard Senate gave the tape to Brian Black, an expert in EVP, electronic voice phenomenon. Black has spent nearly twenty years recording and analyzing ghostly sounds on otherwise blank tape and has developed special computer software to help him determine the origin of the sounds. (See Photo 12.) Brian's first step was to visit the Whaley House and eliminate the possibility that the sounds had a logical, earthbound explanation.

"I found that at the Whaley House the floorboards creak like crazy. I did several recordings of those, but they didn't match at all. They were far too dynamic," says Black. "It would have to be something from a sophisticated mechanical system that would produce sounds like the ones on Sandy's tape."

Using a spectrograph, Black drew a computer picture of the unknown sounds on Sandy's tape. He then compared it to pictures of known sounds. "I did spectrograph comparisons with just about every imaginable sound that's implosive, even cracking knuckles and popping gum." Finally, after analyzing more than two hundred sounds, Black determined that the sound was very similar to billiard balls hitting each other. But it was not a perfect match.

As part of his research, Brian Black went to AAA Billiards in North Hollywood, California, which houses one of the largest collections of billiard balls in the world. He learned that billiard balls are made out of many different materials. Most modern balls are phenolic resin, a high-impact plastic. Older balls are made out of other plastics, Bakelite, and even clay. None of these balls sounded like the ones on Sandy's tape. The owner of AAA Billiards, Terry Moldenhauer, had been looking on curiously as the man with the tape recorder went through rack after rack of billiard balls. He asked Brian Black what he was doing and seemed amused by the answer.

With just a hint of sarcasm, Terry Moldenhauer told Black that if the recording was of a ghostly turn-of-the-century billiard game, then that game would have had to have been played with ivory billiard balls. A wealthy, prominent family like the Whaleys wouldn't have anything but the best, and until the 1940s, ivory was the best. No ivory balls were made or sold after the early 1940s, and today very few remain, except in the hands of collectors. Brian Black made one final recording using antique ivory billiard balls.

When he compared the spectrograph of the ivory balls with the spectrograph from Sandy's tape, it was a perfect match. He called Terry Moldenhauer to tell him that his hunch had paid off. "When Brian told me that he had proved that it was the actual sound of a billiard game with balls that had not been in use since the turn of the century, I was really surprised. I was shocked," Moldenhauer says.

These sounds, recorded by Sandy Stokes, appear to be the best evidence of residue haunting. No one has yet come forward with a scientific explanation for the sounds on the tape. Brian Black explains, "The sounds on the tape could be faked, but it would be very far-fetched. It would take a real expert to fake the sounds of ivory billiard balls and have them appear twenty minutes into side two for only three minutes. It would really be absurd."

For Sandy Stokes, the experience has made her reevaluate her beliefs. "When Brian told me that he had proved that it was the actual sound of a billiard game with balls that had not been produced since the turn of the century, I was really shocked. I thought he was just going to analyze the tape and find that it was some weird problem with the tape recorder. I had no idea it would turn out the way it did, because I never thought things like that could happen."

The only person who wasn't shocked or surprised at the sounds on the tape was June Redding. For forty years, she's been hearing the ghostly sounds of a distant past and seeing the familiar faces of the little dog, the fellow in the frock coat, and the hanging man.

> EVP, electronic voice phenomenon, is also known as "Raudive Voices." It is named for the Latvian psychologist Konstantin Raudive, a leading researcher into the phenomenon in the 1960s and 1970s. EVP searches for contact with other dimensions not only through tape recorders, but also televisions and computers.

America's
Most Haunted

Baleroy is a historic thirty-room mansion in the elite
Chestnut Hill suburb of Philadelphia. It is a
treasure-house of Early American furniture, paintings, and silver.
It is also one of the most haunted houses in America.

Baleroy is the ancestral home of seventy-six-year-old George
G. Meade Easby, known to his friends as Meade. A millionaire
philanthropist and fine art collector, Meade has dedicated his life
to preserving the treasures of Baleroy. Every room tells an important story in American history. In the Blue Room, there is the
sterling silver that was used at the celebratory dinner attended by
the signers of the Declaration of Independence. The cannonball
that felled his great-grandfather General George Meade at the
Battle of Gettysburg has a place of honor in the Red Room. And
in every room there are the ghosts. For the past seventy years,
nearly everyone who has come to Baleroy has been haunted by
the past.

Meade knew this place was special from the moment he arrived. He vividly remembers the day his family moved in. Meade
was six, his younger brother Steven was five. (See Photo 13.) The
boys were immediately drawn to a splendid fountain in the courtyard. They leaned over the edge and Meade saw his own reflec-

tion in the clear water. He turned to look at Steven's reflection, but instead of the image of his younger brother, Meade saw a skeleton. "It shook me up quite a bit," he recalls today. "We saw a skeleton where his image should be, and shortly after that, Steven died."

Since his death, Steven has returned to haunt others at Baleroy. David Beltz, a restoration specialist, has worked for twenty years to preserve the historic home. He and a coworker saw Steven appear in an upstairs window while they were working near the courtyard fountain. "I noticed a person looking out the window at me, a young kid with blond hair. He had his hands on the sill and was looking down toward the yard. I said to my buddy, 'Look at that little kid.' Then it just faded off and my buddy said, 'Man, that was really strange.' " Beltz's coworker never worked at Baleroy again. "He would never come back. He was really scared. He just said that he felt somebody stare at him all the time."

David Beltz's son, Dave Junior, still works at Baleroy, but never in the basement. The last time he was down there, he heard a ghostly voice calling his name. "Dave . . . Dave . . . Dave . . . ," it repeated. Dave Junior called up to his father, "Dad, is that you?" It was not. His father was working on the third floor.

Meade believes that his brother is not trying to frighten anyone, but that, like the child he was at the time of his death, Steven just wants a little attention every now and then. That's how Meade explains the flying portrait incident.

Meade was entertaining guests on the terrace when they heard a loud crash coming from the Gallery. No one was inside the house at the time. The party went to investigate and found a portrait of Steven lying on the floor. "The painting had come off the wall and flown fifteen feet across the hall. The nail was still tight in the wall. The wire was tight on the painting. There's no explaining how that could happen, but it did happen," says Meade.

Flying objects are nothing new to Baleroy. Meade recalls a party given in honor of a visiting minister several years ago. In the presence of more than twenty witnesses, a decorative copper pot flew across the room and hit the minister on the side of the head. Needless to say, the minister never returned.

Steven's apparition and his mischievous activity is only a small part of the hauntings at Baleroy. The ghost of Meade's uncle is ever present. His mother is seen and heard. There are loud footsteps, persistent knocking, and strange encounters in the night. "One night I was alone in the house, sleeping," Meade says. "I felt a pressure on the bed as though somebody was sitting there. I thought someone had broken in despite the elaborate alarm system. I felt something grab my arm, so I turned on the light. Nothing was there, but in the morning I noticed that my arm was black and blue. It wasn't a dream. It actually happened."

Meade's longtime confidant and fellow collector Lloyd Gross was skeptical about his friend's tales of a haunted Baleroy, until he experienced the phenomena firsthand. It was while guiding a reporter through the house that Gross became a believer.

"It happened upstairs in the East Room, in Mrs. Easby's old bedroom. The reporter had a little tape recorder in his hand and suddenly the thing flew in the air in a trajectory, not straight down to the floor," says Gross. "I said, 'Wow, did you burn yourself?' He said, 'No, something pulled it out of my hand.' He got so white we had to take him out on the terrace and give him a shot of whiskey."

Although none of the ghosts of Baleroy have ever been captured on film, there is photographic evidence of one inexplicable haunting phenomenon here. It takes the form of a strange blue fog. (See Photo 14.) Lloyd Gross saw the fog while he was helping prepare the house for a charity benefit.

"I looked through the Blue Room doors and I saw what looked like blue smoke. I said to Meade, 'Look, it's getting cold out. You can see the atmosphere.' And he said, 'Oh no, that's not fog, that's the ectoplasm.' " Lloyd Gross was unnerved. "That pretty well scared him," Meade recalls. "I followed him out to his car and he said, 'Why did you hit me?' And I said, 'I didn't hit you, I'm way over here.' So at that point I knew something was following him."

Apparently something was. When Lloyd Gross got home that night, he thought his foyer was on fire. Then he realized that the ectoplasm he had seen at Baleroy was also in his own home.

Three pictures of the bizarre blue fog have been captured on film. (See Photo 15.) It remains one of Baleroy's most persistent phenomena. The appearance of the fog seems to foretell a visit from the malevolent spirit Meade calls "Amanda." She is not a relative, and the reason why she haunts Baleroy is not known. What is known, however, is that where Amanda goes, death will surely follow.

For many years, a chair in Meade's study has been dubbed the "death chair." According to him, several people have been drawn to that chair by Amanda. She appears in the Blue Room and entices them to rest in the chair. Everyone who has seen Amanda and sat in the chair has died. One victim was Baleroy's former curator.

Paul Kimmons had worked at Baleroy for several years and had never experienced any haunting activity. He humored Meade and the other guests who had seen ghosts in the house. When Easby asked Kimmons to escort psychic Judith Richardson Haimes on a tour, he obliged, but was quick to let her know that he was not a believer. Moments later, Amanda appeared, flowing down the staircase. "Paul was quite frightened," Judith Richardson Haimes recalls. "He said, 'I see that woman. She's here.' He was very upset."

A few weeks later, Judith received a chilling phone call. "I'm not an hysterical person," Kimmons told her, "but Amanda is following me. I look in my rearview mirror and she's there. I wake up at home and she's there. I'm walking down the street and I catch a glimpse of her out of the corner of my eye. She's scaring me to death. I think I'm losing my mind." The encounters took their toll. Paul Kimmons sat in the chair in Meade's study to rest. A month later, he was dead.

Since then, Judith Richardson Haimes has been a frequent visitor to Baleroy. She believes that her psychic power enables her to communicate with many of the spirits, both good and bad, inside the home. "I will never forget the first time I walked in the front doors of Baleroy. The first words out of my mouth were, 'My God, I can't believe how many spirits are in this house.' "

Judith believes that Amanda is not malevolent. "There are those who say Amanda killed Paul," Judith says. "I don't believe that was true at all. I believe that Amanda was there to lovingly help him cross over. Several times I have sensed Paul at Baleroy. I have sensed that wonderful warm energy that he emits."

Judith has also had several successful communications with the spirit of Meade's long-dead mother. In life, Henrietta Easby was prim and reserved, a Victorian lady of few words. In death, she is the same. Her appearances are subtle and infrequent, but when she does make her presence known, it's for a reason. Through Judith, Meade's mother has revealed many family secrets.

"One evening on my way to Baleroy, I kept hearing the name Longfellow," Judith remembers. When she arrived at the house for dinner, the echoes of "Longfellow" persisted. Then, she heard Henrietta Easby's voice saying "Children's Hour . . . Children's Hour." Judith asked Meade what it meant. He was stunned. "The Children's Hour" by Henry Wadsworth Longfellow was his mother's favorite poem. No one but him knew that. Later that night, retiring to the study, Meade's mother again made her presence known.

The study is lined with books from floor to ceiling, all neatly arranged in oak bookcases. But on this night, one book was mysteriously out of place. It was sticking out, almost ready to fall. Meade went to push the book back into place. It was a book of poetry. He took it down from the shelf and noticed an envelope inside. Turning to that page he felt a chill run through his body. The envelope said "To my son Meade in the event of my death." The poem on that page was "The Children's Hour" by Longfellow. The envelope was empty.

"From that point forward," says Judith Richardson Haimes, "it seemed as though Meade's mother wanted to use me to get messages to him." In a neglected storeroom, Judith discovered a pair of silver candlesticks hidden in the rafters by Meade's mother. In an Early American desk, the spirit led Judith to a secret drawer. Inside, they found the bullet-riddled flag that General Meade had captured at Gettysburg. It was as if Meade's mother couldn't rest until she had revealed the secret hiding places of forgotten family treasures.

Henrietta Easby also led Judith to an abandoned trunk in Baleroy's attic. Inside, Meade found important family papers, including a strange promissory note that seemed to indicate that he was the heir to a vast unclaimed fortune. "My great-grandfather was born in the Bonaparte Palace in Cadiz. His father was naval attaché to the court of Spain and loaned the Americans the money to buy the state of Florida from Spain. According to this note, we've never been paid back."

Whether or not George G. Meade Easby can claim the state of Florida as part of his multimillion-dollar holdings isn't the point. He feels it is the mere fact that his mother wanted him to know about this secret legacy that is important. What Meade's mother could not say to her son in life, she is revealing to him in death. According to Judith, "I feel I am being used as the instrument to allow mother and son to communicate so that everyone knows that death is not really the end. Death is a continuation of life."

In her most recent communication, Henrietta Easby led her son to an old desk. In one of its drawers, Meade found a letter from his father. M. Stevenson Easby had always told his son to believe in the here and now. He had never admitted seeing the ghosts of Baleroy, and he had taught Meade to only trust what science could explain. But in this letter written just before his death, Meade's father told a different story. "I was brought up not to believe in ghosts," Meade explains. "But my father left me a letter to be read after his death, and he said he had seen the ghosts and for me not to be afraid."

Meade has taken those words to heart. He relishes the ghosts of Baleroy and knows that when his time comes, he too will return to greet the next generation.

Ectoplasm, a frequent characteristic of Spiritualist seances, is a luminous substance that appears during communication with the spirits of the dead. This strange, doughlike substance often flows from the navel, mouth, or nose of certain mediums when trance states are achieved during a seance. Ectoplasm, which manifests as a solidified mist and has a peculiar smell, is said to be molded by spirits to assume a temporary physical presence on earth.

The Real Entity Case

In his twenty-five-year career as a paranormal investigator, Kerry Gaynor has witnessed and documented more than 750 haunting cases. He has seen poltergeist activity, apparitions, and bizarre physical effects. He has photographed, videotaped, and made audio recordings of phenomena unexplained by nature or religion. And when you ask Kerry Gaynor which case stands out as the most important and the most bizarre, he answers without hesitation or reflection. It is the Entity case.

Gaynor began his work as a parapsychologist under the tutelage of Dr. Thelma Moss, who founded and directed the now-defunct Department of Parapsychology at the University of California at Los Angeles. As a young graduate student in the early 1970s, Gaynor did not realize that a chance encounter would launch the most significant haunting investigation in history. The Entity case would later be popularized in both a book and a 1982 film entitled *The Entity*, but what the real-life investigators found when they met the victim of the haunting was more bizarre and more compelling than any movie.

A thirty-five-year-old woman known to this day only as "Doris" overheard Gaynor discussing his interest in parapsychology in a Los Angeles bookstore. She told him that she was being plagued by a ghost herself and urged the UCLA Parapsychology

Department to investigate. Kerry Gaynor and his colleague Barry Taff agreed to interview Doris and her family.

Kerry Gaynor vividly recalls his first visit to Doris's Culver City apartment. "We conducted a two-hour interview, and during that time, she told us a lot of interesting experiences, but I knew she was holding something back. At the end of the interview she finally admitted that she was being attacked and raped by the ghost. At that time, we thought she was probably crazy. We just didn't think that we should pursue the case."

Soon after the interview, Gaynor was awakened in the middle of the night by a frantic phone call from Doris. She claimed that the attacks were continuing, and she was desperate for help. Gaynor visited her the next day and found that her body was covered by black and blue marks. "She had bite marks on her neck and on her breasts. She had definitely been beaten, and I did not believe it was self-inflicted. But whether it was just a person who did this I had no way of knowing," says Gaynor.

Doris's sixteen-year-old son had been a witness to the event. He had heard his mother screaming in the middle of the night. Doris's two younger children had been afraid to run into her room, but the oldest son did run in and saw his mother being thrown around on her bed. He did not see anyone else in the room. He remembered leaning over to try to help his mother, but as he did so something hit him on the back of the head. An unseen force threw him across the room, and his right arm was broken.

It was compelling evidence that something extraordinary was happening in the modest home, but it wasn't necessarily the kind of evidence Gaynor was looking for. He remained skeptical that the source of the phenomenon was paranormal, and he expressed his doubt gently to Doris. Gaynor insisted that it would require independent verification from nonfamily witnesses to convince him that this case was not a hoax.

A few weeks later, Doris called back. She told Gaynor that five people had witnessed the phenomenon in her house. After interviewing the eyewitnesses, Gaynor and Taff agreed to return to the house with a team from UCLA. Within minutes of their arrival, the Entity made its presence known.

"In our second visit to the house, I was standing in the kitchen, and a lower cabinet door slammed open and a pan came flying out," Gaynor recalls. "The trajectory of the pan was elliptical; it literally flew out and landed about four feet from the cabinet. At that point, I thought there might be some kind of fraud going on, so I ran over to the cabinet and tried to see if there was some kind of mechanism—or even a very small person—throwing pans at me. I didn't find anything."

It was the first time Gaynor had experienced firsthand the phenomenon known as psychokinesis, or PK. He was shocked and intrigued. But the investigator had only moments to note his encounter before a scream from the bedroom sent him running toward Doris. What happened next is an event best described in Gaynor's own words. It was real, it was terrifying, and it was captured on film:

"Doris screamed out, 'It's in my bedroom!' We [Gaynor and Taff] ran in there and she shouted, 'It's over in the corner!' We fired our Polaroid camera in the direction that she said it was coming from. We didn't see anything, but the picture came out bleached out white completely. [See Photo 16.] She shouted out again, 'It's in the corner!' Again, we fired our camera and it was bleached out completely. At that point I thought the camera was malfunctioning. I waited until Doris said it was gone, and I took two control pictures. Those pictures were perfectly normal. The only difference was that in the first ones she said it was there. In the second ones she said it was gone. [See Photo 17.] A few moments later, we felt a cold breeze coming through the door, accompanied by a horrible stench, a stench so foul some people were vomiting.

"We fired the camera in the direction that the breeze was flowing toward us, and again the picture was bleached out completely, except at the bottom of the door, where there appeared a little round ball of light. [See Photo 18.] A few minutes later, she screamed out, 'It's right in front of my face!' We fired the camera, and the face was completely obliterated, but in the picture you could see her dress and the curtains behind her. [See Photo 19.] Again, I wanted a control picture. I waited until she said it was gone and I took a final picture. It was a perfectly normal picture."

For the next ten weeks, the UCLA team returned to the house many times, bringing new eyewitnesses with them each time. Initially, most of Gaynor's colleagues were skeptical. They accused him of hallucinating. When Gaynor had accumulated an impressive list of witnesses, they suggested that the Entity was a case of mass hallucination. Gaynor needed more concrete proof. He needed evidence that this was no normal haunting. His proof came late one night. The Entity put on what can only be described as a light show in front of more than twenty onlookers. Again, Gaynor recalls the fantastic events of that night:

"We started seeing balls of light lighting up the walls. Everybody in the room could see it. The lights got bigger and bigger and brighter and brighter. At some point I started talking to it and I said, 'If you're really here, come off the wall,' because what I was concerned about was that somebody in the room was faking it, that they were projecting the light onto the wall. When I asked that question, the light lifted off the wall, floated into the middle of the room, and started spinning and twisting and expanding in different directions simultaneously. It had full parallax. We could see it from all sides. I had nine professional photographers set up in the room and they were shooting it from all sides."

Dick Thomson was one of the photographers who witnessed the stunning light phenomenon. He recalls that the light took on a personality, that it seemed to express a state of anger. "It was as if it was saying 'All right, here I am. This is me,' " Thomson says. Many of the pictures Thomson took that night were disappointing. The light was so bright, nearly every shot was overexposed, although he was shooting with high-speed film in near darkness. One picture, however, did capture some of what the assembled group had witnessed that night. (See Photo 20.)

"What we see in this photo," Gaynor explains, "are reverse arcs of light. The reason this picture is so important is that the arc on the wall, if it really were on the wall, would be bent, because the two walls are perpendicular to each other. The arc is not bent, which means it is floating in space. The significance of that to researchers is, of course, that that means it's dimensional. This is not somebody with a flashlight shining it on a wall. That light is in empty space."

The negative of that photograph was sent to *Popular Photography* for analysis. After several weeks of examination, the magazine's editorial staff concluded that there was nothing known to photography or optics that could explain the phenomenon. "They told us that you cannot photograph reverse arcs of light; they will always be facing the same direction," Gaynor says. "They published our picture in the magazine. They have never before or since published a picture from a haunted house in *Popular Photography*."

Frank De Felitta was another witness to the Entity's light show. His firsthand experiences on that strange and terrible night would later inspire him to write a book about the case: "All the instruments started clicking, so I knew everyone was seeing this at the same time I was." De Felitta remembers that as the light ball moved into the center of the room, people started ducking and shouting, "Oh my God, oh my God!" Doris started screaming as the light moved toward her. She howled, "I don't want to see your light, show us yourself! Damn it, show us yourself!" The beleaguered woman starting cursing and crying, and there, in front of twenty eyewitnesses, the light transformed.

"Lo and behold, at that point it started to appear," De Felitta recounts. "It sort of developed. A kind of arm was articulated, then you could see a neck, and then of all things a bald head. Now this could have been our imagination, but collectively we saw the same thing, every one of us. We saw the same thing." (See Photo 21.)

Gaynor was also present during the materialization. "It all coalesced into a head, and then shoulders began to form. They extended all the way down to the ground, and a whole body formed, and at that point it just went out of existence. It's almost as if somebody pulled the plug. There seemed to be some kind of massive effort to manifest, and then it just ran out of energy. Whether it was an actual independent being we don't know, but it certainly seemed that way."

That night would be the climax of the haunting activity. Once the vague figure of the Entity had appeared, the ghostly phenomena inside Doris's house gradually began to diminish. There would be more violent episodes, and even after Doris and her family fled the house, the Entity continued to appear periodically. But its activity would never again match that of that one terrifying night.

According to Gaynor, this is typical of haunting cases. Constant, high-intensity phenomena over many years has never occurred in any of his paranormal investigations. This is the struggle that parapsychologists face when they try to document phenomena that by its very nature defies documentation. But rare cases like the Entity case (and the Heartland Ghost, described in a later chapter) sustain the hope that one day mainstream science will accept the reality of a fifth, paranormal dimension.

"During our investigations," Gaynor says, "we spend thousands of hours trying to be in the right place at the right time. In the Entity case, for some reason, we were there. We were there at the right time and we experienced the phenomena over and over. Although some of the people there found it frightening, I found it very exciting and exhilarating. That's what I'm in this for. It's an opportunity to witness things that we've been told all our lives cannot be. It's a connection with the unknown."

Psychokinesis, or PK, is the ability to move an object at a distance without any physical force. PK is most often associated with poltergeist activity.

The Entity is not the only one of Kerry Gaynor's investigations to be turned into a feature film. The 1982 movie *Poltergeist* was also based on a real case in Gaynor's files. The term poltergeist was coined in Germany in the early 1900s and translated means "noisy spirit." Modern-day parapsychologists have abandoned the word poltergeist in favor of the term recurrent spontaneous psychokinesis, or RSPK.

Hell's Gate

C arl Lawson talked to himself. He saw things that weren't there. He was plagued by demons that interrupted his sleep. People around Wilder, Kentucky, thought Carl was just plain crazy. But then a lot of them started seeing and hearing things too, and suddenly Carl didn't seem so crazy anymore.

Carl was a loner who worked as the caretaker for Bobby Mackey's Music World, a country-and-western nightclub on the outskirts of town. (See Photo 22.) He lived upstairs and took care of the place. Carl spent a lot of time there alone. It was while he was alone that the trouble started.

"I'd make a double check at the end of the night and make sure everything was turned off. Then I'd come back down hours later, and the bar lights would be on. The front doors would be unlocked, when I knew I'd locked them. The jukebox would be playing 'The Anniversary Waltz' even though I'd unplugged it and the power was turned off," Carl says. "At first, I thought maybe I was working too much."

Then the ghosts arrived. First, there was the dark, angry man Carl would see standing behind the bar. No one else said they could see him. Then the figure of a woman who called herself Johanna appeared. She wanted to talk to Carl, and he would talk back. People around him saw and heard nothing. The spirits were strongest in the basement. There was an old sealed-up well down there that townspeople said had been used for satanic rituals before Bobby Mackey bought the place. The well was supposed to be filled with blood. Around Wilder, it was known as "Hell's Gate."

Carl wasn't a particularly religious man, but he wasn't tempting fate either. He sprinkled holy water on that old well one night to see if it would bring him some relief from the spirits. Instead, the ritual seemed to provoke them. "A big cloud started rising up out of there, a fluid-type thing, and I ran. I will never forget that there was something in that well. I wish that somebody else had been with me, because I know it's hard to believe. But there was something terribly evil in there that can't be destroyed."

Of all the spirits that haunt Music World, Johanna is the most persistent. Carl would know she was there because he would smell her rose perfume. None of the customers or the staff wore that kind of perfume, and yet it would hang in the air for hours. Carl came to fear that scent as a premonition of death—and he had good reason.

"I was sitting at the bar one night," Carl remembers, "and I started to pick up that scent, and I felt something bad was getting ready to happen—I didn't quite know what. There was a woman on the dance floor celebrating her birthday, and just all of a sudden she had a heart attack and died right there on the dance floor."

Bobby Mackey wasn't happy about the rumors that were starting to spread around town. "Carl started telling stories, and I told him to keep quiet about it. I didn't want it getting around, because I had everything I own stuck in this place. I had to make a success of it," Mackey says. He did not believe Music World was haunted. He did not believe that the well in the basement was Hell's Gate, and he certainly didn't want his customers believing it, either. "And then my wife started bringing it up," Mackey recalls, "and I didn't know what to make of it."

Janet Mackey revealed that she was experiencing strange, haunting activity too. She had seen the ghosts, she had felt their evil force, and she had smelled the rose perfume. According to Janet, "Whenever Johanna's near I get a warm sensation, I feel her scent. And each time I smell her cologne all these incidents happen."

The worst of these "incidents" occurred when Janet was five months pregnant. She was in the basement. The scent of roses filled the air, and then Janet felt an unseen force swirl around her. "Something grabbed me around the waist, like it was trying to get my child. It picked me up and threw me back down. I got away from it, and when I got to the top of the stairs there was pressure behind me, pushing me down the steps. I looked back up and a voice was screaming '*Get out! Get out!*' "

Once Janet Mackey admitted that she had seen and felt the ghosts at Music World, other people began to come forward. Roger Heath, who often worked odd jobs at the nightclub, was the first to corroborate one of Carl's bizarre encounters. It was a hot summer morning. Roger was removing old lighting fixtures from the dance floor, and Carl was storing them in the basement. Just before lunch, Carl came back up from the basement, and Roger noticed he had small handprints on the back of his T-shirt.

"I stopped him and I said, 'Who's your girlfriend?' And he just laughed. I said, 'Well, who was down in the basement with you?' He said, 'Nobody.' So I said, 'Well, go look at your back in that mirror, because you have two handprints on your back.' They were small, like a woman's. It looked like someone had been hugging him." Roger remembers Carl's reaction vividly. "He was freaked out after he looked in that mirror, because there was absolutely no one in the club but him and me."

Erin Fey, a hostess at Music World, also admitted that she had made contact with Johanna. "Carl was talking to himself one night, and I asked him who he was talking to," Erin remembers about that night. "He said it was Johanna, and I started making fun of him. He told me not to laugh, because strange things happen when people make fun of her. The next day on the way to the club, I smelled rose perfume, and then I wrecked my car."

Douglas Hensley, a writer from nearby Newport, Kentucky,

heard about the haunting at Bobby Mackey's Music World and decided to investigate. He started hanging out at the bar, casually striking up conversations with some of the regulars. He became a familiar fixture at the club, and people started to trust him. Then some of the regulars and staff started to tell him that Carl, Janet, and Erin weren't the only ones who had seen the spirits and felt the sensations of evil.

"When I first talked to these people, almost every one of them refused to be interviewed. They simply lied to me. They denied anything happened," says Doug Hensley. "But after I interviewed Janet Mackey, a couple of people opened up, and then it snowballed. I interviewed twenty-seven people, all of whom hadn't shared their stories with each other until I talked to them, yet they all encountered the same ghosts. They've been attacked by unseen entities. They've heard the jukebox come on and play 'The Anniversary Waltz.' "

Many of the witnesses reported seeing one ghost that neither Carl nor Janet had seen. They claimed to have seen the spectral image of a headless woman moving through the nightclub. Independent of each other, several people told Doug Hensley strikingly similar details about her turn-of-the-century clothing. Hensley was at a loss to explain what was going on at Music World. Was it mass hallucination? The power of suggestion? He needed to find evidence that the ghosts of Music World were real.

Doug Hensley believes he found that proof in the public library. Through old newspaper clippings and historical records, Hensley pieced together the history of the site where Bobby Mackey's Music World now stands. He found strange parallels between the real-life events of the past and the ghostly events of the present.

In the early 1800s, the earliest building that had been on the site was a slaughterhouse. The well in the basement of Music World was the only remnant of the original building. The well was a drain that soaked up the blood of the animals killed there. Even after the slaughterhouse was torn down, the well remained and became a gathering place for satanic worship at the end of the last century.

In 1896, the headless body of a young woman named Pearl Bryan was found near the well. Pearl was five months pregnant; there were indications that she had been murdered after her boyfriend, Scott Jackson, botched his attempt to perform an abortion on poor Pearl. "Two men, Alonzo Walling and Scott Jackson, were convicted and given death," Hensley discovered. "They stood on the gallows, and the judge offered them a life sentence if they would tell where Pearl's head was. Both men refused, and rumors abounded here for years that her head was given as a sacrifice to the Devil and that they would rather die than suffer Satan's wrath." Gruesome depictions of Pearl Bryan's beheading in newspaper accounts of the day (see Photo 23) match the ghostly images of the headless woman witnessed at Music World.

Pearl Bryan's was the murder of the decade, and the property gained so much unwanted notoriety that it remained empty for many years. In the 1920s, a new building went up. It was during Prohibition, and the building became a successful gambling casino and speakeasy. The owner, Buck Brady, got very rich very fast. But when the Chicago gangland syndicate caught wind of his profitable establishment, they wanted it for themselves. Buck Brady got an ultimatum: sell it or die. Brady sold, but swore that he'd be back. The apparition of the man behind the bar that Carl, Janet, and so many others have seen is the spitting image of Buck Brady.

Doug Hensley was unearthing events in the historical past that no one in the present knew about. Pearl Bryan and Buck Brady may have been famous in their day, but none of the witnesses to the ghostly activity knew these people from the distant past.

After Buck Brady left, the casino changed hands many times, and the place seemed to be cursed. In the 1930s, it became a nightclub, first called the Primrose, and then the Latin Quarter. The owner had a daughter who fell in love with one of the singers at the club and became pregnant. The owner was infuriated and had the man killed. His daughter was so distraught that she poisoned first her father and then herself. They were both found dead in the basement. The daughter's name was Johanna. She was five months pregnant at the time of her death.

Janet Mackey was five months pregnant when she felt an evil force push her down the stairs. It was an eerie coincidence. And there was another, stranger link between the past and the present. Johanna's lover was named Robert Randall. Bobby Mackey's full name is Robert Randall Mackey. "Johanna would do anything to get to me in order to get to him," Janet believes. "I feel that she is still lingering here and that she will stay here until her lover comes back to her."

Bobby Mackey remains unconvinced that his nightclub is filled with the unclaimed spirits of the dead. He has never seen one and says he won't believe it until he sees it. And yet he admits that the last place he wants to be is in his own club at night alone. "I won't come here by myself unless I have to. It's not because of any ghost, and I'm not a scaredy-cat, but it just feels weird, and I don't stay in here any longer than I have to."

The death of Pearl Bryan was chronicled in local newspapers, but most people learned of her gruesome murder through song. Here is one of several Pearl Bryan ballads from the Department of Library Special Collections, Folklife Archives, of Western Kentucky University in Bowling Green, Kentucky:

> Deep, deep in yonder valley
> Where the flowers are sweet in bloom
> There sleeps my own Pearl Bryan
> 'Neath the cold and silent tomb.

She died not brokenhearted
Nor sickness caused her death
It was from instant parting
Of a home she loved so well.

One night the moon shone brightly
The stars were shining too
And to Pearl's cottage window
Her jealous lover drew.

Come, Pearl, let's take a ramble
Through the meadows sweet and gay
Where no one can disturb us
We'll name our wedding day.

Deep, deep in yonder valley
He lead his sweetheart dear
It was for thine only
That we should ramble here.

In ramblin' she grew weary
Let's retrace our footsteps home
Retrace your footsteps, never
These woods no more you'll roam.

For in these woods I have you
From me you can not fly
No human 'round can see us
So you, Pearl Bryan, must die.

What have I done, Scott Jackson,
That you should take my life?
You know I've always loved you
And would have been your wife.

Down on her knees before him
She pleaded for her life
But deep into her bosom
He plunged the fatal knife.

The birds sang in the morning
But fatal were their tune
They found Pearl Bryan sleeping
'Neath the cold and silent tomb.

The Blue Lady of Moss Beach

"One night, very late, I was doing the payroll, and my checkbook levitated off the desk and sailed around my office. I just said, 'Put it back.' She put it back and that was that. She only plays tricks. She's never harmed anyone."

"She" is the Blue Lady, a mischievous spirit who haunts the Moss Beach Distillery, a popular restaurant on the northern California coast just south of San Francisco. Dave Andrews and his wife, Pat, who witnessed the levitation of her checkbook, owned the Distillery for eighteen years. For most of that time, they lived below the restaurant. From their cliff-side apartment, they had a spectacular view of tiny Moss Beach and the secluded cove that protects the beach from the Pacific Ocean.

When the Andrews bought the Moss Beach Distillery in 1973, the previous owner, Mike Murphy, lightheartedly warned them to watch out for the Blue Lady. She had a penchant for pranks in the form of falling coffeepots, flickering lights, and strange noises in the night. "When we bought the place, we didn't believe in the Blue Lady," Dave remembers, "until we experienced her for ourselves."

The experience that changed Dave Andrews's mind occurred several months after he and Pat moved into the restaurant apartment. After closing time one night, Dave went down into the wine cellar to put away a few bottles of wine. The room was neat and well organized. To prevent anyone from accidentally being locked in the chilly room, the wine cellar could only be locked from the inside.

The next day, Dave returned to the cellar to stock the bar for the night. He could not open the door. He pushed against it with his shoulder, and, while he could tell that the door was not locked, something was keeping him from getting inside. After pushing against the door for several minutes, Dave went for help. No one else could budge the door. Dave went around to the tiny window in the side of the cellar to see what was wrong.

When he looked through the window he was amazed to see what was blocking the door. Every single bottle of wine had come off the shelves and was piled up against the door, unbroken. There had been no earthquake that night. If anyone had gotten into the cellar, the bottles would have blocked their exit, and the window was too small to crawl through.

Over the years, the Andrews experienced haunting phenomena on a regular basis. The sound of high heels clicking across the dining room floor was commonly heard just before dawn. Candles would blow out and then mysteriously relight hours later. When a computer was installed to electronically track drink orders, orders for wine no one had typed in would appear on the screen. Unlike other hauntings, the Blue Lady was not malicious or vindictive. She just wanted a little attention. The Andrews came to think of her as one of the family.

"When we had our annual Thanksgiving dinner at the restaurant for the family and any employees that didn't have a place to go, we always set a place for the Blue Lady, because we never knew whether she was really there or not," Pat says. "At one of those dinners, a new waitress brought her four-year-old son. When the adults retired to the bar area for after-dinner drinks, her boy came running in from the dining room.

"Mommy," he said, "there's a woman in the dining room." When Pat Andrews went to investigate, there was no one there. She asked the boy what the woman looked like. He said that she was very pretty and that she was dressed in blue.

Children seem to be particularly sensitive to the presence of the Blue Lady. Several times, neighborhood kids playing near the beach-side cliffs have come home and complained to their parents that a woman dressed in blue was shooing them away, saying it was too dangerous to play near the cliffs.

Perhaps the strangest sighting of the Blue Lady occurred after a late-night seance in the restaurant. Among the party were two off-duty sheriff's deputies from San Mateo County. The two men came to the seance on a lark, unconvinced that the Blue Lady was anything but a legend.

Driving home from the Distillery after the seance, the two sheriff's deputies took Highway 92, a notoriously dangerous road through a twisting canyon. Coming out of a hairpin turn, the driver lost control and the car flipped over. Paramedics who arrived on the scene were relieved to find that neither of the men was seriously injured.

The next day, one of the deputies got a call from the tow-truck driver who had picked up the car. According to Pat Andrews, "The driver asked, 'How is the lady that was in the accident?' The sheriff's deputy said, 'There wasn't any lady in the accident.' The tow-truck driver said, 'Yes, there was. There was a lady standing there in a blue dress.' The two deputies never came back to the Distillery. They refused to come in the door."

Sightings of the Blue Lady are extremely rare. There have been less than half a dozen reports of an actual apparition. However, there are hundreds of reports by many different eyewitnesses of the mischief that the Blue Lady has left behind.

Jennifer Towner has been a waitress at the Moss Beach Distillery since 1988. She believes that the Blue Lady is most active when skeptics challenge her existence. It's almost as if she has something to prove. "One of our waitresses was telling stories about the Blue Lady to a new hostess. She was kind of laughing and it was obvious she took it all with a grain of salt," Jennifer recalls. "And right then a chair by the hostess station just flipped over all by itself. No one was standing near it, but we all saw it flip over."

Like the Andrews, Jennifer thinks of the Blue Lady as a family friend. "The Blue Lady is quite comfortable with us, and we're comfortable with her. We'll protect her as much as we can. She just pulls a lot of pranks. The funniest one I remember is that a waitress who was in the kitchen toward the end of the evening got smacked in the rear end with a spatula, but there was nobody else in the kitchen."

Who is the Blue Lady and why does she haunt the Moss Beach Distillery? California historian June Morrall believes the ghost may have been a regular customer back in the 1920s, when Moss Beach was a secret drop-off point for illegal whiskey. The Distillery was a posh speakeasy. "Moss Beach was a notorious rum-running area. It was considered the biggest supplier of booze on the West Coast. Politicians and silent film stars came down here because they didn't want to be seen in San Francisco."

According to customers who frequented the Distillery during the Prohibition years, there was one mysterious woman who came every night to hear the handsome young piano player. The woman always wore blue chiffon. "Apparently they were having an affair," says June Morrall. "The only problem was that she was married, and one night her husband came to the restaurant. He was very jealous. There was a scuffle and a fight broke out."

During the fight, the mysterious woman, her husband, and the piano player ended up on the beach. The woman was stabbed to death. The two men fled and were never seen again. Police records confirm that there was a stabbing on Moss Beach, but the woman who was murdered has never been identified.

Most people who have experienced the haunting at the Distillery believe that the unidentified woman who was stabbed to death on Moss Beach and the Blue Lady are one and the same. Several people have reported hearing piano music inside the restaurant, even though there is no piano at the Distillery. Much of the paranormal activity in the dining room seems to be concentrated around table eight, the table where the real lady in blue supposedly sat.

The Andrews sold the Moss Beach Distillery in 1991. Before

they left, they warned the new owner about the Blue Lady, just as Mike Murphy had warned them nearly two decades before. When John Barbour took over, he too was openly skeptical about the Blue Lady. He certainly didn't mind printing the legend on the back of his menus, but he did not see the phenomena as anything more than a good yarn that would amuse his customers.

But, as she had shown so many times before, the Blue Lady was up to the challenge. To her, John Barbour was just another doubting Thomas she could win over with a few pranks. "I would characterize myself as a skeptic," John says, "but I had one experience myself that is totally unexplainable, and I'm convinced it was the Blue Lady."

When John took over, he installed a new heating and air-conditioning system in the Distillery. The thermostats were all electronically controlled and could be programmed to go on and off at specific times. To prevent tampering, each thermostat was inside a locked box. To John, it was an energy-saving improvement. To the Blue Lady, it was a chance to show her stuff.

"I spent the better part of a day programming those thermostats," John remembers, "so they would go on at precisely the right time. The very next day, I came into the restaurant at ten o'clock in the morning and both the air-conditioning system and the furnace were on. I thought maybe I had made a mistake, but when I unlocked the thermostat boxes, every single setting in every thermostat had been changed." John was the only person who had a key and knew how to program the boxes. He called the manufacturer to get some answers.

"I said, 'What possibly could cause this to happen?' And he asked me a series of questions: 'Did you lock it? Did you do this, that, and the next thing?' And I said, 'Yes, yes, yes.' And he said, 'Then that's impossible. It couldn't be changed.' He said that somebody had to change those thermostats, but there wasn't anybody to do it but me. Electronically it was impossible."

Since John's encounter with the Blue Lady, he has become less skeptical and more open to the possibility that he shares his restaurant with the spirit of an unidentified young woman who lost her life on Moss Beach and remains here in death. "I just have to say there's something extraordinary going on here. I think there is a Blue Lady, I really do. I think she likes to play tricks and she likes to get attention."

The Blue Lady is not the only apparition who has reportedly haunted the Moss Beach area. In the late 1960s, a car accident on Highway 92 claimed the lives of a mother and her two sons. The body of one of the boys was not recovered. For nearly ten years after the accident, people traveling on Highway 92 reported seeing the ghost of a boy standing on the road near where the accident occurred. During a drought in the 1970s, the bones of the long-dead boy were finally found in a nearby creek bed. Since the discovery of the bones, there have been no more sightings of the ghost boy on Highway 92.

The Ghosts
of Gettysburg

A tourist stands on Little Round Top and surveys the historic battlefield at Gettysburg. She soaks up the heady atmosphere and feels the sense of history all around her. Down below in the Triangular Field, soldiers are advancing. It could be a Civil War reenactment, part of the afternoon's entertainment, but it is not. It is the Phantom Regiment of Gettysburg.

The soldiers march shoulder to shoulder across the Triangular Field and up into Devil's Den, rifles poised. Their bayonets are fixed and ready. The faces of these soldiers reflect the bloodiest three days in the history of American warfare. They are the faces of boys, some as young as fourteen, who are marching to their death for a cause more precious to them than life itself. They are seen in the present, but the soldiers of the Phantom Regiment have been dead for more than 130 years.

Mark Nesbitt is an author and Civil War historian who collects eyewitness accounts of the Phantom Regiment and many other ghosts who haunt Gettysburg, Pennsylvania. It was while he was a park ranger at the historic battlefield in the 1970s that Nesbitt first began hearing stories about strange apparitions, the haunting sounds of cannon fire, and streams of dense fog spiraling into the ground. He believes that these visions are not hallucinations;

they are manifestations of psychic energy trapped here since the Civil War.

"A lot of people don't understand how horrific, how bloody it was on the battlefield throughout those three days," explains Mark Nesbitt. "You're frightened to death. Because they recruited parochially, you're marching alongside your brother or your cousin or certainly somebody you went to school with most of your life. If there's infantry fire, there are lots of bodies all around. If there's artillery fire, there would be pieces of bodies." Survivors of Pickett's Charge, a battle within the battle, reported that when artillery canisters were fired at advancing Confederate soldiers, all they could see was smoke and pieces of men flying above the smoke.

"There was a lot of physical energy expended on these battlefields. They fought with such a savagery it's hard to believe that the two sections of the country ever healed," says Nesbitt. "The individuals were fighting for something very important. They were young men whose lives were cut short suddenly and horribly. Perhaps that's why a great deal of psychic energy remains in Gettysburg."

Debbie and Tim Sheads believe that they have a photograph that captures this psychic energy on film. The picture was taken almost by accident. The Sheads were participating in a Civil War reenactment weekend and believe that their period costumes may have fooled more than just the tourists. They may have inspired the appearance of a ghost.

"I didn't believe in ghosts until one showed up in our pictures. It's the first time I actually believed that there is something out there," Debbie says. "I looked at the picture, and I was shocked. 'Tim,' I said, 'I think we captured a ghost.' " (See Photo 24.) The photograph was taken at Devil's Den, which, along with Little Round Top and the Triangular Field, are considered the most active areas of the battlefield.

Most of the soldiers who fought and died there were buried where they fell, making the battlefield at Gettysburg the largest unmarked graveyard in America. The small town of Gettysburg, with a population of less than two thousand, was overwhelmed by the dead and dying. Every house and every building in Gettysburg was overflowing with wounded, suffering men and boys. It is not surprising that many of the ghosts of Gettysburg haunt not only the battlefield, but also the town itself.

Pennsylvania Hall, on the campus of Gettysburg College, was used as a hospital during the Civil War. Today, it is a hub of paranormal activity. Many students have reported seeing soldiers standing sentry on the building's cupola. But it was two administrators who reported having the most frightening ghost sighting in Pennsylvania Hall.

"The two administrators got in the elevator and punched the button for the first floor," recounts sociology professor Charles Emmons. He has also collected many stories about ghost sightings in Gettysburg. "The elevator didn't work properly, so they went to the basement instead. When the doors opened, it was not the basement, but a scene out of time and reason. It was the hospital from the time of the battle. They punched frantically at the buttons to get them out of this hell. One of the surgeons was beckoning to them. They kept punching the buttons and eventually got up out of there."

The two witnesses filed a report about their experience with the campus security officer who was on duty at the time. When Charles Emmons went to interview the administrators, he was unsuccessful. "One woman could not be located. The other refused to be interviewed. She was obviously traumatized by it," says Emmons. "We know it happened because of the security report, but she just doesn't want to talk about it."

Professor Emmons has had firsthand experience with the ghosts of Gettysburg—and more forthcoming witnesses—in some of the area's historic homes and inns. In one home, three witnesses reported hearing a tremendous crash coming from an empty dining room.

Emmons interviewed the witnesses. "They thought somebody had tipped over the china cabinets. They thought there was an intruder. They ran outside and got somebody next door to come over with a baseball bat. When they went in the dining room, there was nothing disturbed. But the strangest thing was that when they walked through the room they could hear the sound of broken glass under their feet, even though it was not there."

The Farnsworth House is a Gettysburg bed-and-breakfast built in 1810. During the Civil War, the Farnsworth House became an ad hoc infantry position for Confederate soldiers. From the attic window, infantrymen fired on Union soldiers billeted in the hotel across the street. They whiled away the hours telling stories, and one soldier played the mouth harp. Many guests have heard the ghostly strains of his music and have reported seeing the figure of a tall, willowy young man stealing down otherwise empty corridors.

Patti O'Day works at the Farnsworth House, often in period costume. Like Debbie Sheads, she believes that her Civil War outfits sometimes fool the ghosts. "Late one January, I was coming down the corridor to the landing above the staircase," Patti remembers. "I was wearing my Civil War dress, and for some reason, I lost my footing. As I started to fall forward, I saw the vision of a woman reaching out for me, and then all of a sudden I was upright again. She actually saved me from tumbling down the stairs."

Among the ghosts that are believed to haunt the Farnsworth House is Mia, a Civil War–era midwife. She haunts the Sweeney Room, one of the antique-filled bedrooms at the inn. It was in this bedroom that Mia helped deliver the stillborn baby of the inn's former owner. It was a tragic moment in time that many people have seen replayed in the present.

"There was a young girl visiting with her mother," Patti recalls. "She was very attracted to the Sweeney Room. There was a Victorian comb case on the dresser, and I let her play with the perfume bottles and brush her hair. Her mother wanted to view another room, so we left the child there." Patti did not tell the child about the room's tragic past. She did not want to frighten her young visitor.

"After about ten minutes, we returned to check on her. I entered the room, and she wasn't there. I went around the bed and she was actually crouched in the corner behind a velvet chair. I went over to her and there was no response. Her eyes were closed. Of course her mother came around the bed and was very alarmed. The child looked up at her and said, 'Mommy, the baby is dead.' It was very sad."

Patti has also seen ghosts on the battlefield. "I was on the field, and I had a stabbing pain in my back. I turned around and there was no one there. I sat down on the ground and closed my eyes and saw what I thought was a soldier from the Irish Brigade being hit in the back. He spoke my name. He said, *'Patti, please tell my wife that I love her.'* " This kind of experience is very common among people who have felt the presence of ghosts at Gettysburg.

While many mainstream scientists dismiss these visions as hallucinations or wishful thinking, Professor Emmons believes differently. "Science as we know it has an awful time dealing with this. We try to be scientific, measuring electromagnetics around sites and taking infrared pictures, but there are other ways of knowing that something is happening here."

Paranormal investigator Dale Kaczmarek struggles to find incontrovertible scientific evidence of the ghosts of Gettysburg. He uses a high-tech arsenal of devices that measure atmospheric changes which might help explain the phenomenon scientifically. He uses a Goss meter, a negative ion detector, a Geiger counter, night vision lenses, and other highly sensitive electronic equipment. While he agrees with Professor Emmons that there may be other ways of knowing ghosts, he also believes that haunting phenomena will never be accepted by the mainstream until it can be measured.

A *Sightings* investigative team accompanied Kaczmarek to Gettysburg for an all-night surveillance. Kaczmarek spent several hours in the Triangular Field, where so many ghosts had been reported. Some of the bloodiest battles of the war took place in this field. "I got a very high reading of static discharge there. There's no reason why static should build up out in the open right there. There's nothing to attract static electricity or negative ions," Kaczmarek reported.

Meter peaks and anomalous readings were also noted in the Devil's Den and on Little Round Top. With subsequent trips to the site, Kaczmarek will be able to chart electromagnetic changes at the Gettysburg battlefield and perhaps correlate those to reported sightings.

Kaczmarek says, "I think it's very interesting out there, especially at the Triangular Field. We got a lot of interesting readings with the negative ion detector. I believe the area is infested by ghosts. It's a location that may lead to scientific proof of the existence and possibility of ghosts."

Professor Emmons believes that there may never be enough proof to satisfy the skeptics among his academic colleagues. He also believes that the human heart is the best way to measure the existence of the ghosts of Gettysburg. "If you have the experience of a ghost, or any kind of supernatural experience, it does something to you. There's a sense of awe that tells you something is happening. I don't know how you study that scientifically. We may have to go beyond science to understand this phenomenon."

Gettysburg is only one of over a thousand battlefields that were used during the Civil War. Most of these sites do not survive as historic monuments. They've been plowed up, paved over, and built upon. But beneath the steel and concrete of the twentieth century, many people believe that the echoes of the past remain. If you listen closely, you may hear them, too.

More than 620,000 Americans died during the Civil War, more than in the Spanish-American War, World War I, World War II, the Korean War, and the first three years of the Vietnam War combined. And no single battle exacted a greater human toll than the Battle of Gettysburg. Between July 1 and July 3, 1863, there were 52,000 casualties.

According to Dale Kaczmarek, President of the Ghost Research Society, the five most haunted Civil War battlefields are:
1. Gettysburg, PA
2. Chickamauga, GA
3. Stones River, TN
4. Shiloh, TN
5. Franklin, TN

At Stones River National Battlefield in Murfreesboro, Tennessee, park rangers and visitors report seeing one soldier in particular who was shot while trying to surrender during a bloody battle in January 1863. The soldier is most often seen crouching behind bushes, then moving out into the open and falling to the ground, where he disappears.

Haunting
in the Heartland

I he brutal attacks, the bloody scratches, and the abject terror didn't come until much later.

At first, there was simply a weird, indefinable feeling of dread when they stood at the top of the stairs. The dog started barking and whining and refused to go into the baby's nursery. Lights flickered off and on. The stereo came on in the middle of the night. There were inexplicable cold spots and unpredictable jolts of static electricity.

When a viewer wrote to the *Sightings* offices about a haunted house in the Midwest, the case seemed intriguing but not unusual; however, by year's end, this haunting would become the subject of an unprecedented *Sightings* investigation. Paranormal investigators from across the United States, *Sightings* team members, and hours of raw, unedited videotape would prove that this was a historic haunting.

The house is somewhere in America's heartland. The family—Tony, Deborah, and their young son, Taylor—don't want to reveal their exact location or their last names. For them, the past three years have been a frustrating, terrifying odyssey. They have requested anonymity because of threats they have received and the fear of further persecution. For them, it is time to heal.

Deborah and Tony first moved into their 128-year-old house in early 1993. They were expecting their first child and began converting one small second-floor bedroom into a nursery. The first signs of something out of the ordinary were subtle. "The second week we were in the house, our dog would act real funny around the nursery," Tony recalls. "She was scared to death to go in the nursery. She'd growl and bare her teeth. We thought that was funny because she's such a mild-mannered dog, but we figured that maybe there was something like a cat around that she was sensing."

Deborah didn't suspect any paranormal connection to the dog's behavior either, or to other strange events in the house. Deborah remembers, "We would be sitting watching TV and the TV would turn off, or one lamp would dim real low while everything else stayed the same—and we didn't have any dimmer switches. We would jokingly say, 'Oh, we have a ghost,' but no one really meant it."

That lighthearted attitude changed after Deborah and Tony's son, Taylor, was born. Extraordinary phenomena began to demand serious attention. Deborah recounts the first time she and Tony felt something paranormal was happening to them. "Right after Taylor was born, my sister had come out for a visit to help with the baby. On her last night, we had all gone out to my in-laws' house. When we came back, Tony found all the stuffed animals sitting in the center of the nursery in a circle, all facing out. It wasn't that the cats had run through there or had knocked some off the changing table. Every animal was specifically placed."

Everyone agreed it must be some kind of prank. They put all the toys back where they belonged, including one Teddy bear, who always sat in a tiny toy rocking chair just inside the nursery door. Tony, Deborah, and her sister Karen put Taylor to bed and turned out the light. "When we got to the bottom of the stairs," says Deborah, "Karen turned around and saw the light had come back on in the nursery. We went back upstairs, wondering what was going on, and the one little bear that sat on the chair was lying on the floor in the middle of the room."

The poltergeist activity continued, and the focus seemed to be the nursery. The baby monitor would turn on and off, seemingly at will. Pictures hanging on the wall would be turned upside-down. A windup musical mobile over the crib would play music for several minutes, even though no one had wound the music box. These things would happen just before or just after Tony or Deborah was in the room.

It was easy to dismiss the activity as imagination, forgetfulness, or a prank, until a toy flew across the room in full view of three witnesses. "When it moved right in front of us, it spooked us real bad," says Tony. "We tried to come up with a logical explanation for everything that was happening, and we couldn't. We decided to head to my mom and dad's for the night, just to calm down."

It was while Tony was putting Taylor into his car seat that the first physical attack occurred. "While I was leaning over the car seat, I felt just like a bee had stung me on the back. Deborah said, 'What happened?' and I said, 'Well, a bug must have bit me.' When we got to my parents' house, Deborah lifted my shirt and said, 'Oh my God.'" Tony had four bleeding scratches on his back. Each scratch was more than six inches long.

Tony's parents did not believe the scratches had any connection to the strange occurrences in the house. They encouraged Tony and his family to return to the house and stop worrying about what was probably just a string of eerie coincidences. Tony, Deborah, and Taylor returned to their turn-of-the-century home. It was a decision that would literally haunt them forever.

The supernatural activity intensified. There were a number of unexplained, spontaneous fires inside the home—almost always a toy or stuffed animal that just burst into flames. When a wooden rocking horse was found burning in the middle of the living room, Tony quickly doused the flames. When he tried to test the flammability of the toy, he could not set it on fire, even with a blowtorch. The same was true of a stuffed animal. After the toy's ears burned, Deborah tried to relight it with a lighter. The flame-retardant material would not catch on fire.

Tony suffered more attacks. He was scratched and bitten by an unseen force. The force, whatever it was, seemed to be playful with Deborah and Taylor, but vengeful toward Tony. He recalls one terrifying night, when the ghost began to take a human form. "I was in bed, and it felt just as if somebody was leaning over me with their hands on the mattress. I tried to yell for my wife, but I was so scared nothing came out. Then, I saw a hand come toward my face. It looked like a hand with black lace, like it had a black lace glove on it. It was two inches away from my face and I heard a voice say, *'I'm going to . . . ,'* and that's all I could make out."

A few weeks later, Tony believes he saw the figure of the ghost who was haunting his family. "I walked over to the kitchen cabinet, got out a glass, poured some orange juice, and started to take a drink. As I turned around there was a little girl standing not more than three feet away from me, like she was curious about me, too. I can't explain the feeling I got. I dropped my glass and it shattered, and then as quick as she was there, she was gone."

Tony sketched the little girl he had seen. (See Photo 25.) He asked psychic Barbara Connor, a friend of the family, to see if she could draw any information about the child from his sketch or from the energy in the house. It was Barbara who first gave a name to the haunting agent in the house. Her name was Sallie.

Tony and Deborah tried to photograph Sallie, and several pictures contained unexplained forms. Right after Tony was scratched at the bottom of the staircase one evening, a picture of the staircase revealed an amorphous shape floating in midair. (See Photo 26.) At Christmastime, streaks of light marred a photo of Deborah and Taylor. Tony snapped the picture while Deborah was unwrapping a baby doll she had bought to try and appease Sallie. (See Photo 27.) The pictures were taken with different cameras during different times of day over a six-month period.

It was Barbara Connor who wrote to *Sightings*, enclosing several of the strange photographs and asking for help for the family. The photos were unlike any others *Sightings* researchers had ever examined. In one photo, a crayon appeared to be floating unimpeded above a tablet. (See Photo 28.) In another, menacing blocks of shadow covered Taylor's crib. (See Photo 29.) *Sightings* agreed to conduct an investigation.

Before traveling to the secret Midwest location, *Sightings* asked trick photography expert and photographic analyst Edson Williams to examine the photographs for signs of inadvertent tampering or outright fraud. *Sightings* researchers were skeptical; the photos were just too good to be true.

"Photographic evidence is something I always question, because my job is to create illusions photographically. But the pictures that I was shown by *Sightings* are very difficult to explain. One photo that really caught my attention was the Christmas photo. [See Photo 27.] The highlights that run through the image are localized—they're not throughout the image. They're in very small regions, and they're running at different angles. I initially tried to re-create this simply with a few quick tricks. Unfortunately, they did not work for me. It would be a very difficult shot to re-create. Another photo I found interesting was one that had a blue ghosting image around it. [See Photo 30.] Initially, I thought it was possibly a blue plastic gel that was wiggled in front of the camera, but the density differences were too varied."

Sightings producers spoke with the family and offered to conduct an in-depth investigation. They agreed reluctantly. They did not want media attention, but they did want help in understanding and neutralizing the phenomena. A *Sightings* investigative team led by director Greg Cooke traveled to the heartland of America to meet Tony, Deborah, Taylor . . . and Sallie.

The first step in the investigation was to videotape interviews with the family and other eyewitnesses. It was during this first interview session that the entity made its presence known. Deborah was being interviewed in the kitchen, while Tony was sitting in the adjacent living room with Taylor on his lap. Suddenly, Tony cried out "She's here right now."

The crew turned to see that Tony had four bleeding scratches on his arm. He explained that he had felt a frigid aura shoot through his arm and then he started to bleed. It all happened in an instant. Greg Cooke felt the frigid air, too, and recorded his impressions. "I can feel it," Greg said, his voice quavering. "We're interviewing. It's hot. We've turned off the air conditioner for sound purposes, but it is cold right here in this part of the room."

Deborah explained that this was the common pattern. A cold breeze, a cry for help, and then the attack. "This is the same thing that occurs when she's scratched his face or his forehead or down his back. She does this when she is upset," Deborah told the *Sightings* team.

Greg asked Tony to describe on camera what had happened. Tony seemed to be in pain. He struggled to tell the story. "As you guys were interviewing my wife, I was sitting in the rocking chair with my son and we were tilted a little forward so we could watch the interview through the doorway. This cold just shot through my arm. It's done it before, so I knew the feeling. I can't explain the cold; it freezes your bones. I looked at my arm, and I had four scratches that were bleeding."

Then Tony stopped speaking. He lost his breath. He started to shake. Then he said, "She scares the living daylights out of me. To be honest with you, she's here with me right now. I'm feeling something really cold shoot around my stomach." With that, Tony lifted up his shirt. There, in front of the entire *Sightings* crew, bleeding welts began to form. They grew bigger and bigger, the blood oozed faster and faster. "Oh my God! Look! Look!" Greg Cooke shouted. "It's forming right there!"

No one else was harmed, but everyone felt the cold air and pockets of static electricity. "It was a sensation like the air-conditioning in your automobile," Greg explained. "You feel swirling real fresh air blowing, but if you move your hand just an inch away it's gone." Camera operator Phil Lapkin felt electrical energy swirling around him. *Sightings* microphones picked up a snapping sound along the floor and around his legs, as Lapkin described the feeling as "weird" and "a mild electrical shock."

Paranormal investigator Howard Heim is an expert in the physical manifestation of haunting cases. The day after our initial interview with the family and the stunning paranormal attack, Heim brought in instruments to measure temperature fluctuations, static electricity, electromagnetism, radon, and other environmental factors. When people inside the house claimed to feel cold air, Heim's thermometers registered significant dips in room temperature in just those localized areas.

In the nursery that had been the source of so much haunting activity, field readings of electromagnetism taken with a magnetometer and a Goss meter were normal, until Deborah felt a swirl of frigid air that she felt signaled Sallie's arrival. "Oh, man, she's right here," Deborah said, and the magnetometer needle jumped.

In the living room, Heim examined the stomach scratches Tony had suffered the day before. *Sightings* videotaped the examination. While Heim held a magnifying glass to Tony's stomach, a new scratch began to form right before his eyes and the unerring lens of the camera. The camera remained trained on Tony's torso for nine minutes, the entire duration of the bizarre event. What first appeared as a small scratch grew into a long, thick, bleeding welt. The other scratches that had appeared the day before also welted and bled. (See Photo 31.)

Howard Heim recounts the most significant moment in his career: "It just simply appeared. He lifted his shirt, I put the magnifying glass to his stomach, and all of a sudden blood started to ooze out. This is the most profound thing I've seen in all of parapsychology."

In the months that followed, *Sightings* returned to the midwestern home many times, bringing additional investigators to the site. Paranormal researcher Al Rauber was particularly interested in examining the items that had been allegedly thrown, touched, and, in some cases, burned by Sallie. He felt the heartland haunting was a case of psychokinesis unwittingly produced by Tony. "Understanding his feelings here, and his intense fear, he's very frightened and uncomfortable in this environment.

That's not to say there isn't a little girl ghost here, because in cases when we do have a poltergeist, they draw off the same energies."

Sightings host Tim White also came to the house. Tim did feel a sense of cold air circulating in small isolated patches but remained unconvinced that this was a supernatural phenomenon. In and of itself, the sensation of cold was intriguing, but not proof of the existence of Sallie. But cold usually signaled something more sinister. Tim White saw Tony's arm begin to bleed. Later in the day mysterious welts formed on Tony's forehead. (See Photo 32.) Tony confided in Tim, "This whole spirit thing scares me. Some of the things she's done—she's lit fires—and I think, well, if she wants to hurt me, why doesn't she just light me on fire? But this is as far as she goes."

Al Rauber recommended removing any encouragement that the family was offering to Sallie. He felt they had to get rid of the toys they kept in Taylor's room to appease Sallie. Relatives recommended they move out completely. But Deborah and Tony wanted to stay, and they explained why to Tim White. "I'm scared, but at the same time, I'm curious," Tony said. "To see things and feel things like this, it does something to your mind. You have to know. Why is this happening to me? Why is this little girl here?"

Sightings asked parapsychologist Kerry Gaynor to look at the field tapes of the heartland ghost investigation. He was particularly intrigued by the tape in which a new scratch appeared as the camera rolled for nine minutes. "The exciting thing for me is that the camera didn't pull away, it was there the whole time," Gaynor says. "That severely reduces the possibility of some kind of hoax. Most other cases we come across are playful, bizarre, weird, and a lot of them have normal, natural explanations. This case is more frightening, and we should be very cautious about studying the phenomena."

Gaynor agreed to attend an all-night surveillance in the house. *Sightings* brought in electronics specialists and over a half-million dollars' worth of monitoring equipment. Remote-controlled cameras were strategically placed throughout the house. Frequency counters and oscilloscopes were set to monitor any electronic interference. A thermal imaging system was brought in to record temperature changes. The house was monitored for twenty-four hours, while Gaynor kept vigil with the family.

The electronic surveillance turned up several unexplained environmental and electrical anomalies. In the area at the top of the stairs, where the dog's barking had been the first clue to this mysterious haunting, a frequency counter suddenly and inexplicably jumped from 399 to 575 megahertz. A video camera picked up large amounts of interference in the living room, even though the cameras were on a closed circuit and could not be picking up interference from the outside. In the nursery, the video signal drifted and then disappeared completely. There had been no break in electrical power or the video cable.

Producer Craig Armstrong was in charge of the surveillance. He himself was the first to capture scientific proof of the frigid air phenomenon. Armstrong felt a pinpoint of cold air swirl around his arm. He directed Thermovision imaging of the area, and indeed the normal orange and red tones that thermal imaging shows for flesh came through the scanner as a cool blue. The technical support for the family's claims was impressive, but it was Kerry Gaynor's eyewitness account of his evening with Tony and Deborah that proved most compelling.

"I spent fourteen straight hours in the house investigating the case. During that time, Tony was attacked eleven separate times. There were eleven separate instances of scratch marks on his body. Some of the scratches were thin and some of them were very thick, welt-like scratches that were really quite frightening. He was sitting within two feet of me, and I had him under my supervision at all times. If he got up and walked away, when he came back I asked him to take his shirt off so that I could examine what marks were there to make sure there was no trickery involved. In the last twenty years, I've never come across anything like this. I think we've got something here that's potentially really dangerous."

EVP, electronic voice phenomena, was also recorded during that extraordinary night. It was not audible, however, until Craig Armstrong and editor Mark Quinn Anderson heard an anomalous rumble during a review of the field tapes later that week. On the tape Tony could be heard telling Sallie, "I'd like you to show them that you're really here." As if in response, a low-frequency moan followed.

Sightings asked forensic audio specialist Ric Wilson to analyze the tape. His company, Digisonics, works routinely with the CIA and the FBI and also analyzes black-box recordings for the FAA. Wilson reported that "We looked for a lot of characteristics that would immediately identify it as a mechanical sound, and those were ruled out. One thing that makes this sound interesting and eliminates a lot of possibilities right off the bat is that above 500 hertz, there's nothing. It's all low-frequency and that's it. We can't in our own bodies make that sound. My best bet is that it's something magnetic. How that magnetism is introduced is anybody's guess."

EVP expert Sara Estep was also given a copy of the suspect tape. Her conclusion was similar to Ric Wilson's. "I've been taping for eighteen years, and I've investigated hundreds of haunted homes, properties, and locations, and I've never heard anything quite like it. It sounds more like an energy sound, perhaps put out by the other side. It's interesting that it came right after Tony asked Sallie to let them know she was there. It is an energy sound produced at his request."

The scientists and researchers supplied important data and opinions about the nature of the haunting, but the family's concern was not how but why. They needed the relief an explanation would provide. *Sightings* invited psychic Peter James to come to the heartland location and attempt communication with Sallie. Peter claims he has had the ability to communicate with the dead since childhood. "The first thing I look for is to visually see if there are any ghosts in the area," Peter explains. "If they're there, they generally make their presence known, and these entities do communicate with me."

Peter James came to the haunted house with no information about what he might find there. He had not seen the videotapes, did not know about Sallie or her psychokinetic hallmarks, and had no knowledge about the scratching and bleeding. He was only told that a family needed help with a haunting.

Peter arrived at the house on a cold, crisp autumn afternoon. He stepped out of his car and stopped. He looked up at the second-floor window. "I got just a glimpse of the face of a little girl in that upper window," he told the *Sightings* team. "I don't know who lives here, but I saw the face of a little girl."

Inside the house, Peter was introduced to Tony and Deborah. Before they could even shake hands, Peter was distracted. From the foyer, he pointed up the stairs and said, "There's a little girl up there right at the top of the stairs. Hello? Hello? Can you speak to me? Sallie? Is your name Sallie?" Deborah and Tony were speechless. Peter had called the entity by name, the same name they had been using for over a year.

Peter followed the vision up the stairs, with Deborah and Tony close behind. At Deborah and Tony's bedroom door, Peter stopped. "I'm getting a lot of resistance right here at the door," Peter said. "Whatever is in this room wants me out." Peter called out to the spirit he sensed inside the bedroom. Suddenly, Tony began to feel the frigid harbinger of an attack. Deborah lifted up his shirt. On his back, fresh scratches spelled out the letters "MC." (See Photo 33.)

Later, after Tony had a chance to recuperate, Peter revealed his psychic impressions of the haunting. "I do feel that over the years at least three people have died in this house. Sallie was one. She tells me that there was something wrong with her lungs, her breathing." In the town's Hall of Records, *Sightings* researcher Amber Benson found the 1905 death record of a child named Sallie.

Peter also sensed other people influencing the haunting. "There was a medical person in this house. I feel a medical person with a strange lifestyle." Again, town records substantiated Peter's psychic impressions. A city directory from 1900 showed that the house was occupied at that time by a doctor, a doctor whose lifestyle eventually lead to his arrest and removal from office as mayor. In 1906, just after the death of Sallie, the doctor moved out of the house. Peter James believes there is a connection. He determined that Sallie was one child the dishonored doctor could not—or would not—save.

During his visit to the Midwest, Peter was drawn to one particular graveyard not far from Tony and Deborah's house. It was there that he had a vision of a little girl dying of pneumonia and the doctor who stood by. As he wandered among the headstones, Peter heard a small voice cry out to him from one particular grave. He felt an overwhelming sense of grief. "Here lies Sallie," Peter cried.

The headstone was so old and weather-worn the lettering had disappeared. Amber Benson checked the cemetery's records and discovered that this grave, Plot I, 4th row West, was the final resting place of Sallie Isabel Hall. Peter James spoke to her softly, and then returned to see Tony and Deborah. Peter was able to help the family understand a little bit more about the haunting in their house.

In 1994, the family moved out. When they did, Tony continued to be scratched but the incidents became increasingly less frequent. A new family moved into the house. Sallie has not appeared to them. Father Edd Anthony, a religious advisor who counseled Deborah and Tony, believes that he knows why the haunting has subsided. "I think what's happened here is that a lost soul or spirit was trying to communicate. When you try to communicate with somebody, and if they're not listening, not paying attention to you, you're going to do all kinds of things to get that person's attention. I think the spirit is doing the same thing. The danger comes in when we refuse to do that."

Life in their small town has been difficult for Tony and Deborah since several people learned about the ongoing ghost investigation in their home. "People are calling my husband 'Demon Boy' and refusing to work on his shift," Deborah says. "The town is terrified. This is something that you don't speak about in this small town. It is something that is not discussed. It's taboo."

But Tony and Deborah have to speak out. If they don't, Sallie might just go looking for attention again.

Dermatographism is a medical condition in which a person can scratch himself and nothing will appear until ten to fifteen minutes later. This condition has been offered as an explanation for the scratching phenomenon in the heartland haunting. However, there has never been a single case of dermatographism in which welting or bleeding has occurred.

Stigmata is spontaneous bleeding of the palm, feet, or head; areas of the body associated with the crucifixion of Jesus Christ. In the heartland haunting, these regions remained unscathed. In addition, the appearance of stigmata is usually accompanied by the reported scent of violets, another factor which did not occur in the heartland case.

One in four Americans believes in ghosts.

Forty-two percent of all Americans believe they have had some form of communication with the dead.

UFOs

The Avebury
Mystery Lights

A group of amateur sky watchers gathers on Milk Hill above the town of Avebury in southwestern England. They sit in camp chairs, armed with notebooks and video cameras. It's a cold and windy night, but the sky is clear. A three-quarter moon barely illuminates the corn and wheat fields below. The group waits and watches, and on this night they are rewarded. Suddenly, seemingly out of nowhere, a bright orange orb appears high above the horizon.

John Holman vividly recalls his first sighting of the phenomenon known as the Avebury Mystery Lights. "On June 22, 1991, we videotaped an extremely large ball of orange light. It was only very short-lived, but for five seconds it was tremendous. It was like looking at something that was half the size of the moon just sitting in the sky, brilliantly glowing orange." (See Photo 34.)

John took his videotape to Britain's Ministry of Defense, and they confirmed that the orange UFO was not a military jet, balloon, or experimental craft. "Various video experts in the U.K. analyzed the tape," John says, "and they've been able to triangulate the size to roughly seventy feet in diameter. Analysis shows that it's pulsating to half its size over about five frames. Now, an object over seventy feet in diameter, pulsating with such a rapid and dramatic change in size, has got to be quite an energetic source. It confirms that something very strange is going on in this area."

Avebury residents have known for a very long time that something strange is going on in the skies over their town. Sightings of anomalous balls of light in this ancient hamlet date back to the seventeenth century. But it was not until the early 1990s that ufologists began to sit up and take notice. The sightings have increased dramatically in both scope and scale, and hours of videotape have been collected and analyzed.

"They looked like orange balls of light. You could see they were mushroom-shaped, revolving, and emitting orange light out from the bottom," explains UFO researcher Tom Blower. His videotapes of several Avebury sightings are among the best examples of the phenomenon. (See Photo 35.)

The Avebury Mystery Lights are not conventional or military aircraft, planets, or radio towers. When aeronautics expert Andy Buckley made his own sighting in 1993, he looked for telltale signs that the lights were man-made. "I was aware of a bright light in the sky that was moving from south to north. The object did not show any conventional aircraft navigational lights or wing taillights. It was spherical, oval-shaped, silvery-white, with a slight orange tinge—and completely soundless. That struck me; there was no sound whatsoever."

To solve the mystery of the Avebury lights, many researchers are looking at another supernatural phenomenon that has settled in Avebury. Since 1990, more than three hundred crop circles have been discovered in the fields surrounding the town. (See Photo 36.) According to paranormal researcher Colin Andrews, "The crop-circle activity in this area has been quite considerable. Of all the major patterns in Great Britain, over ninety percent of them are in the Avebury area."

Crop circles vary greatly in size and shape. Some are amazingly complex, often resembling spider webs or intricate Celtic designs. These have almost all been ruled out as hoaxes. The crop circles that continue to fascinate researchers are the simpler designs, which illustrate complex mathematical and geometric formulas. There are only a handful of crop-circle formations that researchers, called cereologists, can agree may have an extraterrestrial origin. Nearly all of these formations are in the Avebury area.

Colin Andrews began to suspect that the two phenomena—the Avebury Mystery Lights and the crop circles—might be connected, after several reports were made of small white lights hovering over fields where crop circles had recently appeared. To date, Colin says, "We have seventy eyewitnesses who report— and many have it on film—lights that are moving from one crop-circle formation to another. My belief is that there is a link. I resigned my position in the government to study this phenomenon full-time, to prove there is a connection."

Avebury ufologist Reg Presley also believes there is a connection. He has seen and photographed numerous UFO events on the hills ringing Avebury. Watching from Woodbury Hill, Reg saw a mysterious light form hover overhead for nearly three minutes. "I saw a light about the brightness of a star, but it was pulsating and moving up and down," Reg recalls. "It moved slowly across the valley, then dipped toward earth and disappeared. But then it came up again, this time four or five times brighter than a star, and changed to orange in color."

The next morning, Reg Presley examined the site where he had seen the light dip toward the ground. He observed, "There was a pattern formed in the crop exactly where this thing was stationary for three minutes. Now, you can say that's a coincidence, but I'm not the only one who has witnessed this."

Ever since he was a child, Stephen Alexander has been fascinated by aircraft, space, and UFOs. What began as a boyhood flight of fancy has become a full-time obsession. For Stephen, weekends and vacations are an opportunity to visit paranormal hot spots and stake out the night sky with his video camera. Over the years, he has recorded several UFO events throughout Great Britain. On July 26, 1990, he traveled to Avebury to see several new crop-circle formations. Standing on Milk Hill looking down at a wheat field, in broad daylight, Stephen witnessed and video-taped what many ufologists believe is the best evidence ever recorded of an Avebury Mystery Light forming a crop circle.

Stephen describes his historic sighting: "My wife and I were actually about to leave when I saw an intense glint, and I started filming straightaway. It was glinting and flashing, and my wife said, 'What's that?' and I said, 'I don't know.' And then this object curved round and dropped into the crop and disappeared for a while. Then it started maneuvering through the crop. It was a very intense energy source. It stayed static in the field for several minutes, then the object suddenly took off.

"It flew across the field at a fantastic rate of speed and went over the top of the hill. I knew it wasn't a bird or a balloon or something blowing in the wind. It was intense, glinting and flashing, and I knew this was something very important here." (See Photo 37.)

Stephen brought his videotape to Colin Andrews for analysis. "Under enhancement, this is a disc as opposed to a ball. It is a solid object seen moving through the crop and across the field," Colin says. He was particularly interested in another object captured on Stephen's video, a tractor driver who appeared at one point to be less than thirty feet away from the glowing disc. Colin tracked down and interviewed the driver, who was reluctant to admit he had seen a UFO.

"Leon Bessant, the farmer who was driving that tractor, said he had never seen anything like it before. The object was really bright—about the size of a beachball—and he thought it was a UFO. When he got back to his farmyard that evening, he described what he had seen to his mates and they made fun of him," Colin recounts. "They were saying things like, 'Oh, beam me up, Scotty,' and so he just dropped the subject. When I tracked him down, I took Stephen's footage with me, and he was very uplifted, because then he could go back to his friends with the tape and show them he was not crazy. They said, 'Wow, he really did see something that day.' "

But what are Leon Bessant, Stephen Alexander, Colin Andrews, and so many others actually seeing? Are the mysterious lights being generated by an extraterrestrial craft, or could they be the result of some unknown natural phenomenon?

Cereologist John A. Burke believes that the glinting and flashing of the Avebury Mystery Lights indicates a natural source. Burke says, "It's quite possible that those balls of light are a glowing plasma involved in the crop-circle formation, plasma being very simply electrically charged air particles. If you have plasma coming from high in the earth's atmosphere, you should expect that it's likely to be swirling by the time it gets anywhere near the ground, and that's completely consistent with what we find with crop circles."

"But what is so strange," Colin Andrews counters, "is that these lights appear to be moving purposely and that's, for me, what sets it aside from a natural phenomenon to one that may be controlled by an intelligence of some sort. Plasma may be moving in sympathy with them, but these lights have total awareness of their surroundings, and on occasion we have reports of an interactiveness between the UFOs and the people observing them."

Dr. Chet Snow, a psychologist specializing in the paranormal, has studied the Avebury phenomena. Like Colin Andrews, he believes there is an extraterrestrial connection between the lights and the crop circles. Dr. Snow says, "The light phenomenon most often associated with the crop circles has seemed to be small, brilliant white objects between the size of a baseball and a pie plate. They exhibit characteristics that couldn't just be a passing headlight or natural activity in the atmosphere, like St. Elmo's Fire. They come down from the sky at virtually a vertical angle. They can make right turns, go at extremely fast speeds, and wink on and off."

The size of the Avebury Mystery Lights seems to belie the possibility that they are piloted craft of any origin, let alone extraterrestrial. "They're much too small to have, let's say, a person inside," explains Dr. Snow. "But maybe they are what we call a drone or a probe that could have been sent down from a ship flying high above."

This theory is bolstered by an intriguing sighting made in 1992 by UFO researchers Gillian and Stephen Trench. The Trenches taped not only a cluster of large lights but also what appeared to be a smaller, brighter white light shooting out from the cluster. (See Photo 38.) Gillian observed that the impressive lights "came over from the left to the right of the trees, then went out, and then came back again. Then, all of a sudden, they tripled in size and changed color to orange. After that, the white ball came out of the side of it and went off to the left, and we never saw it again." Her husband, Stephen, adds, "Through binoculars, I observed a large clear sphere, orange inside, with thousands of lights spinning and rotating. The speed with which it was darting in and out of the trees was unbelievable."

Dutch photographer Foeke Kootje came closer to one of the small "drones" than anyone else in 1994. He was hang gliding off Milk Hill, filming the English countryside as he flew. Directly in front of him, a ball of white light shot into view then hovered in front of him as if to say, "Go ahead, take my picture." Foeke did. (See Photo 39.) "It was a very strange light," Foeke remembers. "I didn't hear a noise at all. At first there was one light, then three in a triangle shape, depending on the angle you were looking at it. I was just so amazed. I have no explanation for what I was filming."

Apparently, hang-gliding photographers and UFO researchers are not the only ones interested in capturing images of the Avebury Mystery Lights on film. Several eyewitnesses have reported seeing military helicopters flying near or hovering above farm fields where Mystery Lights are present. According to Reg Presley, "On several occasions, the army is in the area when the lights are present."

While videotaping one light episode, Colin Andrews had his own encounter with the army. "What appeared to be happening," Colin explains, "was that we had walked into a situation that was undesirable. Two army helicopters approached us and appeared to be harassing us. One was so close it was unbelievable. The other helicopter broke away across the field toward what you can see on my film is a small, white, pulsating object identical to Stephen Alexander's video and very similar to Foeke Kootje's film.

"This helicopter went directly to the light, overshot it, and on the film you can actually see the helicopter backing up to get a full view of this white light pulsating underneath it." (See Photo 40.)

Sightings contacted the British Ministry of Defense for a statement. An M.O.D. spokesperson stated that the helicopters in Colin Andrews' videotape were on a training exercise, and that no one involved with that exercise reported any unusual phenomena.

It's a stance that ufologists like John Holman are familiar with. He has seen the Avebury Mystery Lights, the crop circles, and the helicopters. His plea echoes the sentiments of many people who have visited England's greatest paranormal hot spot. "If people in authority know what's going on," John asks, "why can't we come together on this? We've got dramatic crop circles and UFOs; there could be a whole new technology wrapped up in this. To me, it's so exciting, and it could be happening for our benefit."

Groups of amateur sky watchers continue to gather on top of Milk Hill. They continue to wait and watch. A three-quarter moon barely illuminates a strange object on nearby Silbury Hill. It is a giant piece of granite, part of an ancient stone circle erected by an unknown Neolithic culture more than five thousand years ago. It is among the oldest man-made structures in Great Britain, and it is the same size and the same shape as a crop circle.

"Crop circles" is a broad term used to describe any kind of geometric pattern or design created by an unseen force in corn and wheat fields worldwide. Typically, the crop inside the pattern is crushed horizontally but continues to grow. Crop circles appear mysteriously with no tire tracks or footprints around them that would indicate human intervention. (See Photo 41.)

This English woodcut, known as *The Mowing Devil*, dates back to 1648. (See Photo 42.) It depicts a devil with a scythe making an elliptical pattern in a crop field. A fiery ball of light appears to be hurtling toward him. Many cereologists believe this is the earliest known documentation of the Avebury phenomenon.

The Montreal Mothership

O n November 7, 1990, a UFO the size of three football fields, described by some eyewitnesses as a "mothership," hovered over the Bonaventure Hotel in downtown Montreal for nearly three hours. More than a hundred people saw the strange array of lights in the autumn sky, including two patrol officers and the Director of Operations from the Montreal Police Department, two airline pilots, three newspaper reporters, a constable in the Royal Canadian Mounted Police, and several clinical psychologists who were attending a convention in the hotel. It was the largest mass sighting of a UFO in Canadian history, and to this day no one knows what —or who—was visiting earth that night.

At first, Bonaventure Hotel lifeguard Lynn St-Pierre thought the woman in the rooftop swimming pool was in trouble. She had been floating face-up, motionless, for almost ten minutes. Lynn stepped outside the enclosed area where she was keeping warm to make sure everything was all right. The woman in the pool pointed to the sky.

"When I first saw those lights I was stunned," Lynn remembers. "The lights were very bright. I saw yellow lights—I would say six, seven, or eight spots—within the shape of an egg. It didn't move an inch, from what I could see. Every corner of the roof I went to, that thing was over my head. I said, 'Somebody pinch me, because I don't believe what I see.' "

Lynn called the hotel manager and explained that something unusual had appeared in the sky above the swimming pool. The manager came quickly, and soon rumors that a UFO was hovering over the Bonaventure spread like wildfire through the hotel. Staff and guests came to the roof, and Lynn estimates that over one hundred people witnessed the spectacular light show.

The hotel's director of security called the Montreal Urban Community Police Department and reported the UFO. A patrol officer was dispatched to the scene, and when he witnessed the bizarre light phenomenon for himself, the officer called for backup. A second officer arrived, and he, too, was overwhelmed by what he saw. He asked the Director of Police Operations to come to the hotel. After the director witnessed the UFO, he called the Royal Canadian Mounted Police. The Mounties always get their man, but could they get a UFO?

"I've been a member of the RCMP for nineteen years," Constable Luc Morin explained in an exclusive interview with *Sightings*, "and in my experience I've seen a bit of everything. But I never encountered anything like that UFO. Above the pool I observed three shades of light. I stayed on the scene for approximately two hours, fifteen minutes, and after a while the lights began to move slowly from the west to the east."

The police calls were picked up by an editor at *La Presse*, Canada's largest French-language newspaper. Reporter Jules Beliveau was getting ready to go home for the night when he was told to go the Bonaventure and file a story. "I had already finished my day at work," Jules recalls, "and I didn't want to go there. I said, 'I'm not interested, I don't want to do the story,' but the editor said, 'Go. Just go and see if it is anything special.' "

When Jules arrived at the Bonaventure, he stood in the street and looked at the sky. "I saw nothing," he recalls. Years of chasing false leads and interviewing unreliable eyewitnesses had made the reporter an ardent skeptic. He reluctantly took the elevator to the roof. "When I arrived at the top of the hotel, I saw the lights very high in the sky. The lights were glimmering, and to me they looked like a crown in the sky."

Marcel La Roche, another reporter for *La Presse*, joined Jules on the rooftop, and the two men agreed that they needed a photographer right away. Marcel called the city desk and said, "Please, please, we need a photographer. It's important. We see something up here. We really see something." But all the newspaper's photographers were out on assignment. Marcel had to take pictures with a small pocket camera he carried for emergencies.

Jules remembers his colleague telling him, "I cannot do this. It's too dark and too far away." But when Marcel's photographs were developed, they clearly showed the magnitude of the UFO. (See Photo 43.)

While the two reporters interviewed the eyewitnesses at the hotel, Constable Morin tried to determine what could be causing the light phenomenon. "It did not appear to be the aurora borealis or any other natural phenomenon, so I called the airport tower," Morin explains. "They had nothing on radar, so I called the military to ascertain if there was any operation in that location, and they replied in the negative as well. In order to make sure it wasn't a reflection of some sort, in cooperation with the Montreal Urban Community Police we asked all the construction sites in the area to shut down their lights.

"After those lights were shut down, the phenomenon remained in the sky. It was an object directly in the sky. It was not a reflection. I talked to some airline pilots who were on the roof, and they had no idea—even with their experience—what this light phenomenon could be."

Around 10 P.M. heavy snow clouds began rolling into Montreal. Within a matter of minutes, the slow-moving UFO was no longer visible from the hotel roof. There was an air of disappointment among the group who had gathered and stood together for nearly three hours in the cold Canadian night. Constable Morin remembers, "We didn't know what it was, but I never felt it was a threat. People were very calm. There was no panicking any-where."

When Jules Beliveau's article and Marcel La Roche's photo-graph appeared in *La Presse* the next morning, people through-out Montreal called in to say that they had also seen the mysterious mothership. Pierre Caumartin, a Montreal television-commercial producer, realized that the strange lights he had wit-nessed while driving home the night before were from this same UFO. He had seen the lights around 10:30 P.M. hovering over Montreal's Olympic Stadium, approximately ten miles away from the Bonaventure Hotel.

At first, Pierre thought the lights were coming from an advertis-ing blimp or were part of a promotional stunt put on by the Montreal Expos, who make their home in Olympic Stadium. "The lights intrigued me. They were coldish, bluish, and very bright, like lights we use for filming. It was not the kind of light you would ever see on a plane or a chopper, so I just thought it was something for the Expos. Then I realized, hey, this is Novem-ber. The stadium's covered and there's nothing going on there. What the hell is this?"

Pierre continued driving, keeping the lights in his field of vi-sion. "I noticed that the object went right over the stadium and continued going east. Then it appeared to stop above a power station that's on a military base near my home. I got out of my car and started analyzing the thing. I could even hear the sound it was making. It was a definite purring sound, but not at all like a blimp. The lights were very specific; the beams were very strong. It will always stick in my memory as strange and very exciting."

Pierre had a hard time convincing his friends and family that he had seen a UFO. His wife, who did not see the phenomenon, asked, "Did you have a drink or are you going nuts?" Neither of those options described Pierre's condition on the night of his sighting, and he decided to keep quiet about his experience. Despite the newspaper article and subsequent television cover-age, Pierre told no one he had seen the lights until his friend

Bernard Guenette confided that he had seen the so-called mothership.

"I was coming out of the office very late," Bernard recalls. "I looked up in the sky and saw this greenish light. It was like a pencil of light. It looked very odd. I had the feeling that it was not from here, that it was different." Bernard, a computer graphics designer specializing in visual simulation, decided to see if he could create a composite drawing of the UFO based on eyewitness accounts. He consulted with world-renowned aerial anomalies expert Dr. Richard Haines.

"According to the witnesses' testimonies and an analysis of their estimations by Dr. Haines, we believe the object was hovering at approximately six thousand feet altitude and that it was probably no less that fifteen hundred feet in diameter," says Bernard. What had started for Bernard as an interesting way of experimenting with some of his new computer software became a full-scale investigation. He found Pierre Caumartin's description of the UFO hovering over the power station particularly important.

"I talked with Hydro Quebec about the sighting," says Bernard. Although they did not see anything in the sky, they reported that between 10:40 and 11 P.M. there was a power breakdown at the electric station. It was quite interesting, because only the twelve-thousand-volt line that goes to the military base experienced a power failure."

Constable Luc Morin also conducted an investigation into the mothership phenomenon. He gathered meteorological data from the Canadian Weather Service and sent his complete RCMP report, including eyewitness testimony and photographs, to the National Research Council. "They made a scientific analysis of what they thought the phenomenon was, but it is inconclusive. They analyzed angles, distances, and so forth and could only say the phenomenon appeared to be an object," Constable Morin explains. Why this object did not appear on any radar screen sweeping the area is unknown.

"I think there are only two possibilities," Pierre Caumartin surmises. "It was either some kind of prototype that no one wants us to know about, or it is coming from somewhere else. From being a totally skeptical person, I've switched to a more open mind about these things. I didn't see an atmospheric event. I saw an object in the air. I heard it. There is no way that anyone is going to convince me that I've seen some kind of tricky lighting. There was an object there, and it corresponds to the descriptions of many other people. I'll never forget it."

Bernard Guenette continues to pursue an investigation. He does not ascribe a sinister motive to the lack of interest in the case by government officials. Instead, he believes that the Montreal mothership incident has simply fallen through the cracks, and its global import may never be fully explored. "Many actions have been taken in this case," Bernard says, "but the police say this is not a criminal act, so it is out of their scope. The RCMP says they have no department to study it more. National Defense says they would become involved only if there is a threat to national security, and there was no threat. They simply keep the reports in their archives and do nothing."

> The aurora borealis, also known as the northern lights, is a series of luminous bands of light sometimes visible in the far northern latitudes. The lights appear in different colors and appear to move rapidly across the sky. They are caused by electrically charged particles colliding with the earth's magnetic field.

The Uninvited

"**K**ecksburg is just a quiet little town in the middle of western Pennsylvania, where all the neighbors know each other. If someone sneezes, ten people holler out the window, 'Bless you.' You've got neighbors that have known each other all their lives, but now they won't talk to each other. This town is split into two groups. You've got the Believers and the Nonbelievers," says James Romansky, Sr. James is a Believer.

"There've been friendships lost," says lifelong resident Jim Mayes. And for Robert Binter, a forty-three-year veteran of the Kecksburg Fire Department, the dispute hits very close to home. "I have a brother-in-law who hasn't spoken to me in two years. We used to be close buddies, but now he just ignores me. He said I lied about everything, but I never lied about a thing."

Kecksburg, Pennsylvania, is a town divided, all because of what did—or didn't—happen here on December 9, 1965.

In 1965, John Murphy was a reporter who covered south-western Pennsylvania for WHJB Radio News. On December 9 of that year, he was out working on a story about the search for two sailors who had gone AWOL in New Stanton. On the way back to the station, around 4:45 in the afternoon, Murphy got a call over his two-way radio asking if he was on the scene. "On the scene of what?" he asked.

Hundreds of people were calling the radio station to report an explosion of orange flame in the sky. Thousands more people were calling in to police stations throughout the area. Many people believed it was an airplane that had gone down somewhere near Greensburg, Pennsylvania. John Murphy drove around that area and saw nothing. He stopped a state trooper and asked if he had heard anything about the midair explosion. The trooper confirmed that they were looking for a downed airplane but so far had found nothing.

John Murphy called the Greensburg Airport. The air-traffic controller was unable to explain what people were seeing. The Greater Pittsburgh Airport also had no explanation, although they did confirm that they were receiving numerous reports of a downed airplane. However, their logs showed that all aircraft within their purview were present and accounted for.

While John Murphy was driving around on what was looking more and more like a wild-goose chase, Bill Bulebush was in Kecksburg working on his car. "I saw this ball of fire coming from the northwest and headed toward the mountain," Bill remembers, "and it seemed like it was controlled. I watched it make a turn and swoop down in the trees." Bill grabbed a flashlight and started down into the woods.

"I crossed the creek and fell in," Bill says, "but I went on, because I saw a little bit of smoke and an orangeish arc, like a welding arc. Then I went up to *it*." Bill Bulebush believes that what he saw in those woods was an extraterrestrial spacecraft. "It looked like an acorn. It didn't have any opening, no rivet marks, only a ring around it with writing—like backwards writing—on it. I had never seen lettering like it. The color is pretty hard to describe. It was a real dark color, like a burnt orange."

Back at WHJB, John Murphy was interviewing a woman who also claimed that she had seen a flaming object land in the woods in Kecksburg. Something in her voice made the veteran reporter believe that this was not a prank call. Murphy called two photographers and told them to meet him in Kecksburg. They rendezvoused on a ridge road above the woods. State Police Officer Paul Shipcoe and State Police Fire Marshal Carl Metz arrived at about the same time and took off into the wooded ravine below. (See Photo 44.)

Bill Bulebush had been staring at *it* for ten minutes when he heard voices and saw two men coming through the trees. "I was shaking," Bill recalls. "I was really scared. I thought maybe they'll think I have something to do with this." Bill ran home. By the time he'd calmed down and returned to the area with his son, the state police had set up a roadblock, and the woods had been cordoned off. He never saw the UFO again.

According to John Murphy, Shipcoe and Metz were in the woods for sixteen minutes. When they came back up to the road Murphy asked, "Did you find anything down there?" "I'm not sure," Carl Metz reportedly said. "You better get your information from the Army." It was the first official indication that this was not a plane crash.

James Romansky, Sr., remembers December 9, 1965, like it was yesterday. He was an eighteen-year-old volunteer firefighter with the Lloydsville Fire Department. "You have events in your life that you never forget," James says. "That very same week my father had died. When the fire alarm went off, my mother said, 'Please, you can't go.' She was very emotional. But I had taken an oath that when that whistle blew, I would do my best to help in any way, shape, or form. I really believed that, so I answered the call that night. And I'll never forget what happened. It's burned in my mind."

According to James, his six-member volunteer team was assigned to search and rescue operations in the Kecksburg woods. Their primary job was to aid any survivors they might find trapped in what they assumed would be aircraft wreckage. "But that didn't take place," James says, "because what was on the ground was not a conventional aircraft.

"There were no wings, no tail section, no motors, no doors, no windows. It was like a giant acorn lying on its side. It was made of metal, like bronze, copper, and gold all mixed together. I've been a machinist for twenty-five years now, and I've never come across this kind of metal since. It was ten to twelve feet in length, big enough for a grown person to stand up in, but had no visible means of entry. It had like a bumper around the bottom, maybe eight to ten inches wide, with something like writing or symbols on it. None of us were brave enough to touch the object."

Less than a quarter of a mile away in a small white frame farmhouse, ten-year-old John Hays was listening to the radio. His mother, Lillian, was in the kitchen looking out the window. "There was a fireball fell in Acme," he told her. "I started laughing," Lillian recalls today. "I was looking out the back window and I told him, 'It ain't up in Acme, it's in our backyard.' "

John remembers that within half an hour, there was a knock at the front door. "Military people came to the house, Army and Air Force and a couple of people with NASA patches. The one guy from the Air Force seemed to be in charge, I think he was a colonel, but I was pretty small and it was hard to distinguish the rank. They wanted to use the phone. They stayed in a group and were whispering back and forth. They took over the house and told my mom and dad to send us to bed."

James Romansky also remembers the presence of military personnel. At the crash site, his search team was approached by two men. "The one gentleman was ramrod straight, very authoritative voice, crew-cut hair. I mean, he reeked of military. He said to us, 'All right, this is now a restricted area. You are all ordered out of here.' We turned to leave, and coming down through the woods was a group of military personnel, uniforms, lights, the whole nine yards. Our group going out and their group going in never exchanged words. We had been ordered out, and so that's what we did.

"We went down to the Kecksburg fire hall to see if we could get some coffee or sandwiches. It was getting late, and it was cold and wet. The fire hall was wall-to-wall military. They had armed guards at the door. The town was a virtual military takeover."

Jim Mayes was another volunteer firefighter working search and rescue on December 9. He also remembers a military operation. "They had the firehouse set up as a command post. I had to haul some of them up to the site in one of our trucks. When we got to a certain location in the field, they said, 'That's as far as you go.' So that's as far as we went."

John Murphy was at the State Police Troop A Barracks in Greensburg, waiting for an official statement to broadcast on the evening news. Members of the Army's 662nd Radar Squadron and two men in Air Force uniform, one wearing a lieutenant's bar, arrived. A state police captain announced, "The Pennsylvania State Police have made a thorough investigation of the woods. We are convinced there is nothing whatsoever in the woods."

The official version of the incident was broadcast over radio and television and printed in the next day's newspapers. The media made a lot of people around Kecksburg look like liars. But many of their neighbors came forward in the days that followed and admitted that they, too, had seen a UFO and a military operation. Some of them gave interviews to John Murphy, but when he announced that he would be broadcasting their first-hand accounts on WHJB, they told him that they did not want their statements aired. According to Murphy's follow-up report on the incident, "One person said that they were afraid of the state police. Another person said that they did not want to get in trouble with the Army." The Believers kept quiet, and the Non-believers, who claimed that nothing at all had happened that night, liked it that way.

James Romansky kept quiet about what he had seen for almost twenty years. "I was afraid to say anything," he says "because back in the sixties, when you talked about stuff like this, they'd have you as a candidate for the loony bin." It wasn't until James saw a display about the Kecksburg incident in a shopping mall in 1987 that he went public with his story. Looking at pictures of the wooded ravine set up by UFO researcher Stan Gordon, James leaned over and said, "I was there."

Stan Gordon has been investigating the Kecksburg UFO since he heard John Murphy's original broadcasts in 1965. When he met James Romansky, Stan was startled at the amount of detail

James could remember and how much of that detail corroborated the statements of other witnesses he had already interviewed.

Stan asked James to show him where he had seen the acorn-shaped craft. Stan thought he knew where the site was, because he had traveled there already with another supposed eyewitness, Jim Ramsey. It was a test, and James passed. He took Stan to the same exact spot where Jim Ramsey said the UFO had landed. Then James told Stan about something else he had seen that night, something he hadn't discussed with anyone before.

"That night, when they turned us away from the fire hall," Jim said, "a flatbed truck came back down off the hill with a Jeep in front of it and a Jeep behind it, and they all had flashing red lights on. There was something loaded on the back of the flatbed covered with a tarpaulin. It was about the same size as the object I saw. And that truck was hellbent for leather. If you'd have walked out on that road, you'd have still been there, because they would have to scrape you up with a putty knife. They weren't stopping for anything or anybody."

Stan Gordon had received almost identical accounts from Robert Binter and John Hays. Robert remembered, "The truck was in the ravine for approximately forty-five minutes. When it came out, that truck was covered with a tarpaulin." And John Hays recalled looking out his bedroom window and observing, "The flatbed went down empty and it come back out with something on the back of it, covered up, about the size of a Volkswagen. They had a Jeep with a light flashing, clearing the way, and they went straight out through everybody and up over the top of the hill." None of these men knew the flatbed's destination, but Stan Gordon found one man who claimed he knew.

Clifford Stone, now retired, was an Army sergeant for twenty-two years. His fascination with military technology, operations, and UFOs began when he was a boy and became a passion on a damp night in December 1965. "I was living in Ashfield, Ohio, roughly two miles from Lockborne Air Force Base. A friend of mine's father worked on the base, and one night he called me and asked if I was still interested in UFOs, which he knew I was. He asked if I'd like to get up very early the next morning and go with him on post. They had something coming in from Pennsylvania that I might be interested in.

"The next morning we got to the post around three-thirty or four A.M. A vehicle entered through the gate to go onto the flight line. I noticed that on the back of the vehicle it had something that was covered by a tarp. It was about ten to twelve foot at the base, twelve foot tall. It looked like a chocolate drop. My friend told me that every question I ever had about UFOs was under that canvas."

Since his sighting, Clifford has made repeated attempts to obtain information from the government regarding that object. As an Army officer, he had access to hundreds of files about Army recovery operations. He learned about recovery of space debris, aircraft parts, foreign technology, even Soviet space probes that had landed in U.S. territory. There was nothing about the Kecksburg UFO.

The reason for that, say the Nonbelievers, is that nothing ever crashed into the woods, the military never came, and nothing was taken away on a flatbed truck. Robert Young is a planetary expert who agrees that nothing crashed in Kecksburg. He claims the UFO was a meteor that was known to have passed over Ontario, Canada, and several northern states the evening of December 9, 1965: "Virtually all of the accounts can be explained by people having looked toward and seen the Ontario meteor. I have signed affidavits from sixty-one local people who say that nothing crashed here. There was no military occupation."

Sightings conducted its own investigation into the Kecksburg incident, recording most of the interviews quoted in this story. It was a study in contrasts. Bolstered by Stan Gordon's research, the Believers were willing to come forward. But not one single person who did not believe the incident had occurred would appear on camera. *Sightings* attempted to visit the site of the alleged crash. The landowner, the same man who had owned the property in 1965—and who many believe knows much more about the UFO than he's willing to tell—turned the crew away.

Videotaping from an adjacent property, Jim Ramsey warned the *Sightings* team "The guy that owns it, man, he's one of the Nonbelievers. He won't let you anywhere near his grounds. He'd probably shoot first and ask questions later, especially if he knew it involved that UFO. His feelings and mine are strong against each other. We'd never dare come face-to-face—we'd end up coming to blows."

Stan Gordon believes that the reason many people do not believe anything extraterrestrial happened in Kecksburg is because they were simply in the wrong place at the right time. "They were in a position where they didn't see what was going on, and if you see the geography of the area and where the majority of the people were that night, they could not have seen the military activity."

James Romansky ascribes a more sinister motive to some of the Nonbelievers. "I really believe the government bought some of them off or threatened them with something. That's my personal opinion." In contrast, based on his experience in the U.S. Army, Clifford Stone does not believe hush money was ever offered. "I don't think that happened after the recovery. The reason I state that is I think the military feels confident that no matter what anyone says about what they have seen, most people are not going to believe them."

"People are saying I'm a liar, I'm a faker," says James Romansky. "I have only related what I saw, what I went through, what I experienced. I'm not begging anybody to believe. I know what I saw. Nobody will make me change my mind. It's like someone took a brand and burned it in my arm. It won't go away unless you cut the arm off. And if you cut my head off, well, then a lot of people are going to be happy, because I'm not going to be able to say nothing to nobody."

The skies over Kecksburg were busy the night of December 9, 1965. In addition to the Ontario meteor, which some claim was visible in western Pennsylvania, a Soviet Venus probe fell to earth that day, time and location unknown. A Soviet probe would have held great interest for the U.S. military during the Cold War. "It would have revealed Soviet heat-shield technology that could have been analyzed to determine how large their warheads were in their ICBMs," says a former NASA flight engineer.

Outback Abduction

It was a long drive from Faye Knowles's house in Perth, Australia, to her sister's place in Melbourne, but Faye had three grown sons, a reliable car, and two weeks' vacation coming. She wanted to drive the 1,600 miles straight through—to save time and money—and her boys, Sean, Patrick, and Wayne, agreed to drive in shifts. They packed up the car around 3:00 in the afternoon on January 20, 1988. The Knowles wanted to hit the Australian desert, four hundred miles to the east, in the middle of the night, when the temperature would be bearable. It was a sensible, but fateful, decision.

By 2:30 A.M., the Knowleses were well into the Victorian Desert, in a desolate basin called the Nullarbor Plain. They stopped at a gas station, fueled up, bought some snacks, and switched drivers. Sean was behind the wheel, and Patrick was sitting to his left in the passenger seat. Wayne and Faye were in the back with the family's two dogs.

The highway was empty, and Sean was making good time. After about an hour, Sean saw a bright yellow light up ahead in the middle of the road. He slowed down, thinking that it might be an accident or late-night construction. As he got closer, the yellow light seemed to be emanating from an egg-shaped object hovering just above ground level. He thought he might be seeing things, until a recreational vehicle—called a caravan in Australia—

coming from the opposite direction swerved to avoid the luminous egg.

"I was sleeping on the passenger side," Patrick recalls, "and Sean says, 'Pat, wake up! Look at this! It looks like a UFO!' and I said, 'Oh, man, stop joking. It can't be.' But the closer we got, the more we realized it wasn't a truck, or a signal, or anything like that." Sean swerved to avoid hitting the object and continued driving. In his rearview mirror, Sean could see the distance growing between the UFO and the family's car.

Suddenly, the object started toward them. It appeared to accelerate with tremendous speed. "We drove on, and this object started chasing us," Patrick explains. "I said to Sean, 'Come on, put your foot down, let's get going.' The faster we went to get away from it, the faster this object went." Sean estimates that he reached a top speed of nearly 125 mph trying to escape the terrifying light, but "it caught up within a matter of seconds," he remembers.

Sean made a U-turn and started traveling back toward the west. The UFO turned also. "I don't know how the hell it was flying," Patrick says. "It didn't have any wings or anything like wings. It just kept on chasing us." Sean made another U-turn, heading again for Melbourne. The UFO turned as well and kept pace with the car. In the backseat, Faye and Wayne were scared. The dogs started barking and whining.

Then they were hit. Patrick explains, "It blew our back tire out with a beam of light. The back tire was on fire. We started sliding." As Sean fought to maintain control of the car, he braked slowly and realized that the family would have to confront whatever it was that appeared to be targeting them.

"It landed on the roof of the car and picked the car up," says Patrick. "It lit up the car like a microwave. The heat was intense. Our hair was standing straight up, and we felt really funny—like we were being dehydrated." Wayne describes the feeling as "awful, frightening, like our brains were being sucked out. My fear was that I'd be taken out of my body."

Faye put her hand out the window and felt for the roof. She

came in contact with something she felt was "spongy," and then she was badly burned on her right hand. "We thought we were going to die," Faye says.

"You could actually feel the car rising in the air, with this object on top of us," Patrick says. Sean remembers, "The car began to fill with a thick, black fog. It was so hot, and all this soot, this junk, starting covering us. Our voices started changing. You know how a tape deck sounds when the batteries go flat? Thats what it was like. Then I blacked out."

Patrick picks up the story. "Sean wasn't moving, just staring out. Grayish-black soot was flying in, covering the whole car, the seats, our clothes. It had a very foreign, glassy feel. And there was a terrible smell." Faye remembers that smell, too. "It was terrible, like dead bodies. I couldn't even breathe."

Then the Knowleses remember hearing a loud bang, a "tremendous noise," and the car suddenly dropped back to earth. "Not long after the UFO dropped the car, that's when I came to," says Sean. "I told them all to jump out and start running. You could see this thing was still above us, looking at us. Mum and them were running out to hide in some bushes off the road, and I turned off the lights on the car. Somehow, the object could not find us without those lights."

The Knowles family hid in the low Australian scrub. A faint glow in the east signaled the approach of dawn. Sean says, "As soon as it started to get light, this thing just took flight, and that's the last we've seen of it."

The dawn light was puzzling. No one in the family felt that the entire ordeal had lasted more than fifteen minutes, and yet over an hour and a half had gone by. There was more than an hour of missing time, which could not be accounted for by Patrick, Sean, Wayne, or Faye.

Sean changed the exploded tire. His mother noticed four dents on the top of the car. Patrick and Wayne tried to sweep out the fetid black soot. A truck sped toward them. They tried to wave it down, but it would not stop. They drove away as quickly as possible, leaving Sean's tools and the car jack on the side of the road. They drove to the nearest open business, a roadhouse fifty miles to the east.

"There were a couple of truckers at the roadhouse, and they asked us what happened to us, because we were all shaken up and pretty frightened. One of the drivers said come inside and have some coffee but we said no. We didn't want to trust anyone," Patrick explains. The trucker looked at their damaged car and offered to tow it to Adelaide in his empty trailer. Again, the family declined any help. Instead, they decided to go to the nearest police station.

Patrick continues, "The strange thing was that the police were actually looking for us, because they'd already had a report about what happened." Police transcripts obtained by *Sightings* offer a strange twist to the story. Someone, perhaps in the caravan, had witnessed the Knowleses' encounter but phoned the police anonymously. The conversation included a description of the event that independently corroborates the Knowleses' story:

CALLER: They were traveling along the road. A bright light appeared in front of the car. Shortly after, the lights appeared behind the car. The car was picked up off the road, shaken violently. The car was covered in ash. Black ash.

POLICE: What about the people? Were they harmed at all?

CALLER: They were not harmed, but visibly shaken up.

"At first the policeman didn't believe it. He didn't know what to believe," Patrick recalls. "He came over and looked at the car and felt the material inside the car and asked about the bad smell. He had a look at the tire, saw the four impressions on the car. [See Photo 45.] Then he was convinced that something did happen."

In Australia, sightings of strange entities and forces from the cosmos is part of a tradition long held by its indigenous people. Until European occupation in the 1700s, the Aborigines lived in separate tribes with separate languages, but the art that survives today speaks of one common belief. According to Australian writer Colin Hayvice, "Their drawings, their dream stories, indicate very definitely that the Aborigines have had experience with UFOs. When you look at old cave paintings, you will see things which aren't of this earth. Even today, many Aboriginal people will tell you, 'Yes, we accept the extraterrestrial, things coming from outer space.' "

But the modern Australian majority is not Aboriginal and does not accept with reverence stories about cars being hijacked by extraterrestrial spacecraft. As soon as the first tabloid reporter heard the UFO report come over the police scanner, the Knowleses were besieged by the media.

"They came to the roadhouse where we were going to sleep that morning," Patrick recalls. "They offered us money and help with a hospital because we were getting sick. They offered to take our car and then fly us to Adelaide for an interview. Well, I mean anyone would be silly not to take the money. We weren't looking for a quid, but the media was after us."

In the weeks that followed, the Knowleses were ridiculed in the Australian tabloids, the mainstream press, and on television. (See Photo 46.) The pinnacle of their humiliating experience occurred when Faye and Patrick appeared on a popular Australian talk show, *Tonight Live*. The following is a transcript of part of that interview:

HOST

Would you please welcome a couple of people who've seen the light, Faye and Patrick Knowles. [*Applause*] Well, what was your first reaction?

FAYE

I thought we were going to die, you know.

HOST

Did you know what it was?

FAYE

Didn't know.

HOST

It didn't look like anything you've seen before?

FAYE

No, that's right.

PATRICK

The object picked the car up, and Mum wound down the
window and put her hand on the roof, and she touched it.

HOST

[*Chuckling*] Let me get this right. You're being picked up by
an alien craft and you wound down the window, Faye . . .
[*Laughter*] . . . and put your hand on the roof.

FAYE

'Cause I was curious to see what was up there. [*Laughter*]

HOST

So you're way off the ground, you've got the alien spacecraft
picking you up, and you've virtually petted it, haven't
you? [*Laughter*]

PATRICK

As this was going on it was like a real loud sound on top of
the . . . [*Laughter*] . . . inside the car it was like a material,
it was like a fog that was coming inside the car and . . .

HOST

. . . It was probably smoke from your mum's skin burning!
[*Laughter and applause*]

"The media treatment of the family was ruthless," says Colin
Norris, a UFO investigator uniquely qualified to analyze the
Knowles case. Norris was a public relations specialist with the
Australian Telecommunications Office for forty-three years be-
fore turning his attention to studying eyewitness accounts of
Australian UFOs. "I don't think one person, reporter, journalist,
asked sensible questions and tried to console these people in
seeing their state of anxiety."

"We just wanted people to know what happened to us," Patrick laments. "We weren't after anything. We ourselves thought it was amazing, and we wanted to let people know what happened." The Knowleses were unprepared for the spate of unrelenting ridicule that followed their encounter. The media made them out to be crazy, or worse yet, money-hungry hoaxers. But when the Knowleses met Colin Norris, they learned that other people had also seen—and experienced—the UFO attack.

"I interviewed people who had reported sightings on that same night," Norris reports. "A man on his farm sixty kilometers north of the Knowleses' car watched a UFO sitting in the yard of his property before dark. He came within, in Australia, a cricket-pitch length—some sixty feet—of the craft, and he was badly burned on his face. Just before the Knowleses' encounter, a trucker five kilometers south of their position was sleeping in his rig. He woke up with laser burns on his arms, completely paralyzed. He looked at his arms. They weren't bleeding, but there was congealed blood."

Budd Hopkins, a world-renowned expert in the alien abduction phenomenon, also offered encouragement to the Knowleses. He believes that their story displays the classic signs of an alien abduction. "In many abductions, people describe being taken into a craft inside their automobile, being put back in the car, the car being put back on the road," Hopkins explains. "There are physical marks, a blown tire, sometimes the car comes down too fast. It all sounds crazy, but the point is that evidence suggests that this is absolutely happening again and again in very similar ways."

Colin Norris searched for the anonymous caller who phoned the police with what appeared to be a firsthand account of the Knowles abduction. He was unsuccessful, but in the search he met a truck driver who had been on the road that night and not only saw the Knowleses' car, but also the UFO.

Colin says, "The truck driver was in front of the Knowleses in an area they call 'the basin,' and he could look in his rear-vision mirror and see over a wide area. He watched this thing, the

1. The messages in the Ghost Writer's photos alternate between English and Latin. (Sightings)

2. The final message from the Ghost Writer translates as "All this is over now." (Sightings)

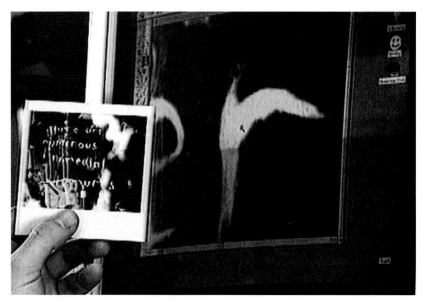

3. Photographic expert Edson Williams examined the photos carefully for signs of a hoax. (Sightings)

4. Williams found duplicating the writing to be an arduous process. (Sightings)

5. In one of the earliest known "ghost" photographs, the specter of Abraham Lincoln stands behind his widow, Mary Todd Lincoln.

6. Sara Estep records what she believes are "voices from other dimensions." (Sightings)

7. The lighthouse at Point Lookout State Park is a hub of eerie haunting activity. (Sightings)

8. This rare photograph appears to have captured a ghost in Civil War–era uniform standing alongside Nancy Stallings. *(courtesy Nancy Stallings)*

9. The infamous Berry-Pomeroy castle in Scotland has been uninhabited for the past three hundred years due to ghostly activity. (Sightings)

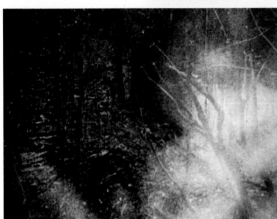

10. Jack Hazzard felt an eerie wind as he snapped this photo on the castle grounds. *(courtesy Jack Hazzard)*

11. The Whaley House has been a fertile haunting ground for over one hundred years. *(courtesy Whaley House)*

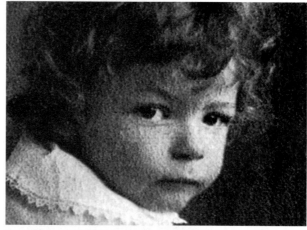

12. Special computer software developed by EVP expert Brian Black pinpoints the source of anomalous sounds. (Sightings)

13. George G. Meade Easby, six *(below)*, and his brother Steven, five *(right)*, shortly before Steven's death. *(courtesy G. G. Meade Easby)*

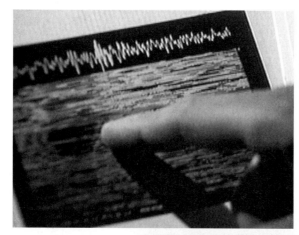

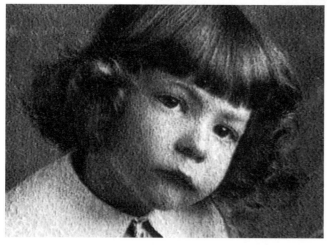

14. Ectoplasm, in the form of mysterious blue fog, as photographed at Baleroy. *(courtesy G. G. Meade Easby)*

15. The blue fog allegedly foretells a visit from the spirit "Amanda." *(courtesy G. G. Meade Easby)*

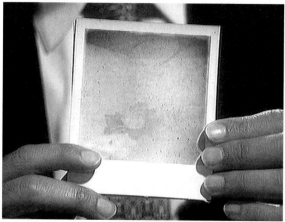

16. When Doris screamed "It's in the corner!" parapsychologist Kerry Gaynor snapped this anomalous hot spot. *(courtesy Kerry Gaynor)*

17. When Doris feels the presence of "the Entity," photographs are inexplicably bleached out. *(courtesy Kerry Gaynor)*

18. A horrible stench and an icy breeze were present when this photo was taken. *(courtesy Kerry Gaynor)*

19. A bright light obliterated Doris's head when she exclaimed, "It's right in front of my face!" *(courtesy Kerry Gaynor)*

20. The reverse arcs of light visible here are significant because they form an arc that floats freely in the air. *(courtesy Kerry Gaynor)*

21. Doris begged the spirit to manifest, and all twenty eyewitnesses saw the shape of "the Entity" begin to appear. *(courtesy Kerry Gaynor)*

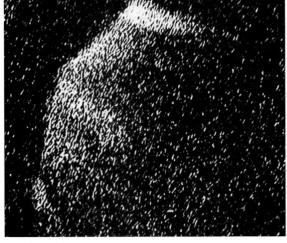

22. Carl Lawson was the caretaker of this Kentucky nightclub when he began to witness frightening paranormal events. (Sightings)

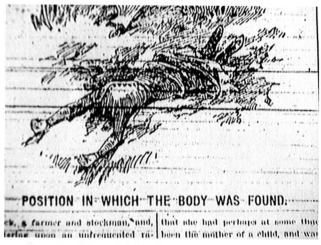

23. The headless body of Pearl Bryan as depicted in an 1896 news report.

POSITION IN WHICH THE BODY WAS FOUND.

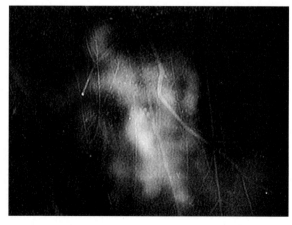

24. Debbie and Tim Sheads were shocked to find this ghostly image in their photo, taken at Devil's Den, where many men suffered and died during the battle of Gettysburg. *(Tim and Debbie Sheads)*

25. Tony's rendition of "Sallie," the young ghost who he claims has haunted his family since 1993. (Sightings)

26. Tony and Deborah believe this amorphous shape is a physical manifestation of "Sallie." (Sightings)

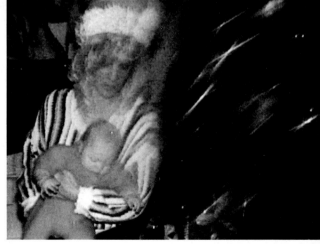

27. A Christmas present purchased for "Sallie" appears to provoke her presence. (Sightings)

28. An unseen hand seems to hold a crayon aloft in the family nursery. (Sightings)

29. Tony and Deborah were concerned for the safety of their baby when menacing shadows appeared around the crib. (Sightings)

30. Photographic analyst Edson Williams was unable to discern the source of this odd ghosting image. (Sightings)

31. Paranormal investigator Howard Heim examines scratches on Tony's torso as they form and bleed sponta-neously. (Sightings)

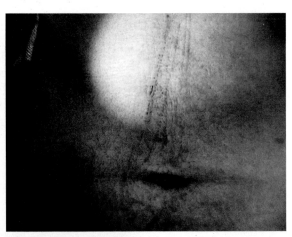

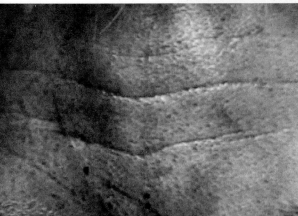

32. Tony and Deborah are convinced that "Sallie" is creating the welts and scratches that appear on Tony's body. (Sightings)

33. The meaning of "MC," which formed on Tony's back, is unknown, but Father Edd Anthony feels that a lost spirit was trying to reach out to the couple. (Sightings)

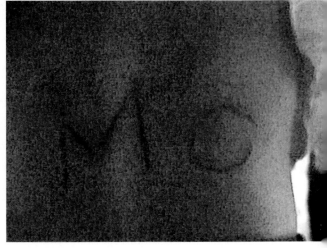

34. John Holman was astounded by the enormity of this bright orange light in the sky over Avebury, England. *(courtesy John and Robin Holman)*

35. UFO researcher Tom Blower has consistently documented his sightings on videotape. *(courtesy Tom and Kerry Blower)*

36. Ninety percent of the numerous crop circles found in Great Britain are in the Avebury area. *(courtesy Peter Sørensen)*

37. Stephen Alexander videotaped this historic sighting of a light allegedly creating a crop circle. *(courtesy Stephen Alexander)*

38. Ufologists believe that this tape may show a probe being sent from a larger unidentified spacecraft.
(courtesy Gillian Trench)

39. Photographer Foeke Kootje captured this ball of light on film while hang gliding off Milk Hill in Avebury.
(courtesy Foeke Kootje, Conny de Bruijn, and Contact Network Int'l)

40. Colin Andrews reports that while he was taping, one army helicopter pursued a light while a second helicopter menaced him.
(courtesy Colin Andrews, Circle Phenomenon Research Int'l)

object, in his rear-vision mirror. He called by CB radio to another trucker who was forty or fifty kilometers behind the Knowleses, but when the light came over the car, the truckers lost contact. The Knowleses tried to stop the second driver when he went past, but they never stop, because out there you never know who's trying to stop you."

The farmer, the trucker burned in his rig, and the trucker who saw the light on top of the Knowleses' car are all good eyewitnesses, but none of them will come forward publicly. They watched Patrick and Faye on *Tonight Live*. They read the papers. They know what happens when you talk about UFOs. They think it's best to keep quiet.

The Knowleses' family car became part of the media frenzy. A promoter who told Faye he would keep the car "safe" for her was found to be charging $3 a head to view the car.

Analysis of the soot found inside the car was inconclusive. Some of the material was consistent with burnt brake lining, but high concentrations of chlorine were also found, an element not usually found in cars, animals, or the surrounding desert environment.

A Russian Top Gun

Maxim Chyrdakov sat with his mother in a cold vestibule in a hotel in St. Petersburg, Russia. They had been waiting for hours, hoping to meet two Americans whom they believed might be sensitive to their cause. Maxim had heard that one of the Americans was a world-renowned psychiatrist, the other was a retired U.S. Army officer—and that they helped people who had seen UFOs.

"Maxim and his mother were camped out in the little waiting area on the floor where my room was," Dr. Rima Laibow recalls. "It became clear that Maxim was in very deep trouble. His mother was desperate to use my experience to help her son." Dr. Laibow was in St. Petersburg working on a project for TREAT— Treatment and Research for Experienced Anomalous Trauma— an organization Dr. Laibow founded to help people who have been traumatized by paranormal events.

Dr. Laibow was in St. Petersburg with Albert Stubblebine III, a retired U.S. Army major general and consultant to TREAT. "Maxim was clearly caught up in a set of events beyond his control. He was searching for someone to believe in what he had done and what had happened to him. He didn't want to go to jail," Stubblebine explains. "When the proposal was made that Rima and I get involved in his case, the last thing in the world I wanted to do was get involved in what was obviously an internal state issue. I said, 'Man, time out; that's not a place where any rational person would go.' But we did."

The only thing Maxim Chyrdakov ever wanted to do was fly. As a boy, he had dreamed of becoming a fighter pilot, but the top flight academies in the Soviet Union were only open to boys whose families had a high position in the Communist hierarchy. Maxim's family was not privileged, and he knew his dream of becoming a Russian top gun was only that—a dream. But by the time Maxim came of age, in 1990, the Soviet Union was a thing of the past, and the military was no longer interested in position. They were looking for talent.

From the beginning, Maxim had talent. He was admitted into Russia's number one flight academy in Yaisk. By his second year, Maxim was the class leader in both technical studies and physical capability. His dream was coming true. (See Photo 47.) If he stayed on track, Maxim would graduate as Russia's top gun. But in August 1991, everything started to unravel.

On August 14, 1991, while he was on a solo training flight, Maxim's generator went out. Despite the mechanical malfunction, he was able to land the plane safely and was praised by his instructors. On August 16, there was another mechanical failure. "I ascended at seven-thirty in the morning, and after the second turn, the engine went out," Maxim remembers. "I reported to the ground. The ground did not respond. I waited twenty-five seconds and reported again. Again, the ground did not hear me. I was losing altitude. At thirteen hundred meters, I ejected. The plane fell into a field and I fell in a reservoir."

Again, Maxim was praised for his efforts. He had done everything according to the book, and one important thing that wasn't in the book. He had not ejected until he knew the plane would land on the ground, not in the water. He knew there would be an investigation to determine the cause of the accident, and he wanted that plane on dry land. "An investigative committee justified all my actions. I was found fit to continue my studies as a pilot for military jets," Maxim says.

But twelve days later, on August 28, 1991, Maxim Chyrdakov

was forced to eject again. This time, it was not a simple mechanical failure. This time, Maxim told his rescuers, he had been forced to eject after a close encounter with an aggressive UFO.

Here, in his own words, is Maxim's account of the UFO confrontation as told to a *Sightings* investigative team.

"Twenty-eighth of August, second shift, I made two flights with my commander and one on my own. During the solo flight I entered Zone Three, not far from the city of Zansk. When I reached an altitude of thirty-nine hundred meters, I was coming out of a spiral. I brought my plane horizontal and saw a reddish-yellow ball in front of me fifteen degrees to the right. The ball was hovering at an approximate altitude of twenty-one hundred meters. I observed the ball for two or three seconds before reporting to the ground.

"When I pressed my radio button, the ball started coming in my direction, jerking to the right and to the left. The sun was behind me. The ball came very close to me and appeared to be about a meter and a half in diameter. I was looking directly at it; the center was yellow with red shade around it. I had the feeling that inside the ball there was maybe not a being, but solid matter. Then I was blinded by a very bright light.

"I bent my head down and closed my eyes. I began to feel a sensation of heat on the back of my head. I was scared. I had never experienced anything like this. I felt that somebody was present and had power over me. Not that somebody was in the cockpit, but that somebody was watching from above and that all my movements were under his control.

"I looked at the instrument panel. The generator was out of order. I saw an emergency light indicating a fire on board. The cockpit was filling with smoke. The plane was very difficult to operate. Speed was dropping very significantly. Ground control did not believe my reports and told me to return to the base. They suggested the only thing wrong was in my head. I told them the engine was not working, the cockpit was filled with smoke, and I was falling. As I was falling, the ball was following me. I reported that the ball was falling with me.

"The flight commander came on and ordered me to eject, but I argued with him, because the plane was over a residential area. He said to eject immediately, but I waited until the jet was beyond the houses and then I ejected. Four seconds later, the plane exploded."

Aeronautic research scientist Dr. Richard Haines has studied the Chyrdakov case in depth. It is only one of more than three thousand pilot sightings he has documented over the last twenty years. "Chyrdakov's description of the UFO moving relative to his own airplane is really quite common," Dr. Haines explains. "I have thousands of cases of pilots describing daylight encounters with structured objects which have flight behavior relative to the aircraft."

"One of the most interesting facts to me," Dr. Haines continues, "is that the airplane seemed to be the focus of attention of the phenomenon. It paced the aircraft. This does not suggest a natural phenomenon, like lightning, for instance. You might expect a short period of attraction, some sort of electrostatic effects, but not over a long duration, as we know occurred in this case."

Russian authorities did not share Dr. Haines' opinions. After his rescue, Maxim Chyrdakov was subjected to four days of intense interrogation by military officials and psychiatrists. "The interrogation was conducted with total distrust toward me, and right from the start, they said the first, second, and now the third incident was all my doing," Maxim remembers. "The interrogation continued until one A.M. At the same time, doctors were conducting all kinds of tests on me."

"Air forces don't like to hire people who lose airplanes," Dr. Haines says. "Chyrdakov was beginning to have a reputation for losing airplanes, but I don't think it was the case that he was making up a story about a UFO to cover up something else. He would just be compounding his problems by doing that. If anything, speaking from a pilot's point of view, he wouldn't say anything about a UFO."

The next morning, the black box recorder was recovered from Maxim's jet. It confirmed that there had been a generator malfunction and a fire on board the aircraft. Maxim felt that this information would vindicate him, but it did not. "Even more strict interrogation followed," Maxim recalls. "Every hour new people would come and ask me the same questions over and over. A general came and told me I had disconnected the generator. I had shut off the engine. I had initiated the fire."

Maxim claims that he was given a written "confession" to sign in the general's presence. "He asked me what intelligence agency I was working for. He told me if I didn't confess he would send me to the Sixth Department—that's a special department of the KGB. I decided that it's better to agree with the general than to be put in the hands of the KGB."

But as he put pen to paper, Maxim had a change of heart. "I understood that if I confessed, it would be even worse for me. So instead of signing the confession, I wrote a report and said that all of the general's words were absolute lies. I did not sabotage the aircraft. I saw a UFO and through its control I was forced to eject."

Maxim was called to Aviation Headquarters. A representative from the Justice Department told him that he was being charged with insubordination and sabotage under Russia's National Terrorist Act and that he could be facing capital punishment. "I was expelled from the academy and demoted to regular soldier. The officers looked at me like I was an enemy of the people," Maxim says.

"From the beginning, I had quite a few doubts about Chyrdakov's truthfulness," says Anatoly Musinenko, one of the military prosecutors assigned to Maxim's case. "Specialists had come to the conclusion that the reason for the destruction of his plane was a premeditated act by the pilot, not a UFO."

Maxim spoke to older pilots who had told him about their own encounters with UFOs during flights. But none of them would come forward in Maxim's defense. He also appealed to the radar operators who had been in the control tower on August 28. "They told me they had recorded an exposure on the radar screen twenty kilometers in diameter," Maxim recalls.

"The radar operators told the commander that it was my plane that made the mark on the screen, but the commander said it could not be me, because the plane could not make a turn of that radius." Maxim asked for copies of the screen exposure to build his case. "Unfortunately, that particular film disappeared, and the commander would not admit he had seen the film with his own eyes."

It was in the days just before Maxim Chyrdakov went on trial that he met with Dr. Laibow and retired Major General Albert Stubblebine. He wanted them to sign affidavits that he was being truthful, that he had indeed had a confrontation with a UFO. "I was extremely reluctant to become involved in this," Dr. Laibow says, "but Maxim was facing criminal charges. He was trembling with fear. Everything he had was in jeopardy, and he couldn't foresee any future other than a prison camp. I agreed to set up a session with him, conduct an assessment of his personality, and through hypnosis help Maxim reexperience what had happened."

Albert Stubblebine was present for the hypnosis session as a consultant and expert in military behavior and terminology. "As she was taking him into the trance," Stubblebine recounts, "he changed from a terrified kid into a pilot sitting in his cockpit. It was impressive to me. You could see Maxim sitting in his plane, using the controls, and you saw when things started to go wrong. In a deep hypnotic state, he described what he saw outside his airplane and the emergency actions he took."

After the hypnosis session and an in-depth consultation with Maxim, Dr. Laibow agreed to sign a statement to the military prosecutor with her diagnosis: "Post-traumatic stress disorder secondary to event of anomalous origin." She believed that

Maxim was telling the truth about what he had seen. Dr. Laibow explains, "The question was, 'Is he fabricating?' and he struck me as a person who in that situation was not fabricating. It is possible to have told a lie so many times that after a while nobody, including you, can tell whether or not it's a lie. I don't think that was the situation with Maxim. He was telling what he believed to be the truth, and he never deviated from that."

Albert Stubblebine also signed an affidavit. He says, "At first I thought there's no way I'm going to write any kind of an affidavit for this kid, but by the time the session was through, you could only come to one conclusion. I don't know what happened up there, but Maxim was telling the truth as he believed that truth inside his own heart."

With these statements in hand, Maxim Chyrdakov was able to marshal the resources of Russia's UFO Center, a state-sanctioned office within the Interior Department. The case was reviewed by the center's director and one of Russia's most famous ufologists, Vladimir Ajaja. "The UFO Center studied all the documents of the Chyrdakov case," Ajaja explains. We subjected him to biomedical testing. We did a critical analysis of his account of the UFO incident. We gathered independent eyewitness accounts. We received confirming information from Dr. Richard Haines of the United States and also Lieutenant General Popov, the highly decorated Soviet astronaut."

The UFO Center concluded that Maxim Chyrdakov did have an encounter with an aggressive UFO, and that he was not responsible for the destruction of his jet fighter. Their report and conclusions were sent to the military court.

According to Prosecutor Musinenko, "Evidence from the military hospital indicated that Maxim Chyrdakov had a very stable psyche. Witnesses were questioned who saw numerous flying objects in the same area. There were also established objective facts and evidence provided by the ufologists."

It's difficult to imagine an American military court accepting reports from ufologists, but the Russian prosecutors found the

UFO Center reports to be thorough and professional. Musinenko continues, "Based on all this information, we came to the conclusion that all the malfunctions that happened on that plane were beyond the control and willing desire of Maxim Chyrdakov. The case was dropped."

Maxim Chyrdakov had been exonerated. He was reinstated in his flight academy with no retribution. Retired Major General Stubblebine, who had been the Commanding General of the U.S. Army Intelligence and Security Command, was astonished. He says, "I could not believe Maxim was not headed to a gulag somewhere. It was so clear that the system was after him that I didn't see how he was ever going to mount a credible defense. The fact that he's been exonerated is amazing."

Although the military court had found Maxim innocent, he felt that his fellow student pilots and training officers still treated him as though he were guilty. The young man who was bound to be Russia's top gun was now the victim of suspicion, rumor, and disdain. "The moral atmosphere of the whole thing and all those surrounding me was very harsh. They will never accept me again," Maxim says.

In 1992, Maxim left the flight academy. Recently, he told *Sightings*, "The attraction to planes and flying remains and will continue to remain. I feel that I am missing something from my soul."

According to Dr. Richard Haines, 15 percent of all commercial and military pilots will report some kind of UFO contact during their career. The actual number of sightings is believed to be much greater, but most pilots do not speak publicly about phenomena that may call their professionalism into question.

In September of 1989, hundreds of residents of the Russian city of Varonya reported seeing UFOs almost identical to the one Maxim Chyrdakov would sight two years later. One of the UFOs reportedly landed south of Varonya in a military factory.

Each year, more than five thousand UFO sightings are reported to Russia's UFO Center.

The Experiments

"**W**hen I went to see *Close Encounters of the Third Kind*, I was the guy sitting in the audience saying, 'No, they got it wrong. They didn't look like that.' And people were going, 'Shhhhhh!' but I knew what they really looked like."

Being shushed in a movie theater was just a minor annoyance compared to the ridicule and disdain Michael Bershad has experienced over the past twenty years. Michael is an Abductee, or Experiencer, as he prefers to be known. And like most Experiencers, he is very careful with whom he shares his story—especially when it comes to memories about bizarre experiments he has been forced to endure.

This is Michael's story:

"I was in my early twenties. I had left my girlfriend's house in Frederick, Maryland, to drive back home to Baltimore. There was this one stretch of road where I had a strange feeling. I looked in my rearview mirror, and lights were coming down out of the sky. My car was ripped off the side of the road. I tried to speed away. It looked like something was following me, like a helicopter—but there was no noise.

"The next thing I remember, I was coming out of unconsciousness. I must have hit my head or something. I staggered out of the car, and there were five little guys standing in the grass on the side of the road. I was so terrified looking into the big black eyes of one of these little creatures that I thought I could just raise my fist and crush his head. And exactly at that moment I became paralyzed. No pain. I just couldn't move.

"There were lights in my eyes. A large clamp came down out of the sky. It fitted over my shoulder and jerked me around and into this flying saucer. There were five or six, I call them guardians, stationed around the room with their hands behind their backs. They put me on a table sort of thing that grew out of the ground. It looked like a mesa, sort of whiteish, almost the color of them.

"One guy took over. I call him the Doctor because he was clearly in charge. We communicated, if you will, although it was pretty much one way. They knew everything I was thinking. To call it ESP doesn't do it justice. I was very conscious that they were probing my mind and were completely tapped into what I was thinking. That's when I realized I was in big trouble.

"My clothes were removed. I was lying on the table, on my back. They passed a sort of wand over my head, my throat, and my chest. They treated this thing very carefully, as though they were taking some measurements. Then I was on my stomach, and I could feel my back being opened up. I have no idea how this is possible, but I could feel the skin and the muscle and the tissue being lifted. I felt a tapping on my spine. There was no blood, no pain. I could tell they were extremely interested in seeing how I worked.

"I never got the feeling that they had any emotion. Whenever I would feel really panicked—and there were times when I was absolutely hysterical—the Doctor would put his hand over my head and I would suddenly feel relaxed and calm. It was somehow psychologically or physically induced.

"One of the last things I remember was humiliating. It absolutely debased me. They took this kind of cylinder and put it over my genitals. It made me have an orgasm in two seconds. There was no pleasure associated with this. It was a disgusting feeling. I really feel like I'm one of those few men who knows what a woman feels like when she's raped. Even now it makes me angry.

It makes me angry that they had that kind of control over me. To take a sperm sample was a complete violation, and they knew exactly how to do it, too."

Budd Hopkins has studied the abduction phenomenon for nearly thirty years: "Psychiatrists and psychologists are the first to say something happened to Michael. This is not a fantasy. This is an event in his life that is truly upsetting." Temple University history professor David M. Jacobs, Ph.D., has interviewed many people who describe experiences remarkably similar to Michael's:

"In most abductions, a person is taken against their will. Procedures are performed on them. A very important part of the phenomenon is that reproductive procedures are carried out upon them," Dr. Jacobs explains. "I believe that the abduction phenomenon is real, that it is extraterrestrial, and that people are basically describing events that are happening to them with an objective reality."

Kim Carlsberg knows about the experiments, too. She is an Experiencer who remembers painful extraterrestrial contact going back to early childhood. "People out there are being hurt. They're afraid and confused, because they have no way of understanding what's happening to them. One day all this is going to come out, and I won't have to feel like an alien myself."

Before Kim and Michael had ever met, their abduction experiences coincided in many significant details, and Kim's memories go a long way toward explaining why Michael was, in his words, "debased." Kim was never interested in UFOs before her first abduction memories. She is a successful commercial photographer who finds it difficult to express the pain she has endured.

According to Yvonne Smith, the founder of the Close Encounter Research Organization, a support group for Experiencers, "We have a lot of wounded people walking around out there. The hurt comes not as much from the experience as from not being believed. It's very difficult for people to come forward to talk about this in public. I admire the people who do, because this information needs to be out there so other people know they're not the only ones."

This is Kim's story:

"I had been working on a *Life* magazine shoot, and I came home really late. I was sitting in my living room thinking over the day's shoot, wondering if the film was going to be OK, and out on the horizon I saw a white glowing light. Well, I lived on the beach in Malibu, and I was used to seeing a lot of white lights, but this light was moving at lightning speed from Palos Verdes to Point Dume.

"The next thing I know, it made a ninety-degree turn and appeared on the beach in front of me. A few seconds later, it took another ninety-degree turn and just shot out of the sky. Two weeks later, I had my first conscious abduction experience.

"I was in a small circular area. I thought it was an elevator. There were two people next to me, and there were two beings behind us. A door opened, and we were pushed through into a huge room I thought was a hospital ward. There were tables, very sterile, and little beings working on people. I remember specifically the first ones were about three-and-a-half-feet tall. They wore no clothes. Their skin was washed out, light gray with no texture. They had large heads and very large dark eyes.

"Then there were what I call the Doctors. They are in the same family, only larger and more intelligent. They seemed to be the guys in control. They wore bodysuits, very tight-fitting clothing. Large heads, again, and very large, intimidating eyes with no facial structure to speak of. They were cold and unemotional. It seems they have a job to do, and they do their job with very little respect for their subjects."

This was only the first in a series of abduction memories that Kim was able to retrieve through therapy. She realized that since childhood, she had been abducted again and again, always by the same creatures, and for the same purpose. Kim came to believe that she was being treated as a model human, one whom aliens could experiment with and manipulate:

"All my memories are at night. They just have a way of appearing in your room. They come over to me—two at my feet, two at my head—and they lift me up. When I hit the ceiling, I go unconscious. I believe they have a way of moving you through solid objects, and I don't believe you can be conscious when they do that. So when I wake up I'm in another place.

"One being I always recognize I call the Praying Mantis Man. He's taller and thinner, with a bigger head and bigger eyes. He's very insect-looking. He can stand in one position and move his head forward; his neck can extend like an accordion. I remember one time being on a table with my head turned away, not wanting to look at this creature. When I looked at him, I recognized him as the one in control, the one with all the power. I said, 'You dragged me out of my bed in the middle of the night and you always get your way. I hate you.' And then he just started manipulating my mind.

"They have several ways of controlling you. I've been drugged with chemicals. I've had a being come up to me and put his hand on the back of my neck, and instantly I feel this anesthesia come over me. They can control you with their eyes. I remember so many times wanting to move my head because I knew as soon as I looked into their eyes they would have complete control over my mind and, you know, eventually they get you to turn your head. [See Photo 48.]

"Their purpose is hybrid experimentation. I've been asked to hold children and babies. I've been asked to give these children affection. These aren't alien children, they're not human children. They're somewhere in between.

"Once, I was on a table and saw something removed from my body that I will call a fetus. It was very, very small. I was asked to hold this baby. It was so small I couldn't believe it could live on its own. I remember putting my finger in the arch of its foot and the arch was the size of the end of my finger. I was afraid to look at the face.

"Much later I was taken into a room and put down on my knees. The creatures stood on each side of me with their hands on my shoulders so I wouldn't stand up. Three children were brought in, two male and one female. The female was very pretty, almost human. It was the first time I experienced emotion out of the beings. They stood back and said, 'Isn't she a beautiful baby?' They were trying to communicate that I had something to do with this child. It was said not with words but it was just a feeling of projection.

"After the abductions, I have a terrible burning sensation inside of me. There's a lot of pain. I have unusual scars in unusual places that I have no memory of getting. These experiences have changed me as a person. I'm not the normal everyday me anymore. I've had bizarre experiences, and it's changed the way I view reality."

Kim has tried to find as many positive effects as she can from the abduction phenomenon: "The experiences themselves have been very painful and frightening, but there have been some things that have come out of it that are positive. I've become a certain kind of person because of the experiences, and I like certain aspects of how they have affected me. I'm very open-minded. I'm very observant, and I've become very psychic."

This is where Kim's story and Michael's story diverge.

"When I was a kid in New York," Michael says, "I saw all these space movies and thought, gee, wouldn't it be really fun to be taken up in a flying saucer and look down over Manhattan and wave to people? But it hasn't been a fun experience. This is not something I would wish on anybody. The only reason I am talking publicly about it is to try to get some kind of control over my life. Talking is the only way I have of grasping ahold of it. The irony is, I can't talk to most people in my personal life and say I've had this experience."

> Ninety percent of all reported abductions involve descriptions of "grays," extraterrestrial creatures with oversized heads, large dark eyes, and almost imperceptible facial features. Reports of reptilian or insect-like creatures are less common.

According to David M. Jacobs, Ph.D., "The abduction phenomenon usually begins in infancy or at least by the age of four. It continues all through childhood, through maturity, and into old age."

According to the most recent survey on the subject (a 1991 Roper poll), one in fifty American adults report having four out of the five most common symptoms of the alien abduction experience.

The five most common symptoms reported by abductees are:
1. Waking up paralyzed with the sense of a strange figure
2. Missing time
3. Feeling of actually flying
4. Balls of light in the room
5. Puzzling scars

Mass Sightings in Mexico City

If you want to see a UFO, go to Mexico City. Hardly a day goes by that someone somewhere doesn't see at least one anomalous disc-shaped craft hovering over Mexico's capital city. On several dates, there have been multiple UFOs witnessed by thousands of people. The continuing activity in Mexico City is considered the largest and longest-running mass sighting in UFO history.

The first mass sighting occurred on July 11, 1991. On that date, tens of thousands of people in Mexico City were already looking skyward before the first wave of UFOs arrived. They were watching a total eclipse of the sun, the last full solar eclipse for three centuries. Astronomers from around the world peered through high-powered telescopes, and, because of the burgeoning home video revolution, hundreds of amateur sky watchers had their new camcorders poised and ready.

By all accounts, the eclipse was breathtaking, but as day turned to night, there was something else in the twilight sky. World-renowned UFO researcher Lee Elders recalls the moment the first sighting occurred. "Exactly at the time of the full solar eclipse, a disc-shaped craft appeared over the city and hovered for over thirty minutes. [See Photos 49 and 50.] At least seventeen people on the ground recorded it on home video. That's never happened before in the history of ufology."

Armando Nicolau is an archaeologist specializing in Aztec artifacts and culture. He wasn't surprised that the first mass sighting coincided with the solar eclipse. "The July 11 eclipse was forecasted thousands of years ago by several Aztec tribes, in particular the Nawa Aztecs," Nicolau explains. "In their Legend of the Sun, this eclipse marks the end of the era known as the fifth sun and the beginning of the era of the sixth sun. According to Aztec tradition, the beginning of the sixth sun is a magical time, and the eclipse symbolizes the opening of a new kind of knowledge."

Many people in Mexico insisted that the UFO which appeared at the time of the 1991 eclipse was a harbinger of the new knowledge predicted by the Aztecs. And in at least one important sense, they were correct. That July 11 UFO was followed by hundreds of others, appearing week after week and year after year, causing even the most ardent skeptics to revise what they thought about UFOs.

Since July 11, 1991, people from all walks of life have videotaped wave after wave of hovering UFOs. One of the first to come forward with his home video was Dr. Marco Antonio Rosas, a respected dentist. He had captured a nighttime flight of an enormous L-shaped craft which moved slowly across the sky in front of his home. (See Photo 51.) It was with wonder, not fear, that he experienced his first UFO. "The people in Mexico City are definitely not nervous or afraid of the appearances of the UFOs," Dr. Rosas explains. "We actually like the idea and feel that these appearances will bring some benefit to the earth."

Angel Toledo is an electrical engineer who has videotaped several significant UFO events. On November 9, 1991, Angel captured the clear image of a revolving craft hovering near an ancient ceremonial site called the Hill of the Star. (See Photo 52.) "It was an object that was flying overhead at a low altitude," Angel recalls. "It was an object in the form of a top, and like a top it was suspended over a tower. It was revolving, rotating at a high rate of speed. When it stopped its rotation, it began to move across the city. I lost sight of it behind a building."

"They say there's a magnetic belt around Mexico City," says television camera operator Cuauhtemoc Alvarenga. He has seen and videotaped several waves of UFOs and finds that the peak viewing hours occur between 5:00 and 7:00 in the evening. Cuauhtemoc has seen single craft and on one occasion, a "flap," the ufologist's term for a formation of individual craft.

"I looked at the sky, and there was something, like bubbles," he says. "To me, it looked like a pearl necklace. While I was taping, I observed through the lens that it split apart." (See Photo 53.) As a professional videographer, Cuauhtemoc is frustrated by the camera's failure to capture the excitement of his UFO sightings. "At the moment I observed the pearl necklace, I thought, They're here. But later, when I watched it on the monitor, I didn't feel the same emotion. The feeling is in the moment. Afterward, it's just a picture."

One journalist who witnessed the original mass sighting during the eclipse has spearheaded a continuing effort to understand the recurring phenomena. Jaime Mausson is one of Mexico's most respected investigative reporters, hosting *60 Minutos*, the Mexican version of *60 Minutes*. "Since July 11, 1991, we have had the most incredible flap that has ever been recorded," Jaime says. "It sounds difficult to believe in a city with almost twenty million people that practically every afternoon you can see a UFO."

In his reports, Jaime Mausson often refers to himself as a *former* skeptic. "What I feel is important as an investigative reporter," he says, "is the fact that the evidence presented has never been questioned. The credibility of the witnesses has been attacked, but not the proof that they have presented."

Credibility is an issue in all UFO sightings, no matter where they occur. But no one has challenged the videotape shot by Padre Ferrer. He is a Catholic priest who has recorded several mysterious craft near his Mexico City church: "I came out of my room to take a video of a pine tree against the setting sun. The light was very beautiful. As I was shooting, I saw a light appear over the mountain. It was not an ordinary light. It was blue and very intense. As it traveled across the sky I was struck by how wonderful it was, not frightening or anything like that."

Padre Ferrer does not believe his UFO sightings are at odds with his religious beliefs. "Christ speaks of his kingdom as not being from this world, that his angels will help him. These writings are very dangerous, and I don't like to use them, but they do say there are possibilities. A philosopher once said, 'If God is outside of the truth, I'll stay with the truth.' Therefore, I feel there is no contradiction."

To date, the largest mass sighting in the world occurred over Mexico City on January 1, 1993. Manuel Lazcano was one of the first to capture the New Year's Day event on videotape. (See Photo 54.) "Just in front of me, approximately fifteen hundred feet up, I was looking at an object that I had never seen before. It was suspended in midair, moving only slightly up and down and left to right for almost fifteen minutes."

According to Jaime Mausson, "Hundreds of thousands of people went to the streets, and all of them looked at very strange things. This was a massive phenomenon. It's very difficult for scientists or skeptics to say, 'No,' or try to invent a story around this. I believe Americans can learn from this sighting. I think we have to look at the skies with an open mind, because if you do, you are going to see things that you never expected before."

With this historic New Year's sighting, journalists throughout Mexico were transformed from reporters to eyewitnesses. Genoveva Ortiz writes for *La Prensa*, Mexico City's second-largest daily newspaper. Her personal observations of the January 1, 1993, UFOs became front-page news. "I arrived at the editorial room around three in the afternoon," Genoveva recalls. "We began to notice a commotion in the street around three-thirty. People were coming out of their homes, all the automobiles were stopping, and everybody was looking up at the sky."

La Prensa reporter Jorge Puig was a lifelong skeptic, until he joined the people in the street and stared skyward. Jorge says, "For a long time, there was disbelief among the media professionals. But now with so many occurrences, we now believe and accept things the way they are. The videos, our observations, eyewitness accounts—they have all shown us that something more exists. Not just us."

Among the skeptical professionals who have been transformed by the Mexico mass sightings are a number of commercial pilots who have had close encounters in the skies over Mexico City. These pilots are naturally reluctant to come forward, and during the course of its investigation, *Sightings* heard tantalizing details from several pilots who would not speak publicly. However, *Sightings* did obtain a partial transcript of control-tower transmissions that verify the existence of at least one confrontation between a commercial jetliner and a UFO:

PILOT

This is Mexicana Flight 180. How is the traffic? On the radar, I have an unidentified object moving very fast, coming up on the right up about a mile.

TOWER

I don't see anything. I don't read anything on my screen.

PILOT

You can't see anything on the screen? Really? What do we do?

TOWER

Maintain altitude.

PILOT

They circled behind us.

Jaime Mausson believes that the pilots' reluctance to come forward may be a result of their close contact with the U.S. Federal Aviation Administration, which does not take UFO contact seriously. But, in contrast to sightings in the United States, where UFO controversy most often takes place outside the media mainstream, the Mexico City mass sightings are discussed openly among government officials and in the media. While not everyone agrees that the UFOs are extraterrestrial craft, healthy debate on the true origins of these anomalous craft is encouraged.

"If you are truthful and you believe this is real, you have to tell," Jaime Mausson offers, explaining Mexico's open policy on UFO investigation. "It doesn't matter if it's risky. It doesn't matter if some people tell me that I'm crazy. It doesn't matter if I lose credibility in the eyes of some, because I am acting as an honest man."

Sightings collected more than twenty of the best videotaped UFO images and presented them to analyst David Froning, a retired chief scientist at a major aerospace firm. He ruled out the possibility that all of the sightings are an elaborate hoax or misidentified conventional aircraft. For one reason, several videos appeared to challenge current aerospace technology. (See Photo 55.)

Froning's analysis concluded that "As far as the pictures of in-flight videos, this is about as good as I've seen. They demonstrate a field propulsion and technology that's far beyond anything that I'm aware that we have today. Most scientists look at these things not as phenomena that violate known physical laws—it's just that they're phenomena that our known laws cannot explain right now."

Bolstered by the results of Froning's analysis and that of many other engineers working in Mexico, Jaime Mausson continues to try to find an answer to the mass sightings. In reporter's parlance, he has uncovered only two of the five "Ws" of journalism. Jaime knows when and where they will appear: weekly, in Mexico City. But he does not yet know what they are, who is piloting them, or why they continue to come.

"I am an investigator. It is my duty to investigate for the benefit of the people," Jaime explains. "If you have the courage and you believe, you will be supported. But to do that is very risky, and I know that is why many of my colleagues in the United States don't do this.

"They are here. They will be here tomorrow. They are proving with their presence that it's possible to travel through the stars. The only reason science has not accepted these things is that we don't know how to travel these tremendous distances between the galaxies. But they are here, and they are telling us, 'Hey, take it easy, it's possible to travel through the stars,' and that's all that really matters at this moment."

According to a sixteenth-century manuscript found in the public library at La Spezia, Italy, the earliest known UFO sighting occurred in 1558. The writer, Antonio Cesena, interviewed peasants in two different areas who all saw "a strange disc, changing from yellow to red, and with red fireballs shining beneath it."

UFO *Tractor Beam*

Now that he's retired, John Healey spends a lot of time discovering America on his motorcycle. It's his reward for a lifetime of community and government service. During his working life, John Healey was a career police officer. He also served as a medic in the Army Reserve. John Healey is what people call a stand-up guy.

When he was a detective with the Cleveland Police Department, John Healey took statements from hundreds of eyewitnesses. He taped the confessions of murderers, rapists, and thieves. But on the morning of October 19, 1973, it was Detective Healey himself who was sitting across the desk from a police interrogator. The tape recorder between them was running as Healey made his confession.

He had not committed or witnessed a crime, but the detective had seen something he wanted to record on tape while the events were fresh in his mind. It had happened the previous evening, when Healey, as a U.S. Army Reserve flight medic, was traveling in a helicopter with three other reservists. The following is a partial transcript of Healey's taped statement:

INTERROGATOR
Today is October the 19, 1973, and the time is approximately 2 P.M. I have with me one of the fellows who

works with me. His name is Detective John Healey. He is
going to describe in his own way an incident that occurred
last night.

JOHN HEALEY

We had all just passed our flight physicals. We were cold
sober and in perfect health. We left Port Columbus Airport at about 10:30 last night, and at about 11, halfway
between there and Cleveland—between Ashland and
Mansfield—the crew chief saw a red light on the horizon.
He asked the pilot if there were any towers around the
area. The pilot said there were not. He told the crew chief
to keep an eye on the light.

As we went along at an altitude of about three thousand
feet, the light seemed to be getting brighter and brighter. It
appeared to be on a collision course. The pilot had to put
the helicopter into a power dive to avoid it. The object
cleared our aircraft by about five hundred feet. We were
looking right through the windshield watching this thing,
and it just damn near came to a stop right over us. We all
got a very good look at it.

It had a steady red light on its nose. It was cigar-shaped.
There were no wings on it. It made no noise, created no air
turbulence. It had a green light shining down out of the aft
end. I've seen aircraft from PT-19s up to C-5As, so I know
aircraft when I see it at night. But this thing scared the
living hell right out of me.

We contacted Mansfield Airport and told them we were
almost in a collision with an aircraft operating at three
thousand feet and six hundred knots. Mansfield never
acknowledged our broadcast. We tried to get ahold of
Cleveland, and we couldn't until the object passed over us.
It continued out to the west, picked up speed, and we lost
it over the horizon. We never saw it again.

INTERROGATOR

Let's go from what actually happened to what you might
think it is. I know this is just your personal opinion, but
what do you think?

JOHN HEALEY

It didn't have wings, but at three thousand feet you have to
have wings to stay aloft. How else do you stay up there? It
wasn't a dirigible or a zeppelin, because those things don't
move at the speed this thing moved. Clandestine aircraft
wouldn't operate at that speed at that low altitude. In fact,
it's against FAA law to fly above two hundred knots at that
altitude. We talked about this thing all the way up to the
airfield, and we just couldn't dope it out.

INTERROGATOR

And the four of you have filed an official report because of
the evasive action you had to take? I'd be interested in
knowing what happens to your reports.

JOHN HEALEY

Oh, no problem. We've got a meeting on the third of November. I'll find out how far the report's gone from there.

The report went nowhere. There was an official investigation
based on the reservists' signed affidavit describing their UFO
encounter (see Photo 56), but the results of that investigation
were inconclusive. The U.S. Army ruled the incident a "near-miss
with an unidentified craft." But more than twenty years after the
event, John Healey is the only one of the four eyewitnesses who
agreed to come forward for a *Sightings* interview. Even after
nearly a quarter-century, there was fear of reprisals.

Today, John Healey still believes that what he saw over Mansfield, Ohio, on the night of October 18, 1973, was a UFO. Details
of the anomalous craft he watched for nearly five minutes are still
fresh in his mind. "We were almost involved in a midair collision
with this object coming out of the east heading west toward us. It

was a clear night—unlimited visibility—and I saw that it didn't have wings, it didn't have windows, it didn't have lights like a conventional aircraft. It was coming right at us. This was an object moving at a fast rate of speed. It saw us probably before we saw it. When it was right in front of us, it stopped and hovered. Maybe it had never seen a helicopter at night."

The U.S. Army apparently felt that the incident was too insignificant to warrant a full-scale investigation; however, legendary UFO researcher Dr. J. Allen Hynek disagreed. Dr. Hynek, author of *The UFO Experience*, coined the term "close encounter" and is the acknowledged father of modern ufology. Shortly after the Mansfield UFO sighting, he began to conduct interviews with the flight crew and collected their own sketches of the event. (See Photo 57.)

In 1976, Dr. Hynek handpicked Jennie Zeidman, an investigator with his Center for UFO Studies, to continue his work on the case and compile a full report. The completed 122-page report, titled "A Helicopter-UFO Encounter Over Ohio," reveals several bizarre details about the event that appear to rule out the possibility that the UFO was a conventional or experimental aircraft.

According to Zeidman's report, the pilot of the helicopter was forced to take evasive action to avoid colliding with the UFO. The helicopter began to dive at a rate of two thousand feet per minute. While the controls were still in a dive configuration, the UFO appeared five hundred feet above, hovered, and cast an ominous green light over the reservists' aircraft. John Healey can confirm this part of the report. He says, "On the undercarriage near the aft end was this humongous green light. It shone down and on us and you could see a definite cone shape. You could actually see the beam of light."

During the time that the light was shining over the helicopter, the pilot reported that something strange was happening to his aircraft. "After the object finally went off to the west," Jennie Zeidman explains, "the pilot noticed that although he had been in a descent and his controls were still in the configuration for a descent, the helicopter had actually risen to thirty-eight hundred feet. After diving for what he recalled to have been several seconds, his altimeter showed that, instead, he had risen eight hundred feet."

How could a military helicopter in a dive configuration gain altitude? The prevailing theory at the Center for UFO Studies, and among other ufologists, was that somehow the unidentified craft was controlling the helicopter. It appeared to be a real-life encounter with an invention of dime-novel science fiction, the tractor beam.

John Healey remembers, "In regard to our aircraft climbing while it was in a dive configuration, if the pilot said he put it in a dive, he put it in a dive. I was between the two pilot seats crouching down looking out the windshield. I was so engrossed in watching that thing, I wasn't looking at the instruments. I didn't feel the force of going into a dive, but I didn't feel the force of us being pulled up either. I didn't feel any kind of g-force. The feeling I had was that this thing was scanning us."

"The climb remains unexplained," says Jennie Zeidman. "The pilot absolutely says the controls were in the mode for a descent. Some people have suggested that the UFO was trying to save the helicopter from crashing into the ground, but there is just not enough evidence one way or the other to prove what really happened."

After the encounter, John Healey recalls that the entire crew was badly shaken. "After we tied up in Cleveland," Healey says, "we stopped at a bar and we were talking about it. We were still in uniform, and a couple of pilots there interrupted us and they said, 'Hey, we've seen weird stuff up there, too.' One of the pilots said he never told anyone about it because he didn't think anyone would believe him."

In her search for evidence to support the reservists' claims, Jennie Zeidman looked for other pilots or eyewitnesses on the ground that could corroborate the sighting. Three years after the Mansfield UFO event, Warren Nicholson, the director of the Civil Commission on Aerial Phenomena, contacted Zeidman about two possible eyewitnesses. Nicholson conducted the first interview with the DeLong family, who claimed to have seen the encounter between the helicopter and the UFO.

"I was a little bit doubtful at first," Warren Nicholson recalls. "I thought that maybe they had just read the one story that appeared in the newspaper in 1973. But they knew things that hadn't been in the article. And quite frankly, they just didn't seem to be the kind of people who could pull off this kind of hoax."

Erma DeLong vividly recalls seeing the Mansfield UFO hovering over what seemed to her to be a paralyzed military helicopter. Erma was returning home from a family birthday party in Mansfield at 11:00 P.M. on October 19, 1973. Her three children and her younger sister were also in the car. "About a quarter-mile from our house, on Lavor Road, we saw a helicopter just sitting in midair with this object over it," Erma remembers. "The kids kept hollering they wanted to stop, but I was scared."

Erma's son Charles recalls, "I can remember hollering at my mom—I was twelve years old then—and finally she stopped the car. I jumped out. I remember the whole sky was lit up a dull, fluorescent green. I looked up and saw this oval-shaped object above the helicopter. It was dark, and from the ground I couldn't really see the size, but it was rather large."

Erma continues, "The UFO looked almost egg-shaped to me. I don't even know if I can describe the color of the light. It was real, real bright and absolutely beautiful. It was wonderful to see, but yet it was also very frightening. I wanted the kids back in the car, to get home as fast as possible. It scared me." Charles says, "Mom wanted us back in the car, but I was excited. I knew it was something I had never seen before and I've never seen anything like it since."

"This case brought together two distinct groups of eyewitnesses," Jennie Zeidman explains. "Because of these two sources, we were able to establish the exact location of the event. We were able to compute the flight path of the helicopter and the flight path of the UFO. And we were able to develop a second-by-second time-line analysis. This makes Mansfield a very credible case, but it is still an unknown."

Despite the concerted efforts of Zeidman and the Center for UFO Studies, there just isn't enough information to reach a conclusion about what appeared in the skies over Mansfield, Ohio, on October 18, 1973. Unless new ground witnesses come forward with revealing details or the military discloses additional information that they may have, the case will remain a mystery.

Perhaps the helicopter itself, now warehoused in an abandoned hangar or rusting on a surplus scrap heap, holds the key to the mystery. According to John Healey, "The strangest part of this whole incident was our aircraft 15444. She was never right after October 18. They would replace radios and navigation equipment, and in a short time nothing would work. There was no structural damage, but she was just never the same. After that night, she was known as the Hangar Queen."

Skeptics contend that the Mansfield UFO was probably a meteor misidentified by John Healey and the other crew members. However, the duration of the sightings, calculated by Jennie Zeidman to be at least three hundred seconds, tends to rule out the possibility that the four highly trained members of the flight crew had seen a meteor.

In the three week period preceding the Mansfield UFO sighting, a wave—or flap—of UFO activity throughout the eastern United States had been widely reported by the news media. More than a hundred individual sightings were reported, culminating in the closest and most reliable sighting by the Army Reserve helicopter crew.

Twin Abduction

J im and Jack Weiner are identical twins, born just a few minutes apart on October 8, 1952. Like many identical twins, Jim and Jack believe that they have shared a strong psychic bond since early childhood. They share many interests; both are Boston-area artists. And they share one experience that has forever changed the way they look at themselves and their place in the universe. Jim and Jack Weiner are the subjects of the only twin alien abduction case on record.

In 1976, the Weiner brothers and two of Jack's friends from the Massachusetts College of Art, Charlie Foltz and Chuck Rak, decided to go on a canoe trip over the summer break. The four friends went to the Allagash National Wilderness in northern Maine. They canoed, they camped, they fished. and when the trip was over, they had a whopper of a fish story. In this case, however, "the one that got away" was an extraterrestrial spacecraft.

All four men related an unbelievable tale of fear, missing time, and later, abduction and bizarre experimentation at the hands of buglike aliens. Yet when the "Allagash Four," as they were dubbed, voluntarily took polygraph examinations, science said they were telling the truth.

"We were just four guys who wanted to do a little camping and fishing," Jack says. "We were excited about getting out of the city and being in the wilderness, going somewhere we'd never been before. The last thing on our minds was any UFOs or anything like that."

The first three days of the trip were uneventful—too uneventful, judging by their empty creel. On August 26, 1976, the four men paddled to Eagle Lake and decided to try some night fishing. "There was no moon," Jack recalls. "It was very, very dark, so we decided to build a fire so we could find our way back to the campsite." Jim picks up the story. "You have to realize that up on those lakes at night, it's absolutely pitch black. You literally cannot see your hand in front of your face. Since we planned on going clear across the lake, we built a very large fire to act as a beacon."

All four men were in the same canoe. They paddled to the opposite shore and dropped their lines into the water. Jack remembers, "We were out there for approximately fifteen or twenty minutes, fishing with no luck, when suddenly Chuck Rak said, 'Hey, guys, that's a heck of a case of swamp gas.' We turned around and 150, maybe 200 yards away at the most, coming out of the trees was this huge ball of glowing, pulsating light."

"I remember it as being a very bright, round sphere of light that had kind of a roiling quality to it," Jim says. "It was yellow-white in color. It was hovering totally silently over the tree tops." Jack says, "It was hovering above the trees, motionless. So we thought, well, it's obviously not an airplane, because airplanes don't hover." The silence of the glowing craft also seemed to rule out the possibility that it was a helicopter.

Jack continues: "Charlie said that maybe we should signal it with a flashlight that we had with us. And we thought, sure, go ahead and signal it—what's going to happen? But the minute Charlie signaled, it started moving toward us. We were beginning to suspect that it was something odd, although I don't remember anyone ever saying, 'It's a UFO.' As it came over the water, somebody said, 'We better get to shore. This thing is obviously coming for us.' So we turned the canoe around, and we could see the campfire burning very brightly on the opposite shore. We started paddling very quickly. I was looking over my shoulder to see where this thing was, and it just kept following us, coming closer and closer. I remember paddling out the side with my hand, because at that point I was in a panic.

"A second later, it was almost on top of us. I remember thinking, How can it do this? It's defying the laws of physics. A beam of light came out of it aimed at our canoe. I knew we were not going to outrun this thing. The beam came right toward the back of the canoe, and then the next thing I remember I was standing on the beach watching it hover over the water with this beam projected directly underneath it.

"It was hovering just twenty or thirty feet above the water, and I remember thinking, My God, this thing is so close I could throw a stone and hit it. It didn't look like a flying saucer or anything like that. It was just this ball of plasmic energy as big as a tractor-trailer truck, maybe sixty feet in diameter."

Strangely, the signal fire that had been raging just a few minutes before was now completely burned out. Jim says, "Elapsed time since we saw the fire from the opposite shore we thought was fifteen or twenty minutes, tops. We couldn't understand why the fire had burnt down so soon." What happened during this period of missing time that all four friends experienced would not be revealed until much later.

The UFO over Eagle Lake disappeared as strangely as it had arrived: "Suddenly, the light went out from underneath it, and it slowly started moving away from us. Then it seemed to turn and blink out. Then, a little higher in the sky, it appeared again. It would seem to go out, then reappear higher, then go out, almost in a steplike fashion. I remember thinking that nobody has anything that can do that. Then, at about a thousand feet up—I can't exactly say what altitude—it just sped away. In a snap of your fingers, it was gone," Jack remembers.

The four men stood on the beach, numbly staring into the sky. Instead of talking about what had just happened, they silently nodded their good nights and went to sleep. Jack explains, "We're all artists. You'd think that we would have spent hours discussing this thing, drawing pictures. The fact that we didn't was very uncharacteristic behavior."

The next morning the Allagash Four moved to another campsite. They spotted a ranger's boat, and Charlie Foltz signaled an SOS. Jack described their UFO encounter to the ranger. He recalls, "We described the ball of light, that we were very close to it, and how it had a beam of light that came out toward us. The ranger acted very skeptical. He said, 'Well, boys, if the campers aren't complaining about the bears or the bugs, it's the gosh-darn Martians.' So we just dropped it."

The ranger's response was typical of the responses the Allagash Four got from their friends and family. "We'd get responses like, 'You guys are nuts' or 'What were you guys smoking out there?' So after a while we just stopped telling people. We kept it to ourselves," Jack says.

The encounter wasn't mentioned again until 1988, when Jim's doctor began investigating the reason why Jim was having so many sleepless nights. Jim explains, "I had been having strange nightmares, but I really didn't want to talk about it. Finally, the doctor got it out of me. I told him I was having terrifying, recurring dreams about being in a room with strange creatures around me and my brother, Jack."

After Jim had confided in his doctor, he confided in his twin. Jack listened in astonishment as Jim detailed what he was seeing in his nightmares. "I said to Jim, 'I can't believe you're telling me this, because I've been having the same dream,' " Jack recounts. "Since 1986 or 1987, I'd been having these horrible nightmares of being on a table somewhere, with my brother and Chuck and Charlie sitting on a bench watching me. I would wake up drenched in sweat and my heart beating really, really fast. It was terrifying, and it just kept recurring."

One of Jim's doctors had an unusual suggestion about who to talk to about his nightmares. "The psychiatrist, who was part of the medical team treating me, asked if I had ever seen a UFO," Jim remembers. "And I said, 'Now that you mention it, I have.'

The doctor suggested there might be a connection. I was shocked by the idea. I'd never read anything about it. I was totally ignorant of the whole abduction phenomenon. I didn't even know what missing time was."

Jim Weiner was referred to Ray Fowler, a paranormal investigator who was conducting research into the burgeoning abduction phenomenon. Ray suspected that the brothers were reliving abduction experiences through their dreams. He was particularly interested in their case, because Jack and Jim appeared uncontaminated by recent books and media reports about alien abduction.

Ray Fowler asked Jim if he and his twin brother would be willing to undergo hypnosis. Both brothers were skeptical and extremely reluctant. "I had never been hypnotized before, and to be honest with you, I didn't believe I could be hypnotized," Jim says. Jack concurs: "I was pretty skeptical, but I said, 'If it'll help, let's do it.' "

Jim's hypnosis sessions were conducted first. Jack's sessions followed several days later. Jack explains, "We weren't allowed to talk to each other about it. That was one of the first instructions; we could not tell each other what came out of the hypnosis sessions until they were all over."

When the brothers finally did compare notes, there were startling similarities in their hypnotic memories. They both described what had happened during that missing time on the shores of the Allagash waterway. Each told the story from their own point of view, and each corroborated the horrifying experiments that were being performed on the other. Here, they describe their independent and unrehearsed memories of the abduction:

JACK: I was inside this circle of bright light that I could not see through. It completely surrounded our canoe. I remember this bizarre feeling that is so difficult to describe. It felt as if I was coming apart.

JIM: I remember pressure, heat, the feeling of my physical body being ripped to shreds on a molecular level. It's difficult to verbalize, but it was an extremely unpleasant feeling. It felt like death.

JACK: I had no idea where I was. I realized that Jim, Charlie, and Chuck were sitting on a bench, naked. I was lying naked, paralyzed, with this thing coming toward me out of the light. My first thought was that it was a person, but when it got closer and I saw what it was, I thought, This is it. I'm going to die of a heart attack. I had no idea what this thing was, but it was definitely not human.

JIM: I was on a bench, and my brother was in the center of this space with creatures examining him. They reminded me of bugs. They had these very large, almond-shaped eyes that were looking right through me. They had very thin necks, and their heads were set on a lateral, not vertically like our heads. They had no ears that I could see, no nose—just a hole in their face with a slight protuberance. They had a strange bony structure coming down over their faces that reminded me of insects.

JACK: Their heads were disproportionately large for their bodies, which seemed thin and delicate. They had very large eyes that seemed to wrap around the sides of their heads, no eyelids. Their hands were not like ours. They did not have five digits, and they didn't have skin. They had four digits, like if you took away my thumb and had a crack down the middle of the back of my hand. They were very dexterous; I was amazed at how nimble they were with this type of fingers.

JIM: One of the creatures was holding something, examining my brother. It was a type of wand, a long, thin instrument maybe the diameter of a pencil, a little over a foot long with a bulbous end.

JACK: It looked pointy and dangerous. I was worried about what this thing was going to do. They seemed to be taking scrapings of skin from my groin area, my stomach, and my ears. They opened my mouth and took scrapings from my tongue and the inside of my cheeks. The next thing I remember was they turned me over and were doing some type of anal exam. I had no idea what was going on. I thought they were going to dissect me. I just kept saying, this is it. This is the last thirty seconds of my life, and I don't know what's going on.

JIM: They walked him through a portal into another area, and they wanted me to go with them. I did not want to go, so one of them took the wand and stuck it into my rib cage. It was quite painful, and from that point on I was absolutely terrified.

JACK: I was sitting in there with my twin brother, just waiting to see what would happen next. I didn't seem to be able to control my body. I remember being able to move my eyes, but I couldn't move my body. I couldn't help Jim when they put him on the table.

JIM: I was on the examination table. I couldn't move my legs. They flooded my mind with lovemaking and sexual visions, which aroused me, but it was all preprogrammed and totally out of my control. I remember them taking a sperm sample. They had such thin necks, I thought I could just reach out and snap it, but I was immobile.

JACK: Then they walked us into this space where our clothing was in a pile on the floor. We put on our clothing in a daze, and then the next thing I remember, we were all standing on the beach and the fire was out.

The brothers' hypnosis sessions were so similar, Ray Fowler questioned their credibility. He sought out Charlie Foltz and Chuck Rak and asked them also to submit to independent hypnosis. Both Charlie and Chuck agreed, and, although not as detailed, their memories matched those of the twins in many significant details. Ray Fowler still suspected collusion among the Allagash Four. He asked them to submit to polygraph examinations.

"I'm sure he was concerned as a researcher about whether we were telling the truth. I wasn't surprised when he asked us to take a polygraph test," Jim says. "I felt that I'd only told the truth about the event, and I didn't feel scared about the test. To me it would be just another form of verification of our story."

Jack had mixed feelings. "I wanted people to know, finally, that I was telling the truth, but I'd never taken a polygraph test, so I was really nervous. I knew they didn't allow them in a court of law. What if the guy makes a mistake, or what if it doesn't work right? What if I look like a liar?"

But Jack Weiner didn't look like a liar. Neither did his twin brother, Jim, nor Charlie Foltz, nor Chuck Rak. The polygraph examiner was Ernest C. Reid: "After administering the examinations, reviewing the charts in detail, there is absolutely, positively no doubt in my mind that they are being absolutely honest with me when they tell me they were confronted with the phenomena in the Allagash region."

This was an important admission from an authority outside of the ufology community. Ray Fowler says, "One person might fool a polygraph examiner, but you have four people all passing the tests and the examiner being convinced that all four are telling the truth. This is very important."

After the polygraph, all four men felt vindicated. The truth of their personal experience had been recorded. But the implications of their truth was also frightening. "It was shocking that we all basically told the same story, gave similar details like four fingers, that kind of thing. When the polygraph results were divulged, you just couldn't deny it anymore. It happened. It was real, and now you had to deal with it," Jack remembers feeling.

Before acceptance, there was denial for the twins. Jack says, "I thought I was nuts, I must be going crazy. There's something wrong with me. This isn't about abduction, this is some kind of brain disorder." Jim was having the same feelings. "Anything but that—I mean, just tell me I'm insane or tell me I'm hallucinating, but UFOs? You've got to be kidding." Jack speaks for both of them when he says, "It took a while to realize that we had to deal with this. It did happen."

Jim and Jack's realization that they had had an alien abduction experience not only answered their questions about the missing time in 1976, but it also explained other strange phenomena they had experienced. "Immediately after the sightings incident in 1976," Jim says, "I started seeing things differently, as if I was being programmed. My artwork changed immediately and very drastically. I was a clay worker, and I had been doing very traditional types of pottery—plates, pitchers, saucers—looking back on it, I would say it was fairly mediocre in design. But after Allagash I started doing very bizarre structural pieces. [See Photo 58.] I became obsessed with this work."

Jack's art changed dramatically, too. He says, "I started out as a very traditional painter. I was interested in still life, landscapes; I did a lot of pretty ordinary paintings. Immediately after the abduction, I became interested in dealing with dualities of space and shape. [See Photo 59.] I became obsessed with mathematics, science, and physics, and it started working into my artwork. I had no idea why."

"I don't know what caused this change in us," Jim wonders. "I don't know whether it is a result of being in a traumatic experience and then working these things out through art, or if it is something that has been programmed into us. Did we pick up something from the aliens that we are now conceptually obsessed about?"

Some of the artwork that the brothers have done are representations of their actual abduction experience. This is not art that they sell or hang in a prominent place. It's one way they can deal with the most nagging question of all. Why them? Ray Fowler believes it was their twinness that attracted the aliens to these brothers in particular. Fowler believes "The entities seem to be conducting genetic experiments with human beings. What happened during the Allagash abduction experience—the kind of interface that took place—there was special attention directed toward the twins."

This notion is disturbing to the twins. Jacks speaks for both the brothers when he says, "It's not over. This is an ongoing thing, because basically, we're tagged. They were scientists here doing a job, and now we're part of an ongoing study. There's nothing we can do to change that. At some point they'll come back to check on us. We have to accept that. Otherwise, what can we do? Go hide? No, they'll find us."

According to abduction phenomenon expert Dr. David M. Jacobs, more than 1 million people worldwide believe that they have had at least one alien abduction experience.

The Strange Death of
Thomas Mantell

O n January 7, 1948—six months after a mysterious crash near Roswell, New Mexico—a Kentucky National Guard pilot radioed in with a strange message. The pilot, a decorated World War II veteran with over 2,800 hours of flight time, told the tower that he was in pursuit of a UFO. Moments later the pilot, Thomas "Tommy" Mantell, was dead.

"Tommy was a wonderful person," remembers his wife, Peggy. "He was a fun guy, but a serious guy. His mind was always up in the air. Flying was his first love, and when he got into the Air Corps in World War Two, he was thrilled to death. I wasn't too thrilled, but if he was happy, then I was happy."

Tommy's sister, Bettye, recalls a boyhood dedicated to dreams of flying fighter planes. She recalls, "Tommy was my big brother. He was three years older than I and awesome to me, of course. He was always interested in airplanes. He made model planes, and he had them hanging all over his room."

The boy who dreamed of flight came of age during World War II. He applied for fighter pilot training, but overshot the height requirement. At six feet two inches tall, his muscular frame just wouldn't fit in the cockpit. But the U.S. Army saw his raw talent and trained him to fly transport planes. Peggy recalls, "He wanted to be a fighter pilot so bad, he was disappointed at first. But then they sent him over to England, and he was very happy because his job was to take gliders and paratroopers behind the line. On D-Day, that's what he did."

On June 6, 1944, Tommy Mantell proved just what kind of a pilot he was. Tommy's top-secret mission was to deliver a glider deep behind enemy lines. Towing the glider behind his unarmed C-24, Tommy came under attack from enemy antiaircraft fire a hundred miles from the drop-off point. His plane was hit, but Tommy pressed on and completed his mission, dropping the glider on target. When he landed his plane safely back in England, no one could believe he had survived. The plane was shredded by gunfire.

After the war, Tommy returned home to Louisville, Kentucky, to a hero's welcome. He was awarded a Silver Star and the Flying Cross for heroism and extraordinary achievement in flight. Peggy says, "When he got out of the army, I was hoping he'd get a regular 9-to-5 job, but he still wanted airplanes. So he started his own flying school and joined the Air National Guard. He liked the Guard because he finally got to fly fighter planes."

It was while piloting one of those National Guard fighter planes that Tommy lost his life. To this day his death remains unexplained, largely because no one has ever determined what Tommy encountered on that last fatal flight. Larry Tabor is a historian and aeronautics expert who has been researching the Mantell case for more than fifteen years. He has amassed hundreds of civilian and military documents related to the strange death of Thomas Mantell.

"When I got into the Guard in college," Tabor explains, "I found out that our squadron at the University of Louisville was named after Thomas Mantell—the Arnold Air Society portion of it. So I began to do research." The more he found out about Tommy's last flight, the more Tabor began to believe that Tommy had died after pursuing a UFO. Based on his review of flight logs, eyewitness interviews, and partial radio transmissions, Tabor reconstructs Tommy's last moments:

"Thomas Mantell was returning from Marietta, Georgia, that day with three other men in a flight of P-51 fighters. They were ferrying the planes to Standiford Field, Kentucky, when they received a call from the tower at Godman Field, Fort Knox. The tower told them to pursue an unidentified flying object that had been observed in the area. One of the airplanes did not participate, because it was short on fuel. The other three aircraft continued on, even though two of the aircraft—including Mantell's—were not equipped to go at high altitudes.

"All three pilots reported seeing some type of flying object. They chased it for a certain amount of time in the early afternoon, but when they reached twenty-five thousand feet, Mantell's wing man turned back to escort the less experienced pilot down. I find that strange, since it's the job of the wing man to stay with his flight leader at all times. Mantell chose to continue the chase and reported to the tower that he was in pursuit of a metallic object going half his speed.

"At some point he said to the tower, 'I see the object. I am going to pursue it a bit further.' That was the last contact that anybody had with Mantell. He went up to thirty-three thousand feet and at that point appears to have died from anoxia, lack of oxygen. The aircraft was continuing its high-power climb. With Mantell dead, eventually the aircraft heeled over from torque and came down in a spin. It crashed in a field in Franklin, Kentucky."

"We were not told or informed of my dad's death by the Air Force," Thomas Mantell III explains. In 1948, Tommy's son was six years old. "They wanted to sweep it under the rug with as little attention as possible, either because they felt they were at fault or because he was chasing something they didn't want to talk about. A neighbor who heard about the crash on the radio came to our house and told my mother what had happened."

Peggy remembers, "Two neighbors came in and said, 'Peggy, we've got something to tell you.' And of course I had no idea what it was. They told me, 'Tommy's had a crash.' And I said, 'Oh, is he all right?' and they said, 'No, he was killed.' " Peggy left the home she and Tommy and their two boys had just moved into and never returned. She moved in with her mother, and as her sister-in-law, Bettye, recalls, the loss was unimaginable. "The main thing I recall," Bettye says, "is standing in my mother's home with Peggy and the boys, and we were all standing in a circle holding hands. My mother said, 'The circle's been broken.' And I would say she was broken also." Grief quickly turned to rage after days of waiting for some explanation from the military.

Thomas Mantell III says, "I do believe and I always will that it was a cover-up, because they never came to talk to anybody in my family about what happened." Peggy still harbors a deep resentment. She says, "I'm very angry at the Air Force. I feel like they know more than they're telling us. It's affected my children. They never knew their daddy."

After the crash, the military's silence also contributed indirectly to a flood of contradictory rumors: Tommy's body was found riddled with bullets/the body was missing; the plane had disintegrated/large chunks of recovered wreckage were radioactive; Tommy's P-51 was ionized/the plane was knocked down by an extraterrestrial spacecraft. Finally, perhaps in response to several sensational stories in *True* magazine, the Air Force suggested that Thomas Mantell may have died while in pursuit of either the planet Venus or a high-altitude balloon.

In the hours before Tommy's UFO sighting and subsequent death, several military bases had reported seeing a UFO overhead traveling at approximately 250 miles per hour. One university professor viewing the object through a telescope described it as round and white, resembling a parachute with something solid hanging below.

"The Navy Skyhook balloon program was aimed at carrying cosmic ray experiments into the stratosphere," says Professor Charles B. Moore. He was present at the launching of a supersecret Skyhook balloon from a General Mills testing facility on January 6, 1948. Moore believes that this balloon was directly responsible for Tommy's death on January 7, 1948. "We heard reports of a large white object being seen in the sky over Illinois," Moore explains. "And later we heard reports of a similar object seen over Kentucky. This was the first time anyone in the central United States had ever seen such a high-flying balloon."

But there are serious discrepancies between the actual shape, size, and flight pattern of a Skyhook balloon and what Tommy reported seeing. He described an object traveling up and forward and said that the UFO was metallic. Larry Tabor has reviewed recordings of Tommy's radio contact with Godman Field, but communication was spotty, and only partial transmissions were picked up.

"I feel that Mantell was intelligent and experienced enough not to have made the mistake of chasing a balloon. On several occasions, he said he couldn't gain on the object—it appeared to be going faster than he was," Tabor says. "The wing man maintained to his dying day that they were chasing a large golden iridescent object. He said that there was no way that it was a balloon."

Perhaps the most compelling evidence that the UFO was not a balloon was the fact that Tommy risked his personal safety to chase the object. According to Tommy's sister, Bettye, "He was not what you would call a flyboy. He didn't take risks unless he had to."

Larry Tabor agrees. He explains, "It is my opinion that Captain Mantell must have seen something that he felt was a threat to the security of the United States. He risked his life, knowing the inherent risk of going to that high of an altitude without air. He was a very experienced pilot, highly decorated and aggressive. He chose to risk his life, and it cost him his life. Whether as a direct result of that object or as a result of some mechanical or human error, he saw something that constituted a threat. And I believe that threat was a UFO."

In an effort to perhaps find answers to the Mantell mystery and bring some measure of closure to the family, *Sightings* sent an investigative team to the crash site in Franklin, Kentucky. *Sightings* found Glen Mays, a local resident who had witnessed the crash forty-six years earlier while waiting for a school bus. He thought he remembered the exact location where he had seen military personnel bury wreckage from Tommy's plane. After so many years, our team had few expectations. But Tommy's surviving family, visiting the crash site for the first time, had high hopes.

Larry Tabor and the *Sightings* team searched the area with metal detectors and a Geiger counter—with no success. As the light dwindled, so did the possibility that anything could be found after so long. But at twilight, one of the metal detectors went off. The team began to dig, and within minutes, over two dozen pieces of aircraft wreckage were recovered. (See Photo 60.)

"Fortunately, there were serial numbers on several pieces of the aircraft that we recovered, and these have been traced to ensure that they did come from the airplane that Captain Mantell was flying that day," Tabor explains. Several pieces registered strong levels of radiation, which, after being buried for forty-six years underground, is highly unusual. Apparently the recovery of this wreckage has generated more questions than it answered. Why the high levels of radiation? Why was it found buried in an unmarked trench by the same military that had promised to do a thorough investigation?

"I've been asked on several occasions if I feel that there's a military cover-up in this case," Tabor says. "I feel that it is more the government's ineptitude. I don't think the investigation was treated with the right respect at the time. The military looked at this more as an airplane crash than the fact that the aircraft had something to do with a UFO. The possibility of pilot encounters with UFOs wasn't even considered until the late 1950s, but by then, in these older cases, the aircraft parts were gone and most of the eyewitnesses had dispersed. Memories fade with the passage of time."

For Tommy's family, faded memories came into vivid focus at the crash site. During the long daytime search in the field, Peggy, Bettye, and Tommy III talked about cover-up and disappointment and grief. But as night fell, they talked about a husband, a brother, and a father. Peggy says, "Coming here after so many years has been very traumatic, but I would have to say it really did help a lot. Tommy was a good man, and he was too good of a pilot to hurt his family to go chasing after something that wasn't there."

Larry Tabor, who continues to search for answers, was reflective at the crash site. "We never want to forget Tommy Mantell. Not because he chased a UFO, but because he laid his life on the line to protect us from what he saw up there. That is a debt which we cannot repay."

The crash of a mysterious object near Roswell, New Mexico, on July 2, 1947, is the most widely researched and hotly debated of all UFO incidents. Early reports, including a press release issued by the U.S. Air Force on July 8, 1947, described the object as a "saucer." Later, officials rejected any implications that the object was of an extraterrestrial nature and stated that it was a downed balloon—the same explanation offered six months later in the Mantell case.

UFO Confrontation: Iran

In 1978, the CIA was directed by the U.S. District Court in Washington, D.C., to turn over to Ground Saucer Watch—a private UFO investigation group—all UFO data unrelated to national security. Although the CIA had maintained that it had had no involvement with UFOs since 1953, 879 pages of declassified UFO information, some dated as late as 1977, were turned over after the court order.

Among the documents was a cable sent from U.S. Army Intelligence in Tehran, Iran, to the CIA detailing an apparent confrontation between an Iranian F-4 Phantom fighter jet and a UFO on September 19, 1976. The four-page communiqué was also sent to the White House, the NSA (National Security Agency), the Secretary of State, and the Joint Chiefs of Staff, among others. (See Photo 61.) The document describes in frightening detail a UFO encounter that remains unexplained to this day.

In 1976, Iran was ruled by Mohammed Reza Shah Pahlavi, the "King of Kings" of the Qajar dynasty. After his ouster by the Ayatollah Khomeini in 1979, the Shah and many of his political and military charges went into exile in the United States, and with them went the secrets of the world's only known military engagement of a UFO.

Beginning in 1994, Essy Niknejad, a *Sightings* segment director, was able to track down many of the highest-ranking officers in the Imperial Air Force who had been eyewitnesses to the UFO confrontation over Iran. These men had remained silent for more than fifteen years, until they agreed to be interviewed by *Sightings*.

"I don't have any doubt about UFOs. I have seen them with my own eyes, and I can't ignore it. UFOs exist." This statement was made not by a UFO buff or an amateur sky watcher, but by Amir Kamyabipour, a former deputy commander of operations in Iran's Imperial Air Force. Because of what he experienced first-hand in Iran, Kamyabipour believes "UFOs are trying to find some way to make contact with our world. I am positive of this, and I will never change my idea because it is in my heart, it is in my blood. It will be in my mind until the day I die."

The first in-flight observation of the Iranian UFO was made by Imperial Air Force pilot Yaddi Nazeri. He now lives in California, but in 1976 Nazeri was stationed at Vatiti Air Force Base in southern Iran. His mission was to monitor and engage enemy helicopters coming from the border with Iraq. When Nazeri heard the siren on the night of September 19, he assumed it was an incoming Iraqi aircraft.

"The operations officer told me that there was a target very close to the base, and I must find out what type of target it is— and, if it's a helicopter, shut it down," Nazeri recalls. "I took off and saw a foreign object with a bright rotating light, exactly like a helicopter, but it was moving away from me at a very high speed. Because of the darkness I could not see the shape—only the light and a metal-type reflector. I requested an F-4, because the object was beyond my speed and power. The F-4 came but also could not catch up to the object. That's when I thought, this is a UFO."

Nazeri estimates that the UFO was traveling somewhere between two thousand and three thousand miles per hour. "In the Air Force, we had many briefings about different kinds of aircraft. We knew all the information about the United States, Russian, and European aircraft. That was our job. According to our knowledge, no country had this type of flying object, so I was thinking, this craft is from another planet."

A few minutes after Nazeri's sighting in southern Iran, civilians to the north in the capital city of Tehran started seeing the object. Many of them called Mehrabad International Airport to report their UFO sighting. "I was the supervisor of Mehrabad tower control on the night of September 19, 1976," says Hossein Pirouzi, another exile tracked down by *Sightings*. "I had a call from a lady who said she saw a strange object over her house. She said it had different colors—red, blue, orange, green—and it was like a ceiling fan."

Pirouzi says he dismissed the call as unimportant, but soon the tower was flooded with calls about the UFO. "I got my binoculars and went out on the tower balcony," Pirouzi says. "That's when I saw the object for the first time. I saw a rectangular shape with a flashing red light in the middle. Then it changed, and I saw only blue light. Then I lost it, but after a few seconds it reappeared, quite red this time. I went back into the control tower and I said, 'Yes, they're right; a strange object really is over Tehran, and I don't know what it is.' " (See Photo 62.)

Pirouzi contacted Shahrokhi Air Force Base, two hundred miles outside Tehran, and described the anomalous craft. The acting base commander called his superior, General Nader Yousefi, and requested permission to launch an F-4 Phantom to pursue the UFO. Yousefi, the assistant deputy commander of the Imperial Air Force, authorized a scramble mission after seeing the UFO for himself from the balcony of his quarters: "I looked in the sky and found the object immediately. It was at least twice as large and twice as bright as any star."

The reputed number-three man in the Iranian Air Force described for *Sightings* what occurred after he authorized the scramble mission. From his quarters in northeastern Tehran, General Yousefi was in direct contact with Shahrokhi AFB, Mehrabad tower control, and both pilots in the two-man F-4 Phantom. Yousefi says, "The jet pilots confirmed the direction and location of the object and reported they were in pursuit."

Radio transmissions between the pilots and Mehrabad were obtained by *Sightings*'s Essy Niknejad. "I'm approaching the object," the F-4 lead pilot can be heard to say. "What is this brilliant object?" The tower responds, "We have reports of this brilliant object above Tehran." The pilot responds, "Yes, I can see it now. I'm getting closer to it . . . it's 120 miles away. How shall I proceed?"

General Yousefi ordered the pilot to continue his pursuit, but when he came within twenty-five NM (nautical miles) of the UFO, the F-4 lost all instrumentation and communication. When he retreated from the object, all systems returned to normal. "When I get close to the object, my systems shut down. It's so frightening. Tell me what to do, I'm running low on fuel," the pilot can be heard to say on one transmission tape. The control tower responds, "If you believe it's too dangerous, don't pursue it." The F-4 pilots apparently thought it was too dangerous. They returned to Shahrokhi AFB.

Yousefi asked for a second F-4 scramble mission. Upon reaching the twenty-five NM point, the second F-4 observed on radar that the object appeared to be the size of a Boeing-707, but its intense brilliance made it difficult to visually estimate the actual size. According to the pilot, the UFO displayed a rectangular pattern of strobe lights flashing blue, green, red, and orange.

The F-4 attempted to gain on the UFO, but could not come any closer than twelve NM without major systems failures. From the transmissions, the pilot can be heard to say, "Strange things are happening. I can't catch him. When I get closer than twelve miles, my emergency equipment comes on." Mehrabad is then heard relaying a message from General Yousefi: "Get as close as you can."

It was a tense time for General Yousefi. He recalls, "I asked them to continue their mission and see if they could get more information from the flying object. Then we lost communication, and I heard nothing from the pilot. I was so scared. I didn't know what was happening to the pilots." It wasn't until the following day, when the pilots were debriefed, that General Yousefi found out what had happened during those few minutes of dead air.

As the F-4 closed on the UFO, a brightly lit object detached from the UFO and headed straight for the F-4. The pilot attempted to fire a Sidewinder AIM-9 missile at the fast-approaching object. "They tried to shoot it down," Yousefi explains, "but when they squeezed the trigger, it didn't work. The trigger was inoperative."

The F-4 had no choice but to go into a negative g-force dive to avoid the object. The pilot reportedly watched as the smaller UFO returned to the larger UFO for a perfect rendezvous. Almost immediately, a second UFO emerged from the "mothership" and headed straight down to the ground. The pilots in the F-4 watched the object fall, anticipating a large explosion when it hit the ground. Instead, it landed gently in a dry lake bed north of Tehran.

The F-4 approached Mach 2 in its final pursuit of the UFO, but the craft was moving away at an incredible rate of speed. The F-4 could not match it. The pilots were granted permission to land at Mehrabad. During final approach, seemingly out of nowhere, the UFO was back. Yousefi remembers, "While they were landing, the tower was screaming on the phone to me, 'General, this flying object is following them. It's going to land at Mehrabad. It is in the short final approach bearing red, blue, and yellow lights. It is landing.' I told him, 'Let it land. If it lands, we can study it.' "

With the enormous UFO on his tail, the lead F-4 pilot was in a panic, according to tower supervisor Pirouzi. For reasons he still cannot explain, Pirouzi could hear the pilot, but the pilot could not hear him, and while the F-4 appeared on radar, the UFO did not. "The pilot said, 'Mehrabad, can you hear me?' " Pirouzi recalls. "He was screaming, crying, 'Mehrabad, can you hear me?' I told him I could hear him, but there was no answer. Then, suddenly I saw the object."

According to Pirouzi and other controllers, the UFO performed a low-altitude flyby over Mehrabad. It was described as a cylinder-shaped object about the size of a tour bus, with bright steady lights on each end and a flasher in the middle. After the flyby, the UFO roared off to the west. It was spotted twenty-five minutes later over the Mediterranean by an Egyptian Air Force pilot. Then, over Lisbon, Portugal, the pilot, crew, and passengers of a KLM Airlines flight reported seeing the UFO as it sped westward to the Atlantic. That was the last acknowledged sighting.

The F-4 pilots in Tehran were shuttled by helicopter to the dry lake bed where they had seen the smaller UFO land. A ground crew met them there. Nothing was visible from the air or on the ground; however, the helicopter was receiving a strange beeper signal from a house just west of the supposed landing site. The people in the house were questioned and said that they had been awakened earlier by a loud noise and a very bright light. They thought it was lightning. The source of the beeper signal was never discovered. It lasted for approximately three days before fading.

On September 20, 1976—the day after the UFO event—a meeting was convened in Tehran to assess the encounter. The Iranian Air Force Deputy Commander, Lieutenant General Abdollah Azarbarzin, conducted interviews with all of the principals, and a report of his findings was compiled. The present location of that report is unknown, but in an exclusive interview with *Sightings*, Azarbarzin disclosed previously secret details of his findings.

"The backseater in the F-4, who was responsible for fire control systems, told us that as the pilot came out of his dive, the F-4 passed under the UFO," Azarbarzin tells *Sightings*. "He could see the shape of the UFO, which was, as he explained it, round like a plate with a rounded canopy like a half soccer ball. Inside was a cockpit with very dim orange light, but there was no crew in the cockpit."

Azarbarzin also explained the conclusions his panel reached about the objects that seemed to shoot out of the larger UFO. He explains, "The pilots called them fireballs, but we all thought that they were very powerful waves of electromagnetism, which jammed all the electronics starting from VHF, UHF, fire control system, gun radar, gun communication, everything. Everything was gone."

During the low-altitude flyby, which Azarbarzin says was reported to him as being between 2,200 and 2,500 feet, the control tower at Mehrabad lost all power. This was particularly strange, since no other part of the airport was affected by the power outage. "But Department of Water and Power told us they did not have a power failure. So we assume that since all the electronic equipment and radar was gone, this object was jamming the equipment."

Reviewing all of these factors and the extraordinary rate of acceleration displayed by the UFO, Azarbarzin reached an alarming conclusion: the UFO had outperformed any known aircraft ever built anywhere in the world. This conclusion was relayed to General Khatemi, the Shah's personal military advisor. Khatemi instructed Azarbarzin to give his report to the U.S. Military Assistance Advisory Group in Tehran (MAAG).

According to his official U.S. Air Force biography, Major General Richard V. Secord was the acting MAAG chief on September 20, 1976. He acted as chief advisor to the commander in chief of the Iranian Air Force and managed all U.S. Air Force programs in Iran. Although Azarbarzin would not state publicly which Americans received his report, another former member of the Imperial Iranian Air Force located by *Sightings* did.

Mamoud Sabahat was vice commander of the Second Tactical Fighter Base in Tabriz, Iran. On the night of September 19, 1976, he was in Tehran to attend a meeting. "We had good contact with the United States," Sabahat explains. "We had members of the U.S. Air Force in our Air Force, and the head of the U.S. team was General Secord. This UFO event was the first time in our Air Force's history that anything had happened like this. It would have been a usual and customary part of the military system to put him in that meeting."

Tower controller Pirouzi spoke in the closed-door meeting about what he had witnessed. He recalls a discussion among

Azarbarzin's panel at the conclusion of the meeting. Pirouzi remembers, "They heard our reports and they concluded that no country is capable of such technology, and all of them believed it was a strange object from outer space."

What military authorities in the United States may have done with this information is unknown. Although documents obtained through the Freedom of Information Act indicate that the U.S. government was fully informed of the Iranian UFO encounter, there are no indications that any follow-up investigation was ever conducted. However, all the former Iranian Air Force officers who spoke with *Sightings* agreed that this was an encounter that redefined how they viewed the universe. It seemed to them that if any UFO sighting was worthy of investigation, it must be the one they encountered on September 19, 1976.

"Because of the experience I had on September 19, 1976, I believe there is something up there. We just don't know what it is or where it came from," says General Nader Yousefi. Lieutenant General Abdollah Azarbarzin agrees. "I believe in UFOs. I cannot ignore their existence. They want to find some way of contacting the people of earth. They are trying, and they are going to do it. Period."

Sightings director of research Jonathan Jerald attempted to contact Major General Richard V. Secord through several different government channels. Major General Secord chose not to respond to these requests.

Some of the details of the Iranian UFO encounter used in this story were based on recently declassified material from the October 1978 *MIJI Quarterly*, a publication of the U.S. Air Force Security Service, Electronic Warfare Center. Particularly notable is the opening paragraph, which not only suggests the possibility that military pilots might encounter UFOs, but states *de facto* that they probably will. Author Captain Henry S. Shields, HQ USAFE/INOMP, writes: "Sometime in his career, each pilot can expect to encounter strange, unusual happenings which will never be adequately or entirely explained by logic or subsequent investigation. The following article recounts just such an episode as reported by two F-4 Phantom crews of the Imperial Iranian Air Force during late 1976. No additional explanation of the strange events has been forthcoming. The story will probably be filed away and forgotten, but it makes interesting, and possibly disturbing, reading."

On September 19–20, 1976, an American Defense Systems Program (DSP) satellite operated by the U.S. Defense Department picked up signals from an unidentifiable technology over Iran. A notation on the DSP printout of the event stated "238 Scans, possible SR." DSP employees told *Sightings* the meaning of this notation is top secret. Recently, a retired NASA astroengineer revealed to *Sightings* that "238 Scans" could mean the DSP satellite observed the phenomenon for slightly less than one hour. The meaning of "possible SR" is still unknown.

The Unexplained

A Psychic Solves
the Case

E ight-year-old Victoria was beautiful, sensitive, and fun-loving. She liked to blow kisses and play in the sunshine. Her parents, Joe and Angelina De Santiago, believed that Victoria was a precious gift from God. But someone—more monster than man—did not share in the sanctity of their daughter's childhood. He stole Victoria, tortured her, and left her to die on the side of the road. Her little body may never have been found if it had not been for a psychic, telepathically leading police to the scene of the crime.

Now there are only memories of Victoria's heroic spirit. "I used to pick her up from school on my 1957 Harley-Davidson," Joe De Santiago remembers, his voice straining with emotion. "She'd jump on the back, hold onto her little lunchbox, and wave to her friends. 'See ya tomorrow, Toria,' they'd say, and I remember looking in the mirror and seeing all the kids waving, and Victoria was just as proud as could be. I'd tell her to hold onto my shoulders, and we'd take off. I can still see the way she'd brush her hair back as we drove through the wind."

On February 3, 1978, Victoria and her three-and-a-half-year-old sister, Eva, were helping their mother clean house. It was a beautiful sunny day in Fresno, California, and Angelina encouraged the children to go outside and play. The sisters played outside for a while, and then Victoria took Eva to the corner store just a block away to pick up some bread for her mother. Their little dog tagged along.

"The counterman said that he remembers the girls coming into the store, and he told them to go out because they couldn't bring the dog inside," Joe says. "What we figured is that perhaps whoever took the girls was there in the parking lot." Fresno police theorize that a stranger may have grabbed the dog and used him to lure Victoria and Eva into his car.

When the girls didn't return from the store after a few minutes, Angelina was worried. After an hour had gone by, she was hysterical. Joe recalls the moment he knew something was desperately wrong. "Angelina said, 'I can't find the girls. The girls are gone,' and I'm trying to think and saying, 'Are you sure they're not just next door?' My heart started pumping, and I was getting scared. How could this happen? We felt totally desperate."

Joe called the police but wasn't content to sit at home and wait. He organized his large extended family into car and truck patrols. Linked by CB radio, they combed the Fresno valley in search of Victoria and Eva. Other CBers picked up their calls and joined in the search. Within hours of the disappearance, Fresno had been transformed from a quiet farming community into an active search-and-rescue team.

At seven in the evening, Angelina got a call from the police station. Someone had abandoned Eva in front of an apartment building on the opposite end of town. She was crying and afraid, but she had been released unharmed. "I asked her, where was Victoria?" Angelina recalls, "and she just looked at me and said 'A man took her away.' We tried to ask her all kinds of questions, but at three-and-a-half, she just could not give the police enough of a description to go on."

Eva did provide one detail that at once comforted and terrified the family. Angelina says, "She said that Victoria told the man to let Eva go and that she would stay if he would just not hurt her sister and let her go. I will always remember that, because it showed that Victoria was a very good person, always protective of her sister, and a very beautiful girl."

Day turned into night. Saturday became Sunday, then Monday, then Tuesday. Fresno Police Sergeant Tim McFadden conducted an intense search and investigation, but he was stymied by a lack of physical evidence. Eva was apparently the only eyewitness. Despite an immense law enforcement and community mobilization, Victoria's trail was stone cold.

Then Joe De Santiago had a dream. "In my sleep I was dreaming about what I could do. What other avenues could I take? And then it came to me in a dream. I sat right up and said, 'Kathlyn Rhea.' "

Kathlyn Rhea is a psychic detective. She uses the powers of her mind to help police solve crimes. She claims that she can see missing children, bodies, criminals—and for the past twenty years she has been remarkably accurate. "Intuition is something everybody has," Kathlyn explains. "The intuitive sense is the sense of feeling, and these feelings are something I've educated to where I can use them fully."

Joe had earlier seen Kathlyn on a morning talk show, describing her successful work in an unsolved murder case in southern California. He was skeptical about her claims of supernatural ability, but after the dream, Joe suspended his disbelief: "When there's only one light shining out of the total darkness, you're going to walk toward that light. Whether it's the wrong way or the right way doesn't matter. It's a direction."

Angelina called Sergeant McFadden and asked him to consider using Kathlyn Rhea as part of his investigative team. The police veteran was resistant, but there was intense public pressure to explore every possible avenue. Reluctantly, and on the advice of his superiors, Tim McFadden agreed to accompany Angelina De Santiago to Kathlyn Rhea's home in San Jose, California.

"When I was told that a psychic was being brought into the case and I was going to fly to San Jose to meet her, I thought, OK, I'll fly up there and meet this lady wearing gypsy clothes. She's going to take me into her house, burn some incense; we're going to rattle some bones. She's going to throw some dust around the air and tell me something that's totally irrelevant to the case,"

McFadden says. "The psychic part of this was just way off. It didn't make it for me. How is somebody a hundred and eighty miles away going to tell me how to find a body in my town?"

Kathlyn Rhea is accustomed to the hard-boiled skepticism that police often express on their first encounter with a psychic detective. But she explains, "I do not do what you see in horror movies. I don't suddenly grab my head and fall down and say, 'Oh, they hit me in the head' or 'Oh, this poor person's being stabbed.' I don't do that. It's more like an objective bystander taking in feelings and bringing a whole picture out. It's just like going to the movies or turning on the TV and seeing the picture in front of your face."

Almost from the moment Angelina De Santiago and Tim McFadden entered Kathlyn's home, the skeptical sergeant had a change of heart. "I don't know what exactly changed my mind," McFadden recalls of that first meeting, "but she was just so matter-of-fact. She wasn't searching. She wasn't probing me or trying to get any information out of me. She just started telling me stuff about Victoria and Eva and the dog, things that I knew were accurate, and I didn't have any reason to believe she'd got this information beforehand. After five minutes with her, she told me enough stuff that she had a hundred percent of my attention."

It was the beginning of an unlikely partnership: the sergeant, the psychic, and the De Santiagos. "All I could think of asking her," Angelina recounts, "was, you know, was Victoria going through a lot of pain? I just had to know the circumstances. Kathlyn said, 'Your daughter is safe. She's in God's hands. I don't think that when we find her that you'll have your daughter back, but we will find her.' "

"After that, she asked the mother to leave the room," Sergeant McFadden remembers. "Then she told me the little girl was deceased. She had been killed and died a very violent death. Kathlyn told me that little Victoria had been sexually assaulted and went on to describe details of the death that were later proven to be absolutely true."

Kathlyn told Tim McFadden that Victoria would be found on a

41. Crop circles are geometric patterns created by an unknown force, with no apparent signs of human intervention. (Sightings)

Alſo, How the ſaid Oats ly now in the Field, and the Owner has not Power to fetch them away.

42. "The Mowing Devil," an English woodcut from 1648, depicts a mythical creature creating patterns in a crop field. *(courtesy* The Fortean Times*)*

43. The massive size of the UFO observed over a Montreal hotel prompted many to name it "the mothership." *(courtesy Marcel La Roche,* La Presse*)*

44. James Romansky, Sr., points toward the wooded ravine where he claims to have seen the Kecksburg UFO. (Sightings)

45. The Knowles family claims their car's tire blew out during a UFO abduction. *(courtesy Channel 7, Sydney)*

UFO SUCKS FAMILY CAR FROM ROAD

46. The Australian media dismissed the significance of the Knowles family's alien abduction.

47. Maxim Chyrdakov *(top row, center)* **at the Soviet Flight Academy.** *(courtesy Maxim Chyrdakov)*

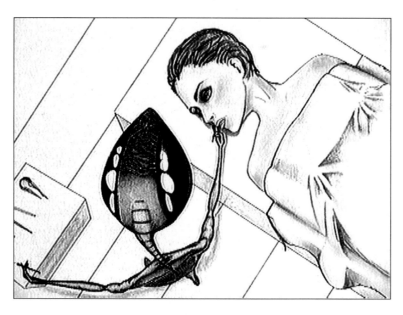

48. An artist's interpretation of Kim Carlsberg's alien abduction experience. *(courtesy Matt Herrington)*

49. & 50. This disc-shaped craft appeared during a solar eclipse and hovered over Mexico City for more than thirty minutes. *(courtesy Lee and Brit Elders)*

51. Dr. Antonio Rosas videotaped this huge craft as it slowly passed in the sky in front of his Mexico City home. *(courtesy Lee and Brit Elders)*

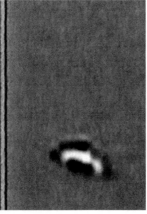

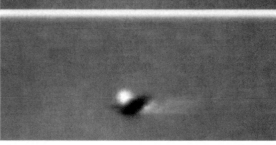

52. This top-shaped craft was revolving rapidly when it was videotaped by Angel Toledo. *(courtesy Lee and Brit Elders)*

53. Professional videographer Cuauhtemoc Alvarenga's attempt to capture the stunning "pearl necklace" UFO over Mexico City. *(courtesy Lee and Brit Elders)*

54. Thousands of Mexico City residents witnessed this January 1993 UFO event. *(courtesy Lee and Brit Elders)*

55. Analyst David Froning has ruled out the possibility that the Mexico City videotapes are hoaxes. *(courtesy Lee and Brit Elders)*

REFERENCE OR OFFICE SYMBOL	SUBJECT
	Near Midair Collision with UFO Report

| TO Commander
83D USARCOM
ATTN: AHRCOG
Columbus Support Facility
Columbus, Ohio 43215 | FROM Flight Operations Off   DATE 23 Nov 73   CMT 1
USAR Flight Facility
Cleveland Hopkins Airport
Cleveland, Ohio 44135 |

1. On 18 October 1973 at 2305 hours in the vicinity of Mansfield, Ohio, Army Helicopter 68-15444 assigned to Cleveland USARFFAC encountered a near midair collision with a unidentified flying object. Four crewmembers assigned to the Cleveland USARFFAC for flying proficiency were on AFTP status when this incident occurred. The flight crew assigned was CPT Lawrence J. Coyne, Pilot in Command, 1LT Arrigo Jezzi, Copilot, SSG Robert Yanacsek, Crew Chief, SSG John Healey, Flight Medic. All the above personnel are members of the 316th MED DET(HEL AMB), a tenant reserve unit of the Cleveland USARFFAC.

2. The reported incident happened as follows: Army Helicopter 68-15444 was returning from Columbus, Ohio to Cleveland, Ohio and at 2305 hours, south east of Mansfield Airport in the vicinity of Mansfield, Ohio while flying at an altitude of 2500 feet and on a heading of 030 degrees, SSG Yanacsek observed a red light on the east horizon, 90 degrees to the flight path of the helicopter. Approximately 30 seconds later, SSG Yanacsek indicated the object was converging on the helicopter at the same altitude at a airspeed in excess of 600 knots and on a midair collision heading. Cpt Coyne observed the converging object, took over the controls of the aircraft and initiated a power descent from 2500 feet to 1700 feet to avoid impact with the object. A radio call was initiated to Mansfield Tower who acknowledged the helicopter and was asked by CPT Coyne if there were any high performance aircraft flying in the vicinity of Mansfield Airport, however there was no response received from the tower. The crew expected impact from the object instead, the object was observed to hesistate momentarily over the helicopter and then slowly continued on a westerly course accelerating at a high rate of speed, clear west of Mansfield Airport then turn 45 degree heading to the Northwest, Cpt Coyne indicated the altimeter read a 1000 fpm climb and read 3500 feet with the collective in the full down position. The aircraft was returned to 2500 feet by CPT Coyne and flown back to Cleveland, Ohio. The Flight plan was closed and the FAA Flight Service Station notified of the incident. The FSS told CPT Coyne to report the incident to the FAA GADO office a Cleveland Hopkins Airport. MR. Porter, 83d USARCOM was notified of the incident at 1530 hours on 19 Oct 73.

3. This report has been read and attested to by the crewmembers of the aircraft with signatures acknowledgeing this report.

FA FORM 2496

---

56. All four Air Force reservists signed this affidavit detailing their UFO encounter.

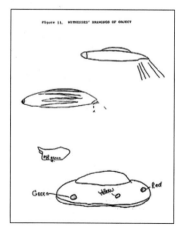

57. A sketch of the Mansfield UFO as drawn by two members of the helicopter flight crew.
(courtesy Jennie Zeidman)

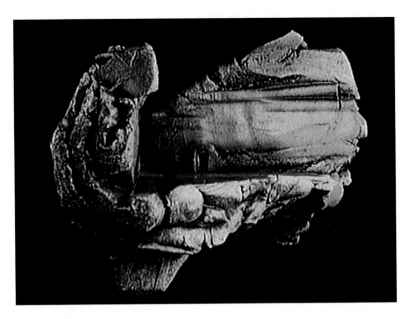

58. Jim Weiner says his sculptures became "very bizarre" after the abduction. *(courtesy Jim Weiner)*

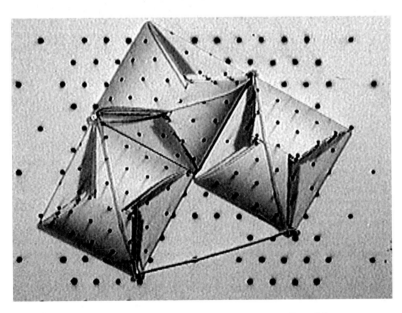

59. Jack Weiner's post-abduction paintings reflect his new obsession with mathematics, science, and physics. *(courtesy Jack Weiner)*

60. Recently, Larry Tabor added Tommy Mantell's watch to the aircraft wreckage recovered during a *Sightings* investigation. (Sightings)

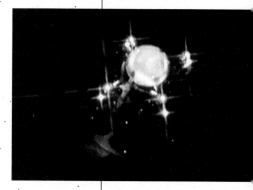

61. The distribution list for a U.S. Army Intelligence communiqué, detailing a UFO encounter in Iran.

PRIORITY

DCT I   MSG654   PAGE   04 267 MA 13

ACTION: NONE
INFO:
PATCZYUW RUFKJC 9712 2610R10 MTMS-CCCC — RUFFHOA.
7NY CCCC
P 230810Z SEP 76
FM JCS
INFO RUEHC/SECSTATE WASH DC
RUFAIIF/C I A
RUFOIAH/NSA WASH DC
RUFADUU/WHITE HOUSE WASH DC
RUFEHOA/CSAF WASH DC
RUFNAAA/CNO WASH DC
RUFADUD/CSA WASH DC
P 2305307 SEP 76
FM USDAO TEHRAN - DEP A HALL
TO RUFKJCS/DIA WASH DC
INFO RUFKJCS/SECDEF DEPSECDEF WASHDC
RUFRBAA/COMIDEASTFOR
RUDOECA/CINCUSAFE LINDSEY AS GE/INCE
RHERAAB/CINCUSAFF RAMSTEIN AB GE/INOCN
RUSNAAA/EUDAC VAIHINGEN GER
RUSNAAA/USCINCEUR VAIHINGEN GER/ECJ-2,
RT
C O N F I D E N T I A L 1735 SEP76
THIS IS IP 6 846 0139 76
1. (U) IRAN
2. REPORTED UFO SIGHTING (U)
3. (U) NA
4. (U) 19 & 20 SEP 76
5. (U) TEHRAN, IRAN: 20 SEP 76
6. (U) F-6
IF. (U) 6 846 0008 (NOTE RO COMMENTS)
8. (U) 6 846 0139 76
9. (U) 22SEP 76
10. (U) NA
11. (U) 'INITIATE' IPSP PI-1640
12. (U) USDAO, TEHRAN, IRAN
13. (U) FRANK B. MCKENZIE, COL, USAF, :DA TT
14. (U) NA
15. (U) THIS REPORT FORWARDS INFORMATION CONCERNING THE
SIGHTING OF AN UFO IN IRAN ON 19 SEPTEMBER 1976.
A. AT ABOUT 1230 AM ON 19 SEP 76 THE
RECEIVED FOUR TELEPHONE CALLS
FROM CITIZENS LIVING IN THE SHEMIRAN AREA OF TEHRAN SAYING

PRIORITY

62. This re-creation of the Tehran UFO was part of an Iranian documentary produced in 1976.

63. A police sketch of Victoria De Santiago's killer, based on Kathlyn Rhea's psychic impressions. *(courtesy T. Macris)*

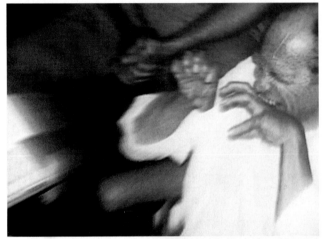

64. & 65. During his exorcism, Bill Ramsey contorted wildly and snarled viciously like a wild animal. *(courtesy Syndication International)*

66. Mutilated animals have been discovered in the San Luis Valley since 1967. *(courtesy Chris O'Brien)*

67. The wounds are surgical and precise, as opposed to the jagged tears left by natural predators. *(courtesy Chris O'Brien)*

68. No tracks are ever found near the corpses, fueling the belief that the animals are abducted by aircraft. *(courtesy Chris O'Brien)*

69. While filming on the set of *It's All True,* Orson Welles fell victim to a macumba curse. *(courtesy Paramont Pictures)*

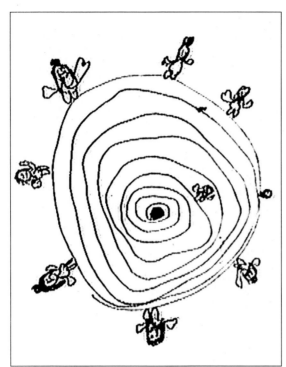

70. The Thronsons believe Katie's final drawing was a premonition of her own untimely death. *(courtesy Julie & Jerry Thronson)*

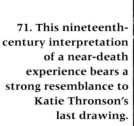

71. This nineteenth-century interpretation of a near-death experience bears a strong resemblance to Katie Thronson's last drawing.

72. Alice Heck and Agnes Nash are identical twins who claim to have hypertelepathy. (Sightings)

73. In Chorley, England, the top half of a suspected victim of spontaneous human combustion is burned to ash while the lower extremities remain intact. *(courtesy Anthony McMunn)*

74. Even during the cremation process, some bones remain, yet in this case nothing was left but three and a half pounds of ash. *(courtesy Larry Arnold, PSI)*

75. Larry Arnold reports that this victim apparently burned to ash within six minutes. *(courtesy Larry Arnold, PSI)*

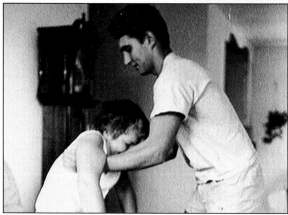

76. Nelda Buss had become completely paralyzed by ALS before being treated by the laying on of hands. *(courtesy Buss family)*

77. Mitchell May credits his healing to Jack Gray, who used hypnosis and a healing touch to rehabilitate his patients. *(courtesy Mitchell May)*

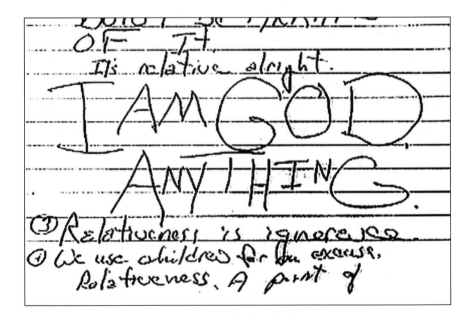

78. David Young's incoherent manifesto.

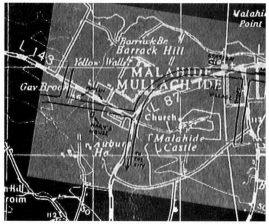

79. Jenny Cockell's childhood map overlaid with an actual street map of Malahide, Ireland. *(courtesy Jenny Cockell)*

80. According to Sonny Sutton, his mother, Mary Sutton, and Jenny Cockell share "the same loving look." *(courtesy Jenny Cockell)*

81. Jenny Cockell with her reunited "children" *(left to right: Christy, Betty, Sonny, Jenny, Phyllis, Frank)* (Sightings)

road that was not well traveled in the northeastern part of Fresno. She would be in a depression, like an irrigation ditch, lying parallel to the road with her face pointing toward the road. There would be a large tree. On one side of the road he would find a plowed field, on the other a poultry ranch. "She said when I found the body, there would be chickens. She said, 'I get chickens around the body, chickens, chickens, chickens.'" McFadden remembers. "She also told me that Victoria would have on only one article of clothing, and that's a sock."

Kathlyn also remembers telling Tim McFadden, "There will be a farmer whose name starts with an *S*. There has to be a street that starts with an *L*. There will be a windmill." Sergeant McFadden wrote down every detail Kathlyn provided. Her psychic visions didn't add up to any of the locations he had already scoured and didn't seem like any place he'd ever remembered seeing in his hometown.

"After my interview with Kathlyn, as I was walking out the door—and I'll never forget this—she stopped me. She grabbed my arm and said, 'Tim, when you find the dog, you'll find Victoria,'" McFadden recalls. "That really stuck with me. And when I returned to Fresno, the first thing I heard was that they had found the dog. I immediately got on the phone with my partner, who was with the dog at the home of a local farmer."

It was an uncanny coincidence. McFadden's partner, Detective Joel Popejoy, verified through the license on the collar that he had indeed found Victoria's dog. McFadden says, "So I asked Detective Popejoy, 'Well, are there chickens out there?'" Detective Popejoy recalls, "I asked the farmer if there were any chickens here, and he said, 'Yes, just south of here there's an abandoned poultry ranch.'"

Tim McFadden was stunned. Kathlyn's prophecy appeared to be coming true. "I asked Joel if there was a windmill, and he said there was no windmill," McFadden says. "He was convinced there wasn't a windmill. And because he was a skeptic he said, 'I've got you. There's no windmill here.' I said, 'Kathlyn says there's a big windmill. Ask the farmer if he has one.'"

Detective Popejoy was beginning to think his partner had gone over the edge. But then the tables turned. Popejoy explains, "It was a situation I will never forget as long as I live. Tim was on the phone telling me about this windmill, and I'm telling him, 'There's no windmill here,' and the farmer who's standing behind me says, 'Oh, yes there is. You just walked by one. It's in the front yard.' "

Tim McFadden remembers his partner's shock and amazement. "He said, 'I'm getting goose bumps; I'm looking at a big windmill right outside this window.' I'm telling him things that Kathlyn said, and he's confirming them right back to me, and I'm getting higher and higher, thinking, 'Wow, wow, this gal does know what she's talking about.' And the rest of the detectives in the briefing room with me are listening to this conversation and feeling the same thing I am. Everybody wanted to go out there and start looking. So we went."

A police response team headed by Sergeant McFadden drove out to Detective Popejoy's location. There was the dog, the abandoned poultry ranch, the windmill, and more. The street name did start with an *L*. It was Leonard Street. The farmer's name, right there on his mailbox, started with *S*. And by the side of the road, in a shallow ditch shaded by a large tree, they found Victoria's body.

"She was just off the side of the road," Sergeant McFadden recalls with great sadness. "Her skull was crushed, just as Kathlyn had described. She had been sexually assaulted. She had one article of clothing on, which was a sock. There was a plowed field on one side, the chickens on the other. Everything was there. It was incredible."

While the incredible events leading to Tim McFadden's discovery of the body were unfolding, Joe De Santiago appeared live on a Fresno television station to plead for his daughter's life. Joe says, "I just pleaded if they could please just let her go and let her come home to her family. And all the way home I was praying, 'Please let her be OK. Please let her be all right. I'll never let them out of my sight again.' Then, when I got home, the family was there, friends were there, people from around the community who had gathered, all had this look on their faces. And then Tim McFadden came up to me and said they found my daughter, and she was not alive."

The Fresno Police Department has searched unsuccessfully for Victoria's killer. Tim McFadden has fought hard to solve this murder, but the solution still eludes him. Thirteen years after the crime, *Sightings* asked Kathlyn Rhea to return to the place where Victoria's body had been found to see if she could provide new psychic impressions of Victoria's killer.

"When I go to the man who did this, he has stubby hands. They're the hands of a laborer. I don't feel like he's here anymore. I want to go further south to a town that starts with an *S*. He's working down there now. This man is not very tall; I would say maybe five foot nine. I feel this man has killed another child since then. There is a wife or a girlfriend he goes back to at times, and I feel like she's frightened of him. I know she knows he's violent." Working with a police sketch artist, Kathlyn believes she has been able to bring out the face of the killer. (See Photo 63.)

Sergeant Tim McFadden hopes the composite will spark the memory of an eyewitness. In the meantime, he continues to believe in Kathlyn Rhea's psychic gifts. "I look at Kathlyn's work as another investigative tool I use. A lot of police officers will not look at psychics this way. But many police officers use intuition. That's the same thing Kathlyn does. Every police department's got a number of officers who just seem to make more arrests, seem to know where to find the bad guys. They're psychic. They don't know it, but they're doing what Kathlyn's doing."

Angelina and Joe De Santiago believe it was Kathlyn Rhea's psychic ability that has given them the small measure of peace they now have. On reflection, Joe says, "Thank you, God. Thank you for finding Victoria's body, and thank you for giving us Kathlyn Rhea. People find it very hard to believe that we have survived, and I thank Kathlyn for helping us have closure."

Despite the good work of some psychic detectives, there are many unscrupulous people posing as psychics, who prey on vulnerable, unsuspecting families. If you do choose to use a psychic detective, make sure it is with the full cooperation of local law enforcement. Check references carefully. Make sure the psychic does not have a criminal record, and never pay any money up front.

Taming of the Werewolf

It was three in the morning. Bill Ramsey lay awake in a strange motel room in rural Connecticut. His mind was racing, filled with conflicting thoughts about why he had come here from his home in southern England and what would happen tomorrow. It had been a long and harrowing journey to this crossroads in his strange life. Back home, Bill Ramsey had attacked and bitten people, including a police officer. He had been accused of being a drunkard, a drug addict, and mentally unbalanced. Now Bill stared at an unfamiliar ceiling and prayed the exorcism would work. He prayed that this would finally be the one act that could quiet the beast within him.

"The story begins when I was nine years old," says Bill. "I was just an innocent kid playing with my little toy soldiers near the garden fence. It was a warm summer's evening. Suddenly, the air went very cold, there was a terrible stench in the air, and I just flew into the most horrendous rage. My mother and father couldn't make out why their little boy was acting like an animal."

Young Bill, snarling and panting, ripped a 3-inch-by-3-inch fence post out of its concrete footing and snapped the solid wood in two. With his teeth, he tore at the wire mesh nailed to the post, spitting out chunks of fencing. "Obviously, my mother and father were frightened, but they didn't say too much to me at the time. They didn't know what it was or what to do," Bill recalls now.

The bizarre incident became a family secret. As the years passed and no further incidents occurred, it seemed the family secret was safe.

Bill grew up, married, and had three children. He began to look at the fence post incident as a strange footnote in an otherwise ordinary life. Bill worked as a laborer in Southend-on-Sea, England, working long hours and many weekends to provide for his family. At the end of one particularly grueling work weekend, the furthest thing from Bill's mind was the specter of his childhood rage. He was simply hungry and exhausted. He was dozing in the back of a fellow worker's van, when something unexplained welled up inside him.

"Suddenly, out of the blue, I started to growl and attacked one of my mates. He thought I was kidding around, until I started biting him in the leg. I just tripped out, and when I came to I said, 'What just happened here?' My friend was very apprehensive. He said it was like having a wild dog sitting next to him. But all of them in the van said, 'Look, don't worry, we're not going to say anything about this. We'll keep it quiet.' They thought I was tired," says Bill.

"During the attack, I was never aware of actually what happened," Bill explains. However, the bite marks on his friend's leg spoke volumes about what had occurred. Bill was frightened, but tried to push the episode out of his mind. He was tired, overworked, under stress. Surely this was not a recurrence of what had happened when he was a small boy in the family garden.

"Nothing happened for a couple of years," Bill says. "Then, around Christmastime, there was another incident that was a little more worrying. I had been working and came home for a bit of dinner before going back out to the job. On my way back, I started getting a chest pain." Although he did not realize it at the time, this kind of pain would later become a signal to Bill that he was about to undergo a ferocious transformation.

"The pain got worse and worse, and you hear so many people in their thirties and forties having heart trouble, I went to hospital," Bill continues. "I hadn't been there more than a couple of minutes when I started to growl and my hands started forming into claws. I picked up one of the nurses and threw her across the room. I only remember that far, and then my mind wasn't mine anymore." Later, doctors, nurses, and police would inform Bill Ramsey of what happened next.

Bill says he was told "Nurses were trying to hold me down, but I was thrashing around and picking up stretchers and throwing them around. I was smashing up the hospital until the police came. They gave me an injection, which should have just knocked me out, but it didn't. I just carried straight on so they had to give me one that would have knocked out a horse, but even that took time."

Once Bill was sedated, he was transported to a mental hospital for observation. A quirk in England's civil law and mental health policy allowed Bill to walk out on his own recognizance less than twelve hours later. "Nobody likes being in a mental institution," Bill explains. "I just phoned up my wife, Nina, to come and get me out of there."

At first, Nina accused Bill of being drunk, but Bill was not a drinker and Nina knew it. "It was totally out of character for me to just attack people that way and to have that disrespect for the law," Bill says. Assuming that he was suffering from some type of mental illness, Bill sought help from a number of psychologists and psychiatrists, but no one could offer an adequate explanation for the physical transformation and the violent animal-like behavior. And despite months of therapy, the terrifying episodes became more frequent and more ferocious.

Bill began to recognize the telltale signs of an impending attack. On a trip to London during this period, Bill felt the familiar chest pains and tightening in his stomach and turned himself in to a nearby police station. "I'm afraid I'm going to kill someone," he warned the officers, and then, before their eyes, Bill transformed. It was a mild attack, and the police were able to control him, but the London tabloids got wind of the event and dubbed Bill Ramsey "The Werewolf of Southend-on-Sea." The Ramsey family secret wasn't a secret anymore.

"I felt ashamed," Bill recounts. "I was the laughingstock of the neighborhood. I was disgusted by it all and bewildered by it all. I think the worst part of the whole thing was not knowing. If someone's got schizophrenia, at least they know what they're up against. But here I was doing these outrageous things and nobody knew why.

"Nina and I even started checking back through my diet. Was there something I was allergic to? Was it maybe too much salt? I mean, it sounds ridiculous now, but when you're desperate for an answer to a problem, you're going to search every avenue. I had a daughter in nurse training, and I went through all her medical books to find something—anything—to explain this thing."

It seemed that the more desperate Bill became, the worse the episodes became. "The attacks started coming a lot closer together. The attacks got longer. I was beginning to feel the end of the world had come. I had no answer to this thing. Every time I went out the door, Nina was frightened to death that she'd get a phone call in an hour saying I'd attacked somebody or that I had killed somebody," Bill says. On July 22, 1987, Nina got the call she had so feared. It was the Southend Police Station. Bill had nearly killed an unarmed police sergeant. He was being held in the precinct's jail on charges of mayhem and attempted murder.

Bill recalls the events of that horrendous night. "It was a hot, dry day. I met up with some people I hadn't seen for a while and, I admit it, I had too many beers. I was afraid of being picked up for drunk driving, so I decided to go home a way I wasn't likely to encounter too many police—which meant along the seafront and through the red-light district. Suddenly, I got this crazy notion in my head. I saw a prostitute on the corner and I thought, She shouldn't be doing that. I'll make a citizen's arrest. I got her in the van and started heading to the police station, exactly where I thought I didn't want to go.

"She said I was crazy. She was frightened. I don't know whether she had a premonition of evil or could read into my face, but as soon as we got to the police station, she opened the van door and ran inside." That was the last thing Bill Ramsey remembers. But for police inspector Tony Belford and patrol sergeant Terry Fisher, it would be a night they could never forget.

"It was eleven at night on Wednesday, July 22, 1987, when Terry and I heard a woman shouting for assistance," Inspector Belford remembers. "She told us that she had been picked up by Bill Ramsey. We were acquainted with the man through the press. We escorted the woman back to his van, and she became quite agitated, so I took her inside leaving Terry out in the yard with Ramsey."

"Ramsey was standing outside his van," Sergeant Fisher recalls. "I told him he'd obviously been drinking and needed to come inside. He clearly didn't want to come with me, and we had a bit of a struggle. He got more and more ferocious, and it became apparent that he was no longer trying to get away from me. He was trying to attack me. I didn't have a weapon on me, so I couldn't defend myself. We just kept fighting, and as I weakened, he appeared to be getting stronger. This was really quite eerie.

"I became alarmed for my own safety, and—I'll make no bones about it—I kneed him in the groin for my own protection, and I really used some force behind it. But he shrugged it off and became stronger. He got me around the throat, cutting off my air supply. I was very conscious of the fact that he had these mad staring eyes and this maniacal expression. I remember lying there on my back in a puddle, covered in blood, my shirt torn and this character on top of me. He was saying, 'The Devil is in me. When the Devil is in me, I am strong. I am strong, and you are going to die.' He said this over and over again in the most menacing, horrible way. It was enough to chill your bones."

It took five officers to pry Bill Ramsey off Sergeant Fisher. "I think mayhem is descriptive of the situation as it was," Inspector Belford says. "Ramsey was dragged into the station and put into the charge room, where we tried to fill out certain forms to warrant his detention. It was at this point that Bill Ramsey started to snarl and growl. He started to salivate. His demeanor was so violent that he had to be removed to a cell."

The door to the cell was solid metal, with a small pass-through window in the center measuring approximately 18 inches by 6 inches. "Within minutes," Inspector Belford says, "Bill Ramsey had somehow managed to get his head and his right arm up to his shoulder outside this opening. He was snarling and growling, and had his hand made up into the shape of a claw. If anybody went near him, he lunged with his clawed hand and attempted to bite them.

"His lips turned up and he showed his teeth, and I can recollect saying in the reports that I filed that he took on the appearance of a mad dog. It was quite apparent that we couldn't get close to Bill Ramsey or think of any method of getting his head and arm back through the hole, so we called the fire brigade, and they decided the only way to get him out was to remove the whole plate around the opening."

Despite the fact that Bill was stuck in that tiny opening, he had to be sedated before members of the fire brigade could approach the door. Inspector Belford recalls, "Having seen the claw and the biting and snarling, we began to associate Bill Ramsey with the suggestion that he was a werewolf. Without a doubt it was a frightening experience. I've been a police officer for twenty-five years, and I've never seen anything like it, and I'm not likely to see it again. We were witnessing something unnatural."

As a result of his encounter with Bill Ramsey, Sergeant Terry Fisher took an early retirement from the Southend Police Force. For his part, Bill remembers nothing of the vicious attack or his attempt to claw and bite his way out of his jail cell. "The next thing I knew," Bill recalls, "I was waking up in the mental hospital back to normal, back to a human being again. There was an attendant at the door, ready with another injection, and he couldn't believe I was the same guy who had caused so much trouble at the police station the night before."

The hospital ran a series of tests to determine the cause of Bill's bizarre behavior. They quickly ruled out schizophrenia, antisocial psychosis, and epilepsy. Brain scans showed no abnormal activity. The final diagnosis was bizarre behavior due to alcoholism. "I openly admitted I was drunk that night," Bill says, "and although I knew the attack wasn't caused by alcohol, I didn't argue with the doctors. They released me from the mental hospital with nothing really resolved. A load of tests had all proven negative."

The one thing that Bill Ramsey did become convinced of after his stay in the mental hospital was that he didn't belong there. "The other patients there would have their troubles all day, every day. Outside of my attacks, I was a normal guy. Being with schizophrenics and people urinating against the walls or excreting on the floor was alien to me. I knew I wasn't like them. I didn't have a mental problem. I didn't have an answer for what I did have, but I knew what I wasn't. I wasn't crazy."

Because of the hospital's diagnosis, Bill Ramsey was again free on his own recognizance. Press reports of this latest attack appeared throughout England and were picked up by the American press as well. Bill Ramsey sank into a deep depression, afraid to leave his house—afraid, even, to be in his house.

"I was terrified," Bill remembers of those dark desperate days. "I had the feeling that ultimately I was going to kill somebody. Nina and I had many a long evening where I would start out quite rationally, thinking 'Is it this? Is it that?' and out of frustration just end up in tears. My children were frightened of this disruption to the wonderful life that they had known. Here was their father, the man they could always turn to should there be any trouble, and now he's the man they have to be wary of. It must have been horrific for the children."

Then a call came from the police station. It was a call that would change Bill Ramsey's life. Bill says, "By this time I thought my world had fallen apart. I was going along a happily married man with a good family around me. Why should this happen to me? What could I do? What was the answer? I was looking for a cure, but I wasn't ill. What was causing it?

"I felt like committing suicide. A phone call came from the police station saying two Americans wanted to see me, psychiatrists. I thought, American technology is sometimes better than ours. We send kids over there for special operations. Maybe their mental health care is better than ours, too. So I agreed to meet these people, and it turned out they weren't psychiatrists at all."

The American couple turned out to be Ed and Lorraine Warren, world-renowned paranormal investigators and lecturers. They had learned about Bill Ramsey through the tabloid press, and Lorraine Warren had instantly read between the sensational lines and had seen a desperate man whom she felt needed her help. After more than forty years investigating claims of paranormal phenomena, the Warrens had never encountered a real-life werewolf.

After learning details of Bill Ramsey's life from the Southend police officers, Lorraine says, "I was driven. Even Ed would say, 'Why are you pursuing this?' I felt that we had to either prove it to be a hoax or that it was a reality, and we had to help Bill Ramsey." Ed remembers their first impression of Bill Ramsey: "I've interviewed thousands of people, and I knew this man was telling the truth. He was such a nice person, we had to help this man. We had to find somebody who could relieve him of this terrible thing that was happening to him."

The Warrens believed that the reason why the police, medical science, psychiatry, and psychology had all failed Bill Ramsey was because he was not sick—he was possessed. Ed explains, "Possession is a state where a person's physical body is totally taken over by something supernatural, something preternatural. The spirit of that person moves away from the physical body, and that body is taken over, just like you would jump in a car and drive it where you want.

"A werewolf is a person who is possessed by the wolf spirit, and this is what happened to Bill. This thing totally took over his whole physical body. And that's what a lot of people don't understand. A werewolf isn't a person that just all of a sudden their hair starts growing out. Instead, they take on the features of an animal. In the wolf state, Bill's hands would claw in an unnatural way. Anybody could do that, but not the way Bill did it. His teeth would actually protrude, the lips would roll up, and the face and the forehead would take on the characteristics of a wolf. In fact, the police officers that we talked to all said he was a wolf, not a man."

A rapport between the Warrens and Bill Ramsey didn't develop right away. Bill was skeptical of their motives and the very idea that he was possessed. Bill remembers thinking "I've been called a drunk, a drug addict, a mental case, and now I'm possessed with a wolf spirit. I knew Americans were a bit eccentric, but this was going one step too far. But I was taught to be polite so I heard them out. They asked if I would come to the U.S. and be exorcised. Exorcised! Come on, I thought, I'm desperate, but not that desperate."

But the Warrens persevered, offering to pay for both Bill and Nina to come to Connecticut and meet Bishop Richard McKenna. Bill remained unconvinced. He says, "I had no faith at all in their exorcism. I thought they were a couple of crackpots. I really wanted to find a cure, but I honestly didn't think this was going to be it." Nina was the one who finally convinced Bill to make the trip to America. "She said we had to give it a try," Bill recalls. "I'd been through all the other avenues with no result, so what else did I have to lose? If it doesn't work, at least we'll see America."

Bill and Nina set out on their journey to Connecticut with a mixture of skepticism and apprehension. Bill remembers, "We were frightened. What if I had an attack on the plane? What if I kill the pilot? All these things were going through my mind. But we had our airline tickets. We had our passports. We had to go."

Bill and Nina checked into their Connecticut motel the night before the scheduled exorcism. Less than an hour later, Bill's worst nightmare came true. "I physically attacked Nina," he tells with great difficulty. "I had got as far as putting my hands around her throat to the point where she almost passed out. But her love tore through, and I came out of the attack. It was very close, very close. Here was the one person who had stood by me, and I had attacked her. That was more painful than anything. No words can tell you how I feel about that."

So there Bill lay at three in the morning, staring at the ceiling, wondering and worrying.

The next day he appeared before Bishop McKenna. Because Bill had shown superhuman strength in the past, six bodyguards with stun guns protected the bishop. "Lord permitted, the devil could easily kill the exorcist," Bishop McKenna offers as an explanation for the intense security. As the rarely performed Catholic exorcism rite began, Bishop McKenna recalls, "As I proceeded with the prayers, he didn't seem to be himself. It was as if another person was taking over. He seemed to go into a kind of daze." Bill remembers, "The bishop came at me with the purple stole he wore around his neck. He put it on my face, and as he put it there, it was as if he'd hit me with a hammer. I don't remember what happened after that."

The memories of the assembled group and the black-and-white photographs are the only record of Bill Ramsey's exorcism. (See Photos 64 and 65.) Lorraine Warren recalls, "I was right behind Bill Ramsey with Nina. Suddenly, the muscles in the back of his neck began to enlarge. The ears began to point, and he howled. Then the hands clawed in such a manner that no human hand could claw like that."

"We were going to make the sign of the cross on his forehead and on his breast. Then he reacted violently and snapped his hand at me. Then he snarled like an animal," says the bishop. Lorraine explains, "His lips rolled up, the teeth protruded, and he tried to bite the priest. But it was as though an invisible barrier existed between him and Bishop McKenna."

"Where did you come from?" Bishop McKenna intoned. "What keeps you here? Begone, Satan. Leave him alone." And then, according to the bishop, "The devil did leave him. He came to himself."

"As I came out of the exorcism," Bill says, "I felt like a new person. I imagine it's the feeling a blind person would get if suddenly he could see, or a deaf person suddenly began hearing. It was the feeling that I was cured. It's nothing you can tell anybody; it wasn't physical, but it was something I knew."

For the Warrens, their professional interest in the case was eclipsed by their personal satisfaction. Lorraine says, "After the exorcism, Bill was free and is free today. The most gratifying part of all is to spend time with them in their home as a family and see the love that the Ramseys have for each other."

Four years after his exorcism, Bill is able to say with great pride "From that day, I've never had any attacks. I've been able to live life to the very fullest."

Bishop Richard McKenna believes that an exorcism should be performed only when one or more of the following abilities are exhibited:

1. Superhuman strength
2. Speaking in tongues
3. Extraordinary perception
4. Levitation
5. Telekinesis

The Mutilations Mystery

I he San Luis Valley is five thousand square miles of fertile pastureland straddling the Colorado–New Mexico border. Ringed by snow-capped mountains, the valley is the largest, cleanest alpine meadow in the world. Generations of cattle ranchers have called the San Luis Valley home. It's the kind of place to build a home, a family, and a successful livestock business. It's not the kind of place you'd expect to find mutilated animals dotting the landscape, but there they are. (See Photo 66.)

Chris O'Brien knows as much as anyone about the strange animal deaths in the San Luis Valley. He has been investigating the bizarre carcasses for more than ten years. "The San Luis Valley is the birthplace of the unusual animal-death phenomenon," O'Brien explains. "It started here in September of 1967. Lady, a horse, was discovered by her owners totally denuded of flesh from her shoulders to the tip of her nose. The spine and skull were bleached white while the rest of the animal looked pristine. The body had a strange type of chlorine smell. A clump of Pacific Ocean seaweed was found nearby. There was a clump of what looked like a gizzard with mane hair in it that burned the owner's hand when she touched it. Bushes in the area were found to have radiation levels higher than normal."

Between 1967 and 1970, several more mutilated animals, mostly cattle, were discovered in the San Luis Valley. Ranchers and livestock inspectors were baffled by the mysterious deaths, but they felt they were isolated incidents, better forgotten. There was a brief lull in the phenomenon between 1970 and 1973, "then all hell broke loose," says O'Brien. "All around the country, thousands of cases occurred during the mid to late seventies. We saw a gradual decrease in the eighties, and now in the nineties, we've had a real increase in reports."

Chris O'Brien has found mutilation cases as far away as Puerto Rico, the Canary Islands, and Australia, "but it's predominantly a North American phenomenon," O'Brien believes. In the United States alone, there have been approximately twelve thousand reported cases of animal mutilation. Investigators are certain the actual numbers are much greater, because ranchers are reluctant to come forward. O'Brien has found that "it is probably only two or three out of ten of these unusual deaths that are actually reported. We are witnessing what could be the greatest unsolved serial crime spree of the twentieth century, and it isn't going away."

The mutilated animals all share certain bizarre traits. O'Brien explains, "Usually, the rectum is cored out and the genitalia are removed. Often an ear or an eye is missing. Blood and body fluids have been completely drained from the animal. The victims are almost always cattle who have had the tongue removed and the mandible—or jawbone—excised and bleached. Some of the more unusual cases feature brains being removed from the skull without breaking into the cranial cavity. Major organs have been removed without any break into the body cavity."

Ernest Sandoval was sheriff of Costilla County in the San Luis Valley for more than sixteen years. During his tenure, he personally investigated seventy-five suspicious cattle mutilation cases. "My deputies and I did everything we could in the investigation of these mutilations," Sandoval recalls. "We took pictures. We looked for evidence. We looked for tracks. We never found anything around the animal. They were mutilated in different fashions. In some instances, the jaw was stripped to the bone, an eye was missing, or the belly button was gone. If it was a bull, testicles were removed. If it was a cow, the sex organs were gone."

While he was sheriff, Ernest Sandoval investigated one multiple mutilation case on the ranch of Emilio Lobato. "I lost forty-nine head of cattle to mutilations," Lobato says. "I lost them in less than three weeks. I've seen a lot of animals that have been torn up by coyotes and other predators, but these cattle had incisions that were just like a doctor would do in a hospital."

Precise incisions are a trademark of the unknown mutilators. (See Photo 67.) The conspicuous lack of blood, teeth marks, or torn flesh is what worries experienced ranchers like Emilio Lobato. He knows that losing cattle to illness and predators is a fact of life when you've got a large productive ranch, but Lobato's animals appeared to have been not so much attacked as experimented on.

"The local authorities were very helpful and supportive," Lobato says. "They helped me guard our cattle on almost a twenty-four-hour basis. But the Colorado Bureau of Investigation was not very helpful, and the FBI didn't react like they do on other cases."

The apparent lack of interest among state and federal officials was frustrating for Sheriff Sandoval. He says, "I was born in the valley. I know all the ranchers. They are my friends. It was difficult when the CBI and the FBI came to investigate. At the first meeting we had, they said it was predators. Many San Luis families were at that meeting, and we just looked at each other and said, 'Bull.' "

In a three-county area of northeastern Alabama, ranchers and local officials have also had to contend with mysterious cattle mutilations and the apparent lack of interest expressed by state and federal agencies. Ted Oliphant III, a Fyffe County, Alabama, police officer, has investigated more than thirty unusual animal deaths in his area. "We're finding the same thing over and over again," Oliphant says. "The sex organs have been removed, the tongues have been cut out. The jaw's been stripped in an oval, clean to the bone—and all without blood."

Again, officials in Alabama insist that the animals are not part of a bizarre experiment, but instead have died from either natural causes or predators. Alabama state veterinarian Dr. Lee Ally concludes, "It may be that the animal is getting mutilated, but it's predators—vultures—that are involved in the process."

Officer Oliphant disagrees: "The indication that predators are not responsible for these deaths is the precision of the cuts and evidence of high heat at the incision site—heat in excess of several hundred degrees, according to a pathologist who studied the tissue samples." That pathologist is Dr. John Altshuler, a hematologist who has spent five years examining suspect cattle tissue.

Dr. Altshuler has found that "a predator, even with the accuracy of gnawing and biting, would have left jagged borders. The fact is that the tissue at the incisional areas is very firm and very hard. Microscopic evidence clearly indicates that heat has been applied, and predators, to my knowledge, cannot do that."

Eli Hronich has been running cattle in northern New Mexico for more than fifteen years. He knows what predators can do to his valuable livestock, and he knows that most of the mutilated cattle on his ranch were not killed by predators. "When animals die of natural causes, there are always flies, maggots, buzzards, crows, coyotes, bears—and in a very short time the animal is gone," Hronich explains. "Most carcasses don't last more than about a day. But with my mutilated animals, you don't ever see any predatory activity. They just lie there and decay away on their own."

Since 1991, Eli Hronich has lost more than seventeen head of cattle to mutilation. "I found the first mutilated animal when my wife said she thought she saw an animal lying in the pasture that might be dead," Hronich remembers. "I went out on horseback, and usually the first thing you notice if you think something's dead are birds. There weren't any birds there. When I rode up to the animal, I saw the eye was gone. The rectal area had a perfect round cut. [See Photo 68.] The scrotum had about the same diameter cut. The sex organs had been removed and the tongue was gone. No blood, no flies, nothing; it was a real clean deal. The buzzards sat on the barn and just looked at it. They never would touch it."

Eli Hronich contacted the New Mexico state livestock inspector for answers. But Inspector Jerry Valerio had only questions.

"It's real puzzling," Valerio says. "A lot of people have said it's varmints, but the incisions are real precise. Every incision we've dealt with has been almost identical in every animal. And every animal is always facing in the same direction. They're always facing east. Varmints couldn't possibly do that in my opinion. We just don't know what's causing it or who's causing it." (See Photo 68.)

Perhaps the greatest mystery is the lack of physical evidence found at the mutilation sites. Officer Oliphant says, "We haven't been able to find footprints, animal tracks, wheel marks, or anything to indicate that anybody's been in there. How do you explain that? We can't."

Chris O'Brien believes the lack of tracks or marks near the carcasses will be an important clue in the eventual solution of the mystery. "All the evidence indicates that the animals are being dropped from the air. It seems to most researchers that the animals are being taken somewhere else, being experimented on, and then being dropped back where they were found. We've had cases of broken horns, broken ribs, and broken branches above the animals that indicate they've been slung in from the air."

O'Brien's theory poses a troubling question. Who would be capable of—or interested in—hijacking livestock for secret experimentation? "The causes behind these mutilations is absolutely unknown. I believe that there are several groups involved in this for various reasons," says O'Brien. Because of the lack of physical evidence, theories about who these groups may be are necessarily based on speculation about who could possibly have a motive for transporting and disemboweling livestock.

Currently, biotech companies are fighting a supersecret war to be the first to find an artificial substitute for human blood. Many of them are using the hemoglobin in cattle blood as a base, because, out of all the animals on earth, cattle have hemoglobin that most closely matches human hemoglobin. The first company to develop this artificial blood could have a $10 billion market all to themselves. The stakes are high, and these companies don't want the competition knowing what they're doing.

The quest for money seems to be behind many of the theories.

Chris O'Brien says, "There is a theory out there that you can detect heavy metals like gold and silver in the types of tissue removed from the cows. In Costilla County, for instance, it's reported that there's a very large gold deposit above the Chama Canyon area, which I believe is the epicenter of these animal deaths. Perhaps someone is monitoring gold levels in the area above the animals that's filtering down to the streams where they drink."

Chris O'Brien is also exploring the possibility that oil companies can find oil based on cattle tissue samples taken from livestock in potential oil sites. And he is considering a coincidental link between locations where mutilated cattle are found. "Because a lot of these animal mutilation cases occur near military bases, nuclear reactors, and uranium mines, there is some evidence to suggest, and many people believe, that the government and/or our military is involved in this," O'Brien says.

The possibility of experimentation at sites located away from where the animals are found is bolstered by numerous reports of flying craft just before—or most often just after—a mutilation. "Whenever these mutilations occur, there are always sightings of helicopters around the area," Ernest Sandoval says.

In more than half of the Alabama cases, farmers reported seeing unmarked helicopters leaving the scene of a mutilation. Fyffe County farmer Doug Segers has lost several steers to mutilators. "They had a chopper in behind my barn," Segers recalls, "and had all my cattle rounded up. The chopper, when it appeared, it was kind of unordinary. It looked like it was setting on a box. It was big enough to get a cow in."

Segers's neighbor, farmer David McClendon, also believes there is a link between these mysterious helicopters and the bizarre death of his livestock. McClendon remembers one particular altercation: "I heard loud helicopter noise. It sounded like it was right over my trailer. I went out the front door, went up to my car, reached under the seat, and pulled out a handgun. I walked to the edge of the trailer and I saw the helicopter. It was light blue with no markings, no numbers, hovering fifteen feet above the trees. I dropped my holster and the helicopter veered off."

Helicopters are not the only flying craft that have been sighted in the vicinity of livestock mutilations. In the San Luis Valley there have been numerous sightings of unidentified flying objects, and many researchers believe there is a significant link between these UFOs and the deaths of hundreds of animals in the valley.

"At the time of the mutilations, we saw many lights in the sky," rancher Emilio Lobato explains. "We could not interpret what they were or where they were coming from. Some of them were very unusual. On the rim of Sanchez Reservoir, my wife and I saw what looked like a round disk—a huge one. It seemed like it had small windows, and they were lighted. It was going around and around. I saw it with binoculars, and my wife did too."

Chris O'Brien is familiar with several reports of cattle coming in contact with supposed UFOs. "There's one case," he reports, "of a rancher who witnessed a group of small alien-type beings carrying a cow toward a craft. They later found the animal in a mutilated condition—thus, the connection between a nonhuman entity or a group of nonhuman entities and a mutilated animal."

Near Eli Hronich's ranch in northern New Mexico, O'Brien heard of a case in which, "a mother and her child witnessed an animal being taken up by a beam of light into a craft. They claimed that they were taken into the craft themselves, and they saw some form of experimentation being performed on the animal."

Whether livestock mutilation is caused by biotech engineers, multinational companies, the government, or an extraterrestrial force, Eli Hronich speaks for many ranchers when he says, "Somebody somewhere knows what's going on. I mean, it just seems like every time we try to do an investigation, it comes to a dead end. We get a lot of publicity, but then it just dies. A lot of people just don't see this as a crime. This is my living, and it's cost me thousands of dollars already. They're taking my living away from me. It's just outright thievery. Why isn't somebody doing something about it?"

Investigators like Chris O'Brien, Ernest Sandoval, and Ted Oliphant are trying, but they believe the bureaucratic obstacles may be insurmountable. Chris O'Brien says, "Until we get the help of state and federal law enforcement officials, we're spinning our wheels. There are no answers. There are just thousands of questions and thousands of dead animals."

Animal mutilations have been reported in twenty of the fifty United States.

Although cattle are involved in an estimated 80 to 90 percent of all animal mutilation cases, there have also been similar deaths reported among horses, goats, sheep, pigs, deer, elk, dogs, and cats.

Popular press reports to this day often refer to the first mutilated animal in 1967 as "Snippy." This is incorrect. Snippy was the sire of the actual mutilated mare, whose name was Lady.

The Curse
on Orson Welles

H undreds of Hollywood movies have been made about the evil power of curses. With titles such as *The Mummy's Curse*, *The Curse of the Cat People*, and *Curse of the Swamp Creature*, these films have made the subject laughable. But there is one real-life Hollywood curse that is deadly serious, and many people believe it is the reason one of the big screen's brightest lights burned out before his time. It is the curse on Orson Welles.

Before Steven Spielberg, before Quentin Tarantino, before any of the contemporary young filmmakers heralded today as Hollywood's *wunderkind*, there was Orson Welles. In four short years, between 1937 and 1941, Welles became the undisputed king first of radio, then film. At nineteen, he was starring on Broadway and producing and directing plays that would later redefine the future of American theater. In 1937, Welles cofounded The Mercury Theater of the Air and produced, among other things, *War of the Worlds*, a landmark radio broadcast that terrified a generation of Americans into believing that flying saucers had actually landed in New Jersey.

In 1940, Orson Welles came to Hollywood at the request of RKO Radio Pictures. The studio wanted this supposed boy wonder to direct a low-budget feature about a fictional publishing magnate. Welles demanded and received total artistic control.

It was the first and only time that any studio anywhere in the world turned a movie over to a director, no questions asked. That movie was *Citizen Kane*, still considered by many to be the greatest movie ever made. Orson Welles was its producer, director, cowriter, and star. When *Citizen Kane* premiered in 1941, Orson Welles was only twenty-six years old.

In 1941, Welles began work on his second film, *The Magnificent Ambersons*. Midway through the production, he was called away to Washington, D.C. Nelson Rockefeller asked Welles to direct a documentary about Brazil as part of an effort to improve Pan-American relations during World War II, and Welles agreed. It would be a fateful decision.

Peter Bogdanovich, the director of more than sixteen films, including *The Last Picture Show*, *Paper Moon*, and *Mask*, describes the effect the Brazilian film, titled *It's All True*, would have on his friend: "Orson had gotten the best deal anybody's ever gotten in Hollywood. He made the picture and got some of the greatest notices ever written about somebody's first movie. He was making another movie—which was probably as good as, if not better than, the first one. And then he went down to Rio, and all hell broke loose. Everything fell apart. He never got another job in pictures anywhere remotely like the kind of opportunity he'd had, nor in theater, nor radio. It was a big black crossroads, and he was struggling the rest of his life."

It's All True was conceived as a three-part documentary (*Carnaval*, *Four Men and a Boat*, and *My Friend Bonito*) capturing the social and cultural panorama of Brazil. "As Orson Welles discovered, you don't make a film about Brazil without including Carnaval and the religion which really lies underneath it," says Professor Don Cosentino, Chairman of the Folklore Mythology Program at UCLA. "Rio de Janeiro is a very powerful center for magic, for curses," Cosentino continues. "The magic-based religion of Rio is called macumba. It has a great reputation for effectiveness. Everybody in Brazil believes in the efficacy of these traditions."

Orson Welles did, in fact, base one part of his documentary on

Carnaval and the samba (the Brazilian national dance), tracing their roots to the black magic of macumba. (See Photo 69.) For *Carnaval*, he negotiated with a macumba priest to allow the priest's ceremonies to be filmed, but he was forced to cancel the filming because the Brazilian government considered the magical practices illegal. There are differing versions about what happened next, but everyone agrees that it resulted in a lifelong curse on the career of Orson Welles.

Welles would claim years later that the priest, whom he referred to as a "voodoo witch doctor," was deeply offended by the cancellation and visited Welles in his office. "The priest didn't take kindly to this. In fact, he objected vociferously," says Professor Cosentino. "He had been insulted, and he said the gods whom he served had been insulted. The next day Welles found a piece of metal with a red ribbon through it stabbing his script."

According to producer/director Bill Krohn, who later completed and released *It's All True* after Welles's death, the director was cursed not by the priest but by members of his cult who were greedy and felt betrayed. "Welles's producer, Richard Wilson, was visited in his office in Rio by three women dressed in white," Krohn explains. "They said, 'We're from the cult. We made all these costumes for your movie. If we're not going to be in it, we want to be reimbursed.' The producer said, 'I don't think that will be possible' and left the room to check. When he came back, there was a ring of needles in the script of *Carnaval*, and the women were gone."

Whether it was the priest or his followers, a piece of metal, or a ring of needles, from that moment on Orson Welles was a changed man. "Orson had a strong belief in superstition, in witchcraft, in black magic and white magic," Peter Bogdanovich recalls, "and I think he took it quite literally. I think he felt the picture was cursed and that he was suffering from that curse. And I think it pursued him to the end of his days."

Perhaps Welles took the curse so literally because this was not the first time he had known the power of a curse. Seven years earlier, in 1935, Welles had directed a groundbreaking version of

Macbeth at the Lafayette Theater in Harlem, starring an all African-American cast. The critics were unanimous in their raves, except for Percy Hammond, the *Herald-Tribune* theater critic. "This one critic had given them a bad review, called it 'the voodoo *Macbeth*'," Bogdanovich explains. "He really panned it, and one of the cast members, a witch doctor in Harlem, didn't take too kindly to this. He put a hex on this guy." Percy Hammond died the day after his review came out.

Orson Welles remembered the curse on Percy Hammond when tragedy struck the set of *It's All True*, soon after he received the needle-pierced script. Welles was filming a re-creation of one of the great moments in Brazilian history, in the part titled *Four Men and a Boat*. "He was re-creating the story of four men who had sailed a raft from Fortaleza in the northeast 1,650 miles to Rio de Janeiro to petition the Brazilian government for social benefits for their people—the Jungaderos—who were starving," Bill Krohn recounts. "Welles was re-creating with the actual people their triumphal entry into Rio harbor. During one of the setups for this, the leader of the raft, Manoel 'Jacaré' Olímpio Meira, a national hero, drowned. Welles was attacked because of this. A national hero had died during the making of his film."

The very same day that Jacaré died, May 19, 1942, Orson Welles got a chilling telegram. RKO was pulling the plug on his project by cutting all funding. Welles tried to complete the picture on his own, but quickly ran out of influence, money, and hope. Bill Krohn says, "Everything that Orson Welles did before 1942 worked like a charm. Everything he did after 1942 was a struggle."

Welles returned to Hollywood with hundreds of rolls of unedited film and a curse on his head. The man who left for Brazil as the most sought-after director in Hollywood returned to find that for unknown reasons he was now box-office poison. RKO had taken *The Magnificent Ambersons* away from him and recut it. "RKO even changed their logo to 'RKO—Showmanship Instead of Genius.' I mean, you can't get much more obvious than that one. Good-bye, Orson," says Bogdanovich. "He didn't direct a film for five years after that, and when he did it was kind of a routine, conventional film, *The Stranger*. He got a reputation as someone who couldn't or sometimes wouldn't finish projects. Eventually, the average public didn't really remember him as a great American director, but rather as a showman or as Johnny Carson's heavyset friend or as a guy who did commercials for wine."

The raw footage from *It's All True*, mislabeled *Bonito*, sat in a forgotten film vault on a lot that now belongs to Paramount Studios for more than forty years. It was rediscovered by accident. Welles's longtime assistant and camera operator Gary Graver called Welles with what he thought was good news. "I said, 'Orson, shall we get it out? Shall we try to finish *It's All True*?' And finally he said to me, 'I can't. I just can't.' He believed the curse on it had affected his career, and he wasn't meant to finish it," Graver remembers.

Bill Krohn, a longtime Welles admirer, was granted permission to finish Welles's film. "When I first heard about the curse, I didn't take it too seriously, but as the years wore on and the movie wasn't getting done, I began to think that maybe there was something to it," Krohn says. "We had found one of the two most legendary lost films in film history, and everyone who should have helped either didn't help or did things to hurt us."

"We'd get a producer," Krohn continues, "and then he'd go bankrupt. We got money raised from the Brazilian government, and then the whole Brazilian government went under. It really seemed as if we were in a chess game with an invisible opponent, and every time we made a move, he made a move. And he was winning. I mean, all film projects are hard to get off the ground— but this one took eleven years."

When Bill Krohn did finally secure enough financial support to begin preservation work on *It's All True*, the curse seemed to wield its ultimate power. He explains, "At just the point when the film was finally donated to UCLA and the American Film Institute for preservation, Orson Welles died." Peter Bogdanovich recalls, "Toward the end of his life, I think Orson was scared of the film. It was a terrible thing to come back and haunt him at the very end of his life."

For Bill Krohn, Welles's death added a new urgency and significance to finishing *It's All True*. Krohn began to explore the possibility that the curse could be removed. "I went to see a man in Brazil who had first introduced Welles to macumba and had taken him to his first macumba ceremony. I asked that man if he could do something with his connections in the local religion to have the curse lifted. He said he would get to work on it. Three months later, I got a letter saying that he had died."

Krohn was later introduced to Lina de Souza, a Brazilian spiritual priestess living in Los Angeles. "When I saw Lina for the first time, we sat down and she threw a bunch of seashells on the table and looked into them to see what had been done. She said, 'Whoever did this did a good job, but I think I can turn it around.' " Lina adds, "When I threw the shells, I read what the shells did, and then I gave him the answer. The god said it could be removed."

Lina de Souza gave Bill Krohn a strange shopping list of items he would need for the curse-removal ceremony. Krohn remembers feeling somewhat foolish about the whole process, until he realized that he was participating in a secret belief system shared by many people worldwide. He explains: "Lina told me to buy eggs, ribbon, black and red candles, a big white bowl, and other things. A guy from Jamaica was working at the cash register, and I asked, 'Do you know where I can get some Brazilian flour and palm oil?' and he said, 'Planning on doing a little cooking?' and I said, 'You know what this is about, don't you?' And he said, 'Yeah, we have the same thing where I come from.' "

Lina performed her curse-removal ceremony, and it seemed to work. A reconstructed *It's All True*, co-directed by Bill Krohn, Richard Wilson, and Myron Meisel was finally released by Paramount Pictures in 1993, more than fifty years after it had been shot. The successful release of the film seemed to indicate that the curse had been lifted, but Bill Krohn feels it wasn't until a film festival in Munich, Germany, that the curse on Orson Welles finally ended. At that festival, *It's All True* won a $6,000 prize. The money was donated to the Jungaderos in Brazil, some of the descendants of Jacaré.

Watching *Citizen Kane* today, it's hard not to wonder what would have happened if the macumba curse had been lifted in Orson Welles' own time. How would movies be different today if there had never been a curse? Peter Bogdanovich says, "Orson was an unusual artist. He was an innovator, controversial, experimental. He was a magical personality, there's no question about it. One of a kind."

> Don Cosentino, professor of African and Caribbean folklore, mythology, and literature at UCLA, warns "Curses can kill people. Curses can make people sick. Curses can ruin people's finances. Curses can certainly ruin people's love lives. How do curses work? There is no answer to that."

A Child's Premonition

Most psychic researchers believe that we are all born with extraordinary powers of ESP, the ability to sense and feel things outside of the physical world. But as we grow older, they warn, this enhanced psychic awareness is weakened by a world that teaches people to rely on empirical thinking. If this is true, it might help explain why six-year-old Katie Thronson had a premonition of death that—tragically—came true.

Just before her seventh birthday, Katie showed her mother, Julie Thronson, a beautiful crayon drawing. It was her vision of a life after this one, and Julie was sure it was nothing more than the creative output of a very active imagination. But less than a week after Katie drew her seemingly fanciful picture, the little girl who was heaven-sent was gone.

"Katie was a beautiful little girl who was really happy, who was always kissing people. She was just really loving," Julie recalls. Katie's father, Jerry, remembers that "She'd always have her arms around other children. She seemed to be the one that always brought the children together."

Of her three children, Julie thinks of Katie as the most creative. "She was always drawing, and I always called her my little artist," Julie says. "Over the course of almost seven years she made hundreds of drawings. She expressed herself by drawing hearts all the time, because she was filled with love."

Julie vividly recalls the day in October of 1991 when Katie came to her with one particular drawing that seemed very different from the rest. Out of the blue Katie asked a very unsettling question. Julie recalls, "She came into the room where I was sitting, holding a tablet that she had been drawing on, and in a real innocent way came up to me and asked me, 'Mommy, am I going to die?' And I said, 'No, honey, of course not. You're not going to die.' And she said, 'Never?' And I said, 'Katie, no, you're not going to die.' And then she just danced off, happy that she wasn't going to die."

It was the kind of question every child asks as they begin to puzzle out the way the world works and their place in it. Except for the death of a great-grandmother when Katie was too young to remember, the family had never suffered a loved one's death. And, as Jerry explains, "We were never overly religious—what you'd call regular churchgoers." It seemed only natural that Katie would have questions.

Katie's simple query took on new meaning two days later. Katie didn't feel well. It seemed like the flu, but her condition quickly worsened, and she was rushed to the hospital. Doctors there suspected, and later confirmed, that Katie had a ruptured appendix. "In the hours after that time and prior to her going into surgery, her prognosis had become extremely grave," Julie remembers.

While Jerry took care of the other Thronson children, Julie stayed by her daughter's bedside. Just before three in the afternoon, as doctors were preparing for surgery, Julie noticed a change in Katie's breathing. Katie lapsed into unconsciousness, and Julie could not wake her.

"I said, 'Katie, Katie, just talk to Mommy,'" Julie remembers of that horrible day. "And she wasn't responding to me at all. And I looked at the clock and it was right at three o'clock. Then I looked back at Katie, and she just sat up in the hospital bed and raised her arms out toward the window. She opened her eyes. It was like she wanted me to pick her up, and yet her arms weren't outstretched in my direction. There was a stillness in the room that is indescribable. It was completely still. It felt like an infinite moment. And in my spirit I knew that my little girl had been taken. I ran out into the hall and I just yelled, 'My little girl just died. I just saw her die.' "

A medical team rushed in to try to revive Katie. Julie was asked to wait just outside the room where her daughter was dying. "And then I noticed a pregnant woman in a hospital gown and hospital slippers walking toward me. And I could tell by the look in her eyes that she was going to say something to me," Julie says. "And she came right up to me and touched me on the shoulder and she said, 'The Lord has spoken to me. You're to be a lioness. Your little girl is OK.' I felt a shiver go through my body. I thought, if the Lord has spoken to her, then Katie must be OK. Whether she is going to live or whether she's gone, Katie's going to be OK."

The woman disappeared as if into thin air. Julie never saw her again. For three days, doctors tried to keep Katie alive with machines, but they were finally forced to pronounce the comatose six-year-old legally brain dead. Jerry and Julie made the agonizing decision to remove life support. The Thronsons' doctor, Dr. Robert Huff, explains what happened: "The autopsy indicated that there was indeed appendicitis, and that there had been extension of this infection locally to other organs that were nearby."

According to the death certificate, Katie Thronson died on October 10, 1991, but both Julie and Dr. Huff believe that Katie was gone much sooner. Julie says, "When I told the doctor that Katie had raised her arms out toward the window, he said, 'I believe that was the time that Katie left her body.' And although they had artificially kept her alive, she had died at three o'clock."

Six-year-old Katie was the first to be laid to rest in the family plot. It was an unspeakable tragedy, from which the Thronsons thought they would never recover. But a few months later, Julie found a ray of hope stuffed inside a cardboard box. She was looking for some of Katie's artwork to include with thank-you notes she was writing and found the tablet that Katie had been drawing on just days before her death. (See Photo 70.)

"She had drawn a picture of these angels, surrounding a light. The clouds and the moon had sad faces and all the angels had sad faces; some of them even had tears coming down their faces. The picture said everything. When I saw it I knew without a doubt that Katie had had a premonition," Julie says. Jerry agrees: "For some reason, she was given this picture in her mind as a sort of premonition. There was something going on between Katie and God, something we don't know about."

Jerry and Julie drew strength from that cherished drawing, and five months after Katie's death, Julie saw a picture in *Life* magazine that confirmed her belief that Katie's drawing was a premonition. It was a nineteenth-century engraving depicting one artist's vision of life after death. The welcoming vortex of light was strikingly similar to Katie's own vision. Both pictures had a spiral pattern that resembled the tunnel of light commonly reported in other near-death experiences. (See Photo 71.) Was it a coincidence, or did Katie receive a message from beyond?

"There was no doubt in my mind that she had never seen anything like this picture before or had ever been told anything like it," Julie explains. "As far as I know, she had never even heard of angels. I never talked to Katie about angels, so for her to come up with this concept of angels flocking toward the light was very unusual." Jerry adds, "Whether or not she knew the meaning of her drawing, I believe her spirit did."

Among the experts quoted in the *Life* magazine article on near-death experience was Dr. Gerald Jampolsky, founder of the Center for Attitudinal Healing in Sausalito, California. Dr. Jampolsky works with families of children with terminal illnesses and counsels bereaved families. Julie wrote to Dr. Jampolsky about Katie's drawing, and when they met, he expressed his astonishment at the clear vision of an afterlife he saw in the simple crayon figures.

"It was very similar to other drawings by children and adults who had returned from a near-death experience," Dr. Jampolsky says. "I pointed out to Julie that there were seven angels in a ring and that, looking at it as a clock, at the three o'clock position one of the angels was going toward the center, going toward the light." Julie also recalls that conversation: "I was amazed for a minute, and as Dr. Jampolsky continued to discuss the drawing, I'm thinking, he doesn't know that Katie died at three o'clock. There's no way he could know that."

Dr. Jampolsky says, "Children can be really wonderful teachers. They've been wonderful teachers to me and have really helped me let go of any doubts that the essence of our being is love. That's our first principle, that life's eternal."

Julie also tried to find the pregnant woman who had comforted her just after Katie's death. Through birth records published in the local newspaper, she contacted every woman who had been in the maternity ward of the hospital during the beginning of October 1991. None of them remembered speaking to Julie. "She was obviously an angel," Julie concludes. "There was some kind of message there about life, death, and birth."

The message came into even sharper focus for the Thronson family on October 7, 1992. One year to the day after Katie died, Julie gave birth to her fourth child, Cody. It was an uncanny coincidence, but Jerry says "I don't believe it was a coincidence at all. I believe Katie's drawing left us with a picture full of meaning about life and death. I believe it was truly a gift, maybe a gift from God." And Dr. Jampolsky concurs: "I was once told the definition of coincidence and I've always found it very helpful. A coincidence is a miracle in which God wishes to remain anonymous. That makes a lot of sense to me."

Now when the Thronsons take Katie's brothers to see her grave, it is with sadness but also a sense of peace. Jerry says, "The picture has brought us into many areas of study about life after death, and it's brought us into contact with a lot of people that maybe we can help through this picture. It has been very inspirational." And Julie adds, "The impact that drawing has had on our lives is beyond words. We have this to share with people. We hope to share with them that there is a beautiful side to all of this. I hope that people will believe in everything their children say." Jerry believes "It has helped us in the healing process. It gives us peace. I feel honored that Katie was given a glimpse from the other side."

Julie Thronson now counsels other families who have had to cope with the death of a child. "I was always terrified of death," she says. "I was terrified of anything ever happening to my children. But Katie's drawing has increased my faith and my perception of life and death. There really isn't a separation. I love Katie as much now as I did when she was alive."

Recently, Katie appeared to once again bring her family closer to the realization that death is not the final ending. The Thronsons were in a serious car accident, broadsided at a busy intersection near the children's school. Julie explains, "It was a high enough impact that it totaled the car. Christopher, our middle son, was injured. On the third night after the accident he said to me, 'Mom, how come Katie doesn't come here?' And I said, 'Because she's dead, Christopher.' And he said, 'No, she's not, Mom. She's in school.' And I said, 'She can't go to school.'

" 'Yes she can, Mom. Katie's in school. I saw her,' he said. And I said, 'Where did you see her?' He said, 'Through the window, through the window at the car crash.' Well, considering his window was completely shattered and the flying glass is what caused his injuries, I believe that Christopher saw Katie. Spiritually he saw her. Spiritually, she is still with us."

> According to the International Association for Near-Death Studies, more than 8 million people have had a near-death experience.

Missing Pieces

Like many sets of identical twins, Alice Heck and Agnes Nash, now sixty-eight, have always shared a special bond that extends beyond the physical. Not only do they look alike, dress alike, and share the same goals and interests, but Alice and Agnes also believe they have a deep psychic connection. They finish each other's sentences. If one of them is hurt, the other feels pain. If Alice's phone rings, she knows without picking up the receiver when Agnes is on the other end. Alice and Agnes's parallel thoughts and feelings have been a natural part of their lives since the twins' birth in Rochester, New York, on April 6, 1926.

"We're exact, identical, mirror-image twins with hypertelepathy," Agnes explains. (See Photo 72.) "Just like in a dream, I can see in my mind what Alice is doing, and she can see in her mind what I am doing. I can always tell what she's wearing. She can tell you what I'm wearing. If I go to the store to buy something, she will see it in her mind and go to the store and buy the same dang thing."

Since as far back as they can remember, the twins, who call each other "Sissy," have felt each other's triumphs and pain. Agnes recalls, "When we were kids, I was roller-skating over at the school one time, and I fell. I really had a pretty bad cut on my knee. Sissy was home, and she told Dad, 'You better go get Sissy.

She's hurt bad at school.' She wasn't with me. She didn't see me leave. She didn't know I was skating. But she knew what had happened."

The deep connection continued into adulthood. "I was living in Florida," Agnes says, "and Sissy was living in New York. I had just finished eating lunch, and all of a sudden, I saw Sissy holding her little boy Jimmy's head like in a dream. And I said, 'Something's happened to Jimmy. Sissy's gone to the hospital with Jimmy.' Well, we called home and she wasn't there, so we called my older brother, and he told me, 'They just rushed little Jimmy to the hospital. They think he's fractured his skull.' I've been able to see things like that all my life."

Along with the experiences of pain, premonition, and extended perception that Alice and Agnes shared growing up, they also shared a deep secret feeling. Agnes says, "No matter what we did growing up, we always felt like we were looking for something. We didn't know what it was, but there was always a void." Alice felt the void most acutely when she was in a crowd. "We'd always be looking around, searching. We didn't know what for."

It wasn't until the twins were much older that they found out there was a reason for their inexplicable feeling of emptiness. There were missing pieces in their identical lives. Alice remembers, "My mother told me when we were fifty-one years old, about two months before she died." Agnes adds, "She called us to her house. She said, 'I've got something to tell you. I don't know how you're going to take it.' " Alice picks up the story. "She said, 'I realize that I do not have much longer to live.' She knew she was very, very sick. And she said, 'I think you better sit down.' "

"We both said, 'What is it, Ma?' " Agnes recalls. "And she said, 'Well, you've always thought you were identical twins.' 'Well, we are!' we said. 'No, you're not,' Ma said. 'You are quadruplets. There are four of you.' Right then, when she said that, it seemed as if a great weight had been lifted, because I always felt there was something missing in our lives."

Alice says, "She said that she hadn't told us before because she didn't want us to have the heartache of not knowing where they were or what they were doing." Alice and Agnes's mother died without revealing any more of the story than that. The twins were half of a secret whole, and the truth about what happened to the missing siblings went with their mother to her grave.

There were many rumors and much conjecture among family members about where Alice and Agnes's missing half might be found. Some believed the pair had been stolen from the hospital, others that they had been given up for adoption. Alice and Agnes's father had died in 1961, and the sisters believe he may never even have known that he was the father of four. "My dad probably never knew, because at the time we were born, Daddy was in the Brooklyn Naval Hospital, and they didn't think he was going to live."

After their mother died, Alice and Agnes enlisted the help of a private detective, various adoption support groups, and several retired members of the local law enforcement community to find their missing half. For seventeen years, they searched for answers using these conventional methods. Nothing worked, until they asked a psychic for help. "In a lot of ways my sister and I are psychic, but I used to think that most professional psychics were quacks," Alice says. "I found out they are not. My feelings changed when I began to realize that what the psychic was telling me was true. She really knew."

Alice had sought out Sandra Sanfilippo, a Rochester, New York, psychic who uses a method called psychometry. "I usually start out holding a person's watch or an object that belongs to them," Sandra explains. "From that I can pick up vibrations and energies. It gives me a tool to connect with their aura. Then I can pick up what look like little movies running through my head."

Before their first session, Alice told Sandra nothing about herself, her sister, or the family mystery she was trying to solve. But Sandra picked up on the reason for Alice's visit right away. Sandra recalls, "It felt like Alice was only part of a picture. I was picking up a void around her heart. During the reading, I picked up a name right away—the name of a missing sister. It just flowed right out of me. But there was also a sense of sadness, because this sister would really be reluctant about meeting them and connecting with them."

Sandra also told Alice and Agnes that they would discover the whereabouts of one missing sister on or by Father's Day. They would meet her in the summer. She would be found within 220 miles of their home. On every point, including the name of that sister, Sandra was right. One month after her psychic reading, Alice and Agnes made the connection.

The twins had appeared on a national talk show, telling their story and hoping someone might come forward as a result. A little boy was watching that show and noticed a striking family resemblance. "And that's when the grandson of our new sister saw us and thought we looked like his grandmother. That's how it all started," Alice says.

The boy's grandmother knew she was adopted and had also been searching for her birth family. She contacted Alice and Agnes on Father's Day and met them that same summer, just as the psychic had predicted. Agnes remembers, "The minute she came to the motel where we were staying and walked in the door, it was just as if we'd always known her. There was no strangeness. We just felt she was our sister, and that was that."

Alice and Agnes felt that now they were triplets. And as they began to learn more and more about their separate lives, they discovered many eerie similarities. Although they had grown up more than two hundred miles apart from this "new sister," their lives had followed parallel paths. Agnes says, "So many of the things our sister's told us about her past match our past. What we did in school and how we were as kids—she was the same way. Even her grades were the same as ours."

Alice says, "Our new sister has a son and a daughter, Mark and Maureen. I have a son and a daughter, Mark and Maureen. Her daughter was born July 12, 1952. My son was born July 12, 1952." And Agnes adds, "Our new sister and her husband lost twin girls back in 1960, and her one boy was born the same day that I lost my twin girls, October 3."

Looking over old family photographs, there was another uncanny coincidence. "My new sister was married a year before I was," Alice says. "She bought her gown in her hometown in a specialty shop. I bought my gown here in Rochester in a specialty shop. They were the same gown. She had hers altered. I had mine altered. Both were changed the same way, with seed pearls added to the neckline. And when I went to her house, I saw her taste is still very much like mine. Even our bathrooms are identical, down to the towels."

Baptismal records seem to support Alice and Agnes's belief that this is their sister. Alice explains, "When she showed us her baptismal, everything fit into place. She was given my mother's first name. She was given a cousin's last name. Everybody on her baptismal was related to us." But despite this one document, the long-lost sister has not completely accepted Alice and Agnes as part of her past. She has no birth certificate, no adoption records, no hard evidence.

"She is still looking for a paper trail. I guess it's overwhelmed her, according to what she says. She doesn't want her name used right now. But she has admitted to us that she knows in her heart that she is our sister. So now we're leaving it up to her," Agnes says. "The whole experience has been awesome and overwhelming."

While Alice and Agnes work to build a relationship with their new sister, there is still another missing piece to be found. There is another sibling out there somewhere, and Sandra Sanfilippo believes it is a brother. "She told me that at this time she sees a brother, that his name is John but his nickname is Jack. Now, my new sister went to a different psychic, and she was also given the name John," Alice says. "I hope that we do find him. He would be sixty-eight years old and might look like us. He may have dark hair, because our hair is naturally dark. His birthday should be April 6, 1926."

Sandra Sanfilippo believes this missing brother wants to find Alice and Agnes. "I feel like the brother would welcome this idea with open arms. He's always wanted to be more connected and loved by people. The sense I get is that he needs love very much. He's out there, and he needs to be found."

Alice and Agnes have come to trust the psychic impressions provided by Sandra. She did help them make a connection with at least one person with whom they share many uncanny resemblances, but they are not sure that it's a brother they should be looking for now. Alice has one persistent vision—one memory that continues to haunt her. She remembers a missing piece of the puzzle that just doesn't seem to fit anywhere.

"Someone told me there was a doctor in town whose daughter couldn't have children, and then later on she turned up with twins," Alice recalls today. That reminded me; when my sister and I were three or four years old, my mother took us down to River Street to see two little girls. The woman there wouldn't let my mother see the girls. She said they weren't hers, they were just visiting. She let us go in and play, while our mother stayed outside. But instead of playing, the four of us just did nothing but hug and kiss, and when we left we cried. The next time we went down there, I think it was a few days later, they were gone."

The remembrance opens up a Pandora's box full of troubling questions. Were those twins the other half of a set of quadruplets? Where did they go and where are they now? Is the "new sister" really that, or could she be someone who has, inexplicably, led a life parallel to that of Alice and Agnes? Is there a brother as the psychics predicted? These are the questions Alice and Agnes must face in the twilight of their lives. What is the answer?

According to Professor Robert Plomin of the London Institute of Psychiatry, identical twins reared apart are even more alike in terms of major life events than identical twins reared together.

Many secondary physical characteristics, such as freckles and facial hair, are genetically predetermined, causing many identical twins to be exact mirror images of each other. In most cases of mirror twins, one sibling is right-handed and the other is left-handed.

Identical twins never have identical fingerprints.

A Burning
from Within

I t was early on the morning of January 6, 1980, when crime-scene investigator John Heymer was called to a small council house in Ebbw Vale, Wales, to examine an unusual death by fire. Heymer had been to hundreds of crime scenes before. It was his job to inspect and photograph crime victims, and Heymer had become inured to the sight of gruesome human remains. But on this cold morning, John Heymer saw something more bizarre and more horrifying than anything he had ever seen before.

"I asked a sergeant, 'Where's the fire?' because there was no smell of fire and there was no sign of smoke," Heymer recalls of his first moments at the scene of the crime. "The sergeant pointed to a closed door and said, 'Through there.' The paint work on the door was pristine white, but when I opened the door, it was like stepping into Dante's *Inferno*. It was the strangest sensation I've ever had. The atmosphere was hot and steamy, lit by a weird, hellish sort of orange-red glow.

"I looked around and saw a misshapen, molten lampshade lying on the floor, lying on top of a pair of shoes. Just beyond the shoes were a pair of human feet clothed in socks with short lengths of trouser above. Then those trousers disappeared to reveal calcified leg bones which went up as far as the knees and then just disintegrated into an amorphous mass of ash. At the other end of the ash was a blackened human skull.

"I was looking at the remains of a seventy-two-year-old man who had seemingly burned to ash, but part of the armchair he had been sitting in remained unburned. The man's ashes were on top of a nylon carpet and the foam backing was unburned. The hearth was perfectly clean; in fact, there was a pile of dry sticks ready to light in the fireplace."

John Heymer had come face-to-face with a controversial paranormal phenomenon known as spontaneous human combustion, or SHC. And, as he was soon to learn, SHC is not something most forensic scientists and arson investigators like to talk about. "Normally at a crime scene I would collect the evidence to be sent to the laboratory," Heymer explains, "but in this case, I called the forensic scientists in the lab, described the situation, and asked them to attend. They treated me in a rather condescending fashion. They said that there is no such thing as spontaneous human combustion, and nothing more was ever said about it. I don't think it was a general conspiracy—it was just each bloke looking out for his job. If you admit that you believe in SHC, that's no way to get a promotion."

Since that cold January morning, John Heymer has investigated other cases of alleged SHC, many of them chronicled in the book *Spontaneous Human Combustion*, by Jenny Randles and Peter Hough. Randles and Hough, noted British paranormal investigators, first got involved in the SHC phenomenon in 1985. "The local police invited us to look at a case that occurred at Halton College in Widnes, Cheshire," Jenny Randles recalls. "A young student was walking down the stairs in the middle of the day surrounded by her friends, laughing and joking, when she literally became a mass of flames. The fire was beat out and she was taken to the hospital where, tragically, she died."

It was an atypical SHC case, because eyewitnesses had been present at the moment of external ignition and were able to smother the flame. More typical is the so-called 1980 "Chorley case," which Randles and Hough have also investigated. "The victim lived alone in a house in Lancashire," Hough says. "The night before she died, neighbors had noticed black smoke coming from the chimney, but they thought no more of it. The next morning, two men called at the house. They got no reply. Neighbors forced their way in, and what they discovered was grisly to say the least. From the waist upwards, everything—including skin, muscle, and bone—had been turned into a fine white ash." (See Photo 73.) There was some oily, sooty residue on the hearth and on the nearby wall, but the carpet and nearby furniture had not burned.

According to cremationist Pamela Byrne, temperatures in excess of 1,500 degrees are necessary to burn a human body. The process takes between three and four hours. Even then, Byrne says, "In my time as a cremationist, I have never seen a body cremated to nothing. There are always skeletal remains left over." Byrne says that human bones are removed from the crematorium and pulverized with heavy grinding stones before they can be placed inside an urn. "So if a body was reduced to ash in a fire, it would be a mystery to me how that occurred," she concludes.

After more than a decade of research, Randles and Hough have uncovered more than seventy cases of unusual death by fire that they believe were caused by SHC. But, they caution, the words spontaneous human combustion may actually be a misnomer. Most victims don't suddenly burst into flames; instead, they appear to have been slowly devoured by intense heat from the inside out. This burning from within is one of the essential traits that SHC researchers have identified as the hallmarks of the phenomenon.

Randles explains, "The overriding factor is the incredible localization of the fire. The fire does not destroy the house, or even the room where the victim is found. We're talking about a situation where the fire is localized to within inches of a body that has largely turned to ash. Apart from a few extremities, there is near total destruction of the body; not just skin and tissue, but bones—which are incredibly difficult to destroy by way of fire."

Larry Arnold is the president of Parascience International, a consortium of researchers studying paranormal phenomena in the United States. Arnold has seen these same circumstances in American SHC cases and notes additional elements common to the pattern in cases of suspected spontaneous human combustion.

"In a classic case of SHC, the center of the body is reduced quite literally to dust and ashes. There may be some extremities left—perhaps a lower leg, perhaps fingertips, perhaps the head. But the main part of the body is burned to dust. You will have the absence of any fueling accelerant that could cause that intensity of fire: no gasoline, no kerosene, no hydrocarbons." According to Arnold, other factors include "a lack of a fuel source outside of the body itself. And you find most often a lack of odor at the fire scene—and if there is a smell, it is described as a sweet or perfume smell. This is very atypical of human incineration."

Larry Arnold observed many of these factors for himself during his investigation of a case of suspected SHC in Essex County, New York. Firefighters there had discovered a puzzling scene inside a modest home. In one bedroom, the center of a mattress had burned clear through the floorboards, while the rest of the room remained unscathed. At first, they didn't even realize a human victim was involved.

Essex County Director of Emergency Services, Robert Purdy, describes the scene as he found it: "I've been to several fatal fires, but I'd never seen anything like this, ever. The individual disintegrated in his bed. There were two pieces of bone, and the rest was powder. [See Photo 74.] There was no residue of accelerant at all, but even with intense fire, you should still wind up with a torso; you might not have any limbs on it, but you still have the bulk of the body. Your organs are there. They might be broiled, but they're there. In this case, there was nothing left but three and a half pounds of ash."

Larry Arnold discovered that "In the victim's bedroom, a TV at the far end of the room had melted down, yet the victim's bathrobe still on the bed itself had not melted or burned. Since heat rises, you would expect to find the area above the point of combustion—in this case the body—to have a tremendous amount of damage. But the wallpapered ceiling was pristine. There was not one scorch mark, not a hint of fire damage what-soever only a few feet above the man himself."

Perhaps most surprising was what investigators found by the bedside. It was an oxygen enrichment device, used by the victim because he had emphysema. It was still operating at full capacity, the singed end of its outlet tube hanging from the nightstand. "The victim was sleeping in an environment that had more oxy-gen than usual," Arnold says. "So when the fire started, with that increased amount of oxygen, the fire from whatever source should have taken the house down, but the blaze was localized to the body and the bed. These are very bizarre circumstances that just defy logic."

It is these apparent inconsistencies with known properties of fire and human incineration that have many experts claiming SHC is a real, scientific phenomenon worthy of investigation. John Heymer says, "Even in the fiercest of fires where people burn, the fire destroys the extremities but never the torso. For instance, there was a fire in a bomb factory, and the whole thing went up, burned through a concrete floor nine inches thick. When they recovered the bodies, the arms and legs were missing, but the torsos were all recognizably human. And there's another thing I suppose I should tell you," Heymer continues. "The liver is the most difficult organ in the body to destroy by fire, yet in all these SHC cases, there hasn't been a piece of liver found. Maybe the liver is the source. Maybe it starts there because the liver is the chemical factory of the body."

Since the first reported case of spontaneous human combustion in 1613, many theories have been offered as to its cause. Most popular among them is the possibility that alcoholism has played a role. "In the Victorian era, SHC was actually taken quite seri-ously," Jenny Randles says, "because it was used as a vehicle for anti-drink laws. Temperance groups argued that if you consumed too much alcohol, you would burst into flames. That, of course, has been shown to be scientifically nonsensical." John Heymer remembers one recent case where alcohol was still being blamed. He says, "It was suggested that the victim had drunk so much liquor that he caught fire. Well, as we all know, you're dead long before you drink enough to do that."

"It's only been in just the last decade that fire officers and forensic scientists have actually started collecting information," Randles says. Most current theories center around the possibility that the body can somehow create a spontaneous internal combustion through various chemical processes. According to Randles, "There are three main theories that try to explain spontaneous human combustion. First, that it's some kind of chemical reaction within the human digestive system which can somehow produce a combination of explosive chemicals, a kind of deadly cocktail. Second is that we're dealing with some kind of interacting energy field, or high levels of static electricity building up in the body. And the third plausible possibility is that ball lightning, a rare atmospheric effect known to occur inside small spaces, might actually be capable of forming inside the human digestive system."

Many scientists and veteran arson investigators dismiss these theories, and the very notion of SHC itself, as pure fantasy. "Scientifically speaking, there is no way the human body can spontaneously combust," says Joe Nickell, who has long contested the paranormal claims of SHC advocates. "Comparisons to a crematorium are false comparisons. It's like comparing a piece of wood you've set on fire with a piece of wood you've put in the oven and baked. Baking and burning are very different phenomena, and so there is no comparison."

As far as the strange localization of SHC fire deaths, Joe Nickell is not baffled. He says, "Anyone who has had any experience with a simple thing like a campfire knows that you can get quite close to a fire laterally, but place things over the fire and they burn easily. So it is not a mystery that the body burns that way without the house burning down. While these may be relatively unusual deaths, they are not unexplainable."

Nickell and others believe that deaths blamed on SHC are actually caused by what has been termed the Candle Effect. This is the theory that a smoldering fire trapped within the confines of, say, an overstuffed chair will burn for hours. A person, perhaps sleeping, in the chair dies from smoke inhalation, and then the fire continues to burn, feeding off the victim's body fat. The victim becomes, in essence, a human candle. His or her bones and organs are the wick, which slowly disintegrates into the molten fat.

Unfortunately for advocates of this theory, the Candle Effect has never been successfully reproduced in any laboratory. And, as SHC proponents are quick to point out, the Candle Effect requires many hours of unnoticed, unattended burning. Larry Arnold points to one particular case in Upper Darby, Pennsylvania, that seems to directly contradict the human candle theory. Henry Lott, who was the township's fire chief at the time of the incident, remembers making the grisly discovery:

"When I arrived at the scene, the remains of a female were in an upstairs sitting room," Lott recalls. "The only part of her that was recognizable was from the knees down. If it wasn't for the legs, you wouldn't even be able to tell it was a human being. The victim was sitting in a chair and the chair was still relatively intact. It was eerie to see a human being completely burned with no real damage to the rest of the room. Why or how that happened, I don't have an answer for it." (See Photo 75.)

Working with Henry Lott, Larry Arnold determined that "From the time that we know the victim was last spoken to [by her granddaughter] until the fire department arrived at the scene, no more than six minutes had elapsed. So, within 360 incredible seconds, this individual had burned herself almost to dust."

There is only one known case in which law enforcement officials have actually reported seeing someone in the midst of an unexplained human combustion. This is what happened in Birmingham, England, in 1967—as told by John Heymer. "Some cleaners waiting at a bus stop noticed blue flames flashing at the first-floor window of a derelict house. When fire station officers responded, they could see the flickering blue flame and smashed a window to get in. There at the bottom of the stairs was the body of a tramp, later identified only as a man named Bailey. Bailey was face down with his head twisted around. His jaws were fastened on the mahogany newel post.

"There was a four-inch slit in his abdomen, from which a blue flame was issuing at force. Now, that blue flame was not burning the stairs, the landing, or a plank of wood Bailey was lying across. There was no burning. There was no electricity on, no gas supply. Bailey was a nonsmoker, and he had no matches or lighter on him. The area was searched for a possible source of ignition, and none was found. They had to put a hose in his abdominal cavity and spray a considerable amount of water in there to stop the blue flame from rolling out. That is not normal burning."

An autopsy revealed that Bailey had died of smoke inhalation, leading to this gruesome conclusion by Heymer: "He died of suffocation, having inhaled the fumes of combustion. Since he was the only thing burning, he suffocated on his own combustion. The pain must have been horrible. They say it took a pry bar to get his jaws off that post, so he died rather hard, to think of it."

Apocryphal stories like this one are tantalizing and give SHC proponents fuel for the fire of their imaginations. But it also may keep some serious scientists with new theories from entering the SHC fray. Larry Arnold acknowledges, "There's clearly a reluctance to admitting the probability of spontaneous human combustion, because it is so bizarre, so atypical. It is surrealistic to think a person can self-ignite. This is so problematic that people in mainstream science can't come to grips with it."

Jenny Randles suggests that researchers look to nature for the answer to the SHC riddle. She says, "There are a number of processes in nature, within botanical systems, where trees, plants, and compost generate heat and cause fires. And we've all seen these little packets of chemicals which you can break open and use as hand warmers on camping trips. These processes are already known to science. We know tremendous amounts of heat can be generated spontaneously out of nowhere."

What we don't yet know, of course, is if these same processes could, or do, take place inside the human body, causing a burning from within.

An early written description of the effects of spontaneous human combustion appeared in Charles Dickens's novel *Bleak House*. Dickens himself was an amateur SHC investigator and used the phenomenon to do away with the evil, drunken character Krook. In this passage, Mr. Guppy and Tom Weevle are searching for Krook. They think he is in his sitting room, but when they go inside they find only that

There is a little fire in the grate, but there is a smouldering suffocating vapour in the room and a dark greasy coating on the walls and ceiling . . .

They advanced slowly, looking at all these things. The cat remains where they found her, still snarling at the something on the ground, before the fire and between the two chairs. What is it? Hold up the light. Here is a small burnt patch of flooring; here is the tinder from a little bundle of burnt paper . . .

And here is—is it the cinder of a small charred and broken log of wood sprinkled with white ash? Or is it coal? O Horror, he *is* here! and this . . . is all that represents him.

The Healing Touch

W hat do you do when medical science gives you a diagnosis that's impossible to live with? People with chronic pain or seemingly incurable illnesses are forced to address this question every day. Some have found miraculous answers from extremely unconventional sources. They have been cured through psychic healing.

Psychic healing is based on the powerful role the mind and spirit can play in making us well. Since earliest recorded history, psychic healing has coexisted with mainstream medicine. In primitive cultures, shamans were the sole healers in their community—selected, not schooled, to perform ritualistic medicine. Their powers were bestowed during secret ceremonies in which sacrifices were made to the gods. In an altered state, the shamans would call the faithful to come to them for a cure, a cure based on the belief in the benevolent forces of the unknown.

While many shamanistic traditions continue today, they seem naive in comparison to the sophisticated medical practices we have come to rely on. But many people are returning to the old ways, usually as a last resort in extreme medical cases. One ancient healing method gaining recent popularity is called the laying on of hands. Healer Dean Kraft uses this primitive method in his otherwise modern office in Beverly Hills, California. Kraft explains that he discovered his unique ability to heal quite by accident.

"My brother-in-law got this headache, and my first response was to go lay my hands on his head. I did, and his headache went away. I really didn't know much about it at the time," Kraft says. "I just started the laying on of hands. It is an intuitive process. It's not planned. Once I start the laying on of hands, my hands just go to areas, and I follow them. I start to visualize. For example, if it's a tumor the size of an egg, I start to picture it in my mind getting smaller. I see myself as a catalyst, like a spark plug, using my energy to trigger the person's own healing system."

Dean Kraft, like many psychic healers, is quick to point out that he is not an alternative to traditional medicine. "I believe that medical doctors are meant to diagnose," Kraft says. "I believe very much in medical science. I basically work on cases after doctors have given up."

Actress Cindy Williams, star of the film *American Graffiti* and the long-running television series *Laverne and Shirley*, believes that she was cured by Dean Kraft. "I had very bad sciatica for about a year and a half," Cindy explains. "It was equivalent to having your teeth drilled on constantly; that's really what the pain was like, what it got to. I couldn't drive, because I couldn't press my right foot down on the gas pedal or the brake. I had to have someone drive me."

More conventional treatments had failed. "I was seeing a chiropractor constantly," Cindy recalls, "and that would alleviate the pain for about an hour, and then it would just slowly come back during the day. I was basically in tears most of the time, and my quality of life was nil. Then a friend of mine took me to lunch and said, 'There's no reason why you should be in this pain. Dean Kraft will heal you. He's real.' "

Kraft describes his healing process as a transference of energy from his hands into his patient. "We know that it can affect things, but we haven't yet been able to determine what this energy is," Kraft says. "I don't even like to use the word energy. It's a very loose term, but it's the best one right now to describe the type of transference that's taking place."

For Cindy Williams, the results were almost instantaneous. She says, "I went to see Dean, and I remember thinking, Well, is this going to work? All these thoughts ran through my head, because I am a person of faith, but there's still that bit of skepticism, I will admit. But after one session with him, I was healed forever and ever. It was like getting out of prison."

In January of 1985, Nelda Buss was descending into a prison of her own, and the sentence was death. Nelda had been diagnosed with ALS, better known as Lou Gehrig's disease. She remembers, "It was my birthday. I was forty-three years old, and they told me I had Lou Gehrig's disease. Actually, they said ALS, amyotrophic lateral sclerosis, and I wasn't real sure what that was. But when the doctors said there was really nothing they could give me and nothing they could do to make me better, I just broke down."

ALS is a medical mystery, a degenerative muscle disease with no known cause and no known cure. Nelda's son Gary recalls the utter hopelessness the family felt after his mother's diagnosis. "The established medical profession just said, 'Good-bye, see you. Have a good life. Live it to your fullest.' "

The disease inevitably progresses from partial to complete paralysis of all the muscles in the body. For Nelda, the decline was rapid. Her husband, Glenn, remembers: "She just kept getting progressively worse, and I guess from the time she was diagnosed until she was basically an invalid was only about six months." In the final stages of ALS, Nelda became a quadriplegic, unable to move but mentally alert and aware that she was about to die. (See Photo 76.) "I gave away most of the good clothing that I had," Nelda remembers. "And I had my dress all picked out for what I was to be buried in." But then Nelda heard about Dean Kraft.

Nelda says, "It was just such a relief to talk to him. I told him that the doctors had said there was no hope, and he said, 'Well, that's not always true.' " Kraft performed his laying on of hands technique with Nelda for three months. Finally, they had a small but significant breakthrough. "Glenn was showering me and I could move my toe. That was so exciting," Nelda recalls.

After her toes, Nelda began to slowly regain movement in her fingers, then her back. Soon she could control her hands, then her arms and legs. In addition to treatment from Kraft, Nelda worked very hard on her own physical exercise regimen. Over the next year, her family videotaped Nelda's miraculous progress as a permanent record of how far she had come, in case no one believed what had been accomplished.

When *Sightings* interviewed Nelda, Glenn, and Gary Buss several years into her recovery, the crew had to interrupt a family snowball fight in the front yard of their Virginia home. Nelda did not seem like the same woman who had once picked out her own funeral clothes. "Everything has changed," Gary Buss says with pride. "She's back and she's doing more than she ever did before. I mean, it's great to have a mother. It really is."

There are other psychic healers, in addition to Dean Kraft, who claim to have reversed seemingly irreversible disease and injury. One of the most famous and widely respected of these healers was the late Jack Gray. In 1972, Jack Gray was called to the bedside of Mitchell May, a gentle, disarming man who had barely survived a horrible car crash in Athens, Alabama.

"When the paramedics got there they thought I was dead," Mitchell says witnesses at the scene later told him. "It took them forty-five minutes to cut me out of the car. From what I've been told, I had about forty fractures. I had a couple of inches of bone actually ripped out of my leg. The nerves were completely severed."

When Mitchell's brother Terry arrived at the hospital, he was horrified. "It really looked to me like a pride of lions had been chewing on his legs, and they'd said, 'We've had enough,' " Terry recalls. "And I didn't have any doubts. I just said, 'Amputate, if you need to.' I mean, it never occurred to me that he would be able to walk or use those legs again."

Unsure if Mitchell would live or die, his family moved him back home to Los Angeles, to the prestigious UCLA Medical Center. UCLA orthopedic surgeon Dr. Edgar Dawson remembers his first look at Mitchell May. "Mitchell was very seriously ill when he got here," Dr. Dawson says. "Most of the skin just below the knee down to the ankle was gone, and there was just bare bone hanging out with no muscle or skin over it. And it was grossly infected. There was green material just sort of oozing out of holes in the bone. It was incredibly painful, and the only way I knew to get rid of his pain was to amputate his leg."

Mitchell also remembers his first consultation with Dr. Dawson. "He was saying to me, 'Mitchell, you are not going to walk on your legs again. That's just how it's going to be.' But inside of me a voice was saying, 'Well, we'll see. We'll see.' " Mitchell resisted amputation in the beginning, but faced with the reality of his infection and an adverse reaction to the heavy painkillers he was receiving, Mitchell almost gave up. "I never said, 'Go ahead and amputate,' but I got very close. I was scared. I was scared of having to live with that pain for the rest of my life. I knew I couldn't," Mitchell says.

Mitchell's mother, Lorraine, watched her youngest son suffer. She sought every conventional method to alleviate his constant pain. In desperation, she turned to the UCLA Neuropsychiatric Institute. Surprisingly, she was referred to Jack Gray. His combination of healing touch and hypnosis had helped others. "I was very skeptical, but I was desperate at that point. Jack Gray was trained in helping people with pain and healing people, but he was not a doctor," Lorraine May says. Dr. Dawson shared her skepticism. "This is ridiculous. It isn't going to work, but it's probably relatively harmless, so why not?" Dr. Dawson remembers telling Lorraine.

Mitchell's condition was worsening rapidly. Dr. Dawson says, "Mitchell didn't know this, but I had already scheduled his surgery to amputate his leg." Jack Gray arrived at the eleventh hour. Mitchell says, "I expected some guy in a purple cape to come strolling in with a magic wand or something. And here came into the room a totally ordinary-looking man. He looked at me and said, 'Mitchell, we can heal you leg. You have whatever you need already in you. It's born in everyone. We're just going to wake it up.' "

Jack Gray used the laying on of hands, a form of hypnotic trance, and worked with Mitchell on positive visualization. "I saw Mitchell for the first time get hope," Lorraine remembers. And after the hope came the healing. "Bones started to grow where they said it couldn't grow," Mitchell explains. "Skin started to regenerate where they said that couldn't be happening. Nerve functions started to happen again, and they're saying, 'But, but, but,' you know, 'that's not supposed to be able to happen.' This all took time. I was in the hospital for a year. I was in a wheelchair for a couple of years. I was in metal braces. And each step of the way the doctors were saying, 'This is incredible, but this is as far as you're going to get.' " But Mitchell fooled them all. He made great strides working on his healing and finally walking—with the help and support of Jack Gray.

A scratchy black-and-white movie reminds the May family of the day Mitchell took his first steps, three years after the car crash. The voice of Jack Gray can be heard on the film. "Say to yourself, I can walk. Recall how you used to. Now I'm going to let go. When I let go, walk, Mitchell, up and back. Walk! Walk, Mitchell, without crutches." On film, Jack Gray is seen removing the crutches. Mitchell walks. (See Photo 77.)

"When I saw him take his first steps, I passed out," Terry remembers. "I mean, I fainted. I'd seen a miracle. I had never seen a miracle." But no one was more astonished than Dr. Dawson, who had followed Mitchell's progress. "All I know is that something happened after the healer came, and nothing happened before. As a scientist, I have to conclude that the healer made Mitchell well, not me. And that's a scientific observation from a pure skeptical scientist."

Today, Mitchell May lives and works in Utah. He himself has become a healer. It is the legacy of Jack Gray. "I racewalk every day," Mitchell says. "I stretch every day. I can run. I can hike for miles. I feel so lucky to be alive. Jack gave me part of himself. I definitely owe my life to him."

Psychic healing has a long and dubious history. It is essential that any form of nontraditional treatment be undertaken only with the advice and consent of a medical doctor. Psychic healing is a complement to, not a substitute for, conventional medical treatment.

Schoolroom Angels

I he sign at the edge of town greets newcomers with
the motto "Cokeville, Wyoming: Like No Place On
Earth." And for the 493 people who live in Cokeville, that was
never more true than on May 16, 1986. That was the day David
and Doris Young, two self-styled "revolutionaries," decided to
take the Cokeville Elementary School by force. It was also the
day, people here believe, that angels came to town.

It started just after lunch. School secretary Christine Cook was
helping a prospective teacher get ready for her interview with the
principal. Two strangers came into the office, a man and a
woman. The man was pulling a small shopping cart behind him.
Christine thought they might be new parents she hadn't met yet.
They weren't.

Christine recalls, "I said to them, 'Is there something I can
do to help you, sir?' And he said, 'Yes, ma'am, there certainly
is. This is a revolution. Your school is being taken hostage.
Don't press any buzzers or any alarms. Just come this way.' I
looked in David Young's eyes and I knew it was no joke. I've
never, ever looked into anyone's eyes that were so cold and
emotionless. I mean, it was like this big void. There was nothing there."

David Young was a walking arsenal. "He opened his jacket,
and he had guns all the way around, stuck in his belt," Christine

252

says. "There were several rifles in the cart. He pointed into the center of the cart and said, 'This is a bomb,' and then he proceeded to show me the triggering device. He had a white cord wrapped around his arm, and that cord was connected to the trigger of the bomb. He said, 'As you can see, if anyone hits me, or bumps me, or tries to do anything, then my arm will pull that cord and the bomb will go off.' "

David Young knew what he was doing. As ATF agents would later discover, Young had detonated an identical test bomb in the Arizona desert just days before he and his wife came to Cokeville. "He said the bomb was capable of blowing up the entire building. He said it would level the building and everyone in it," Christine explains.

During the macabre demonstration, more school staff members entered and were taken hostage. David and Doris Young took the small group at gunpoint and paraded them down the main hallway. They stopped at the door to one of two first-grade classrooms. "He took us into the classroom and told the teacher and the children that they were being taken hostage," Christine recalls. "He said, 'You don't need to be afraid. If you do what we tell you to do, nobody's going to get hurt, but if you children don't listen, we will shoot you.' "

David Young turned the classroom into his command center. He ordered Doris to round up, one by one, every other class in the school. In less than fifteen minutes, all 153 teachers and students of the Cokeville Elementary School were crammed into the one small first-grade room. Ryan Taylor was only eight years old when his class was taken hostage. He remembers that "The lady told us we were being brought down to see a gun safety demonstration, and that's what we had in our minds when we came into the classroom. But when we realized what was happening, we were really afraid."

Amy Bagaso remembers becoming separated from her best friend when her fifth-grade class was escorted to the "gun demonstration." "I saw her come in the door," Amy says, "and I was starting to walk over to sit by her when David picked me out of the crowd and said, 'Wait! Where are you going?' And I said, 'I'm just going to talk to my friend,' and that's when he pulled out a gun and said, 'I don't want to have to use this.' Our principal leaned over and touched my hand and told me to stay where I was. 'What's going on?' I said, and he said, 'Well, Amy, we're being held hostage.' "

When local law enforcement arrived outside the school, David Young delivered his demands. He wanted $2 million in ransom for each hostage so he could carry out his "plan." Christine explains, "He totally and completely believed in reincarnation. The ultimate plan was that after he got the money, he was going to blow up the building, the children, the adults, himself, and his wife, and take us to a place he referred to as a brave new world. In this brave new world, he would raise the children to be his followers, and the adults would be used to help raise the children."

David Young gave each teacher a copy of his bizarre manifesto, outlining his apocalyptic plan for the children of Cokeville. (See Photo 78.) "It said God equals infinity, infinity equals zero; therefore, God does not exist. He really believed he had mathematically and scientifically proved there was no God," Christine explains. David Young was clearly insane—incoherent—and as the hours ticked by, he became increasingly unreasonable. He was a human bomb with a hair trigger.

Christine remembers the fear. "We had children sick to their stomachs, crying and telling their teachers 'I want to go home.' " Ryan Taylor says, "I was getting really scared because he was just talking weird and threatening people that he'd shoot them and stuff like that. He said if he didn't get the money then he'd kill us all and take us to his world."

"We kept asking our teacher what was going on," Amy Bagaso says. "We were asking him some pretty serious questions, you know, which is kind of hard for a teacher to answer. Stuff like, what happens when the bomb goes off? Is it going to hurt real bad? Are we ever going to see our families again? Are we going to die? Our teacher would take turns holding each of us. We all sat around and we cried."

By 3:30 in the afternoon, David Young had become agitated and frenzied. One teacher was concerned that a child might inadvertently get too close, or do something to set off an irrevocable chain reaction. He suggested placing a desk in the middle of the classroom where David and Doris could sit, while the teacher taped off a 6-foot-by-6-foot square around the desk. The Youngs agreed. The teacher dubbed it the "magic square," and told the children that as long as they stayed out of the magic square, they would be all right.

Outside, the entire town was waiting. Everyone either had a child in the school or knew someone who did. Every resource in the Wyoming-Idaho area was being marshaled. State and federal agencies set up a command post a short distance from the school. Attempts to negotiate with David Young were failing. Richard Haskell, the closest bomb specialist to the scene, was called in. He recalls making the one hundred-mile trip from his station in Sweetwater County, Wyoming, in seventy minutes. "I was driving there, not knowing what the device was exactly, but I could just picture it was a high velocity-type bomb—dynamite or black powder—and I could see bodies scattered all over the place."

Glenna Walker had graduated from her EMT training just two weeks before the takeover. 'I had three children at the elementary school," she recalls with emotion. "This was my first real call as an emergency medical technician. I had total fear and panic, but inside I kept thinking, I need to stay in control. I need to be able to respond. But I was so fearful."

As the mobilization continued outside, something strange was beginning to happen inside the classroom. For reasons no one understood at the time, the atmosphere seemed to change. Christine recalls, "All of a sudden, I wasn't afraid. The fear seemed to be more in David and Doris and less in us. I just felt this calmness come over me. I don't know what it was or why I felt that way, but I did."

Amy recalls the feeling as "total peace, this comforting feeling that touched everybody. I know there was something there. It was definitely a spirit that was letting us know that we were going to be all right." At the same moment, Ryan remembers that "Something told me just to be relaxed and not to worry, and I'll make it through. It told me somebody's watching over you who will make sure you get out."

For seven-year-old Katie Walker, whose mother was the new EMT in town, the feeling took on a human form. Katie remembers, "I just kind of looked up and I saw this woman I didn't know. She had short, curly hair, and she had on a long white dress and white slippers. She told me that she loved me and to listen to my brother and everything would be OK. I told her I'd listen, and then I just went back to what I was doing. When I looked up again, she wasn't there anymore. Then my brother came over, and he told me and my sister to stay by the window and everything would be OK. He told us he had the feeling to come and tell us this but didn't really know why he was telling us to get by the window. That's when the bomb went off."

"The room was almost instantaneously black," Christine recalls. "There were boxes of shells in the cart with the bomb, and they started exploding. It was like the grand finale at a fireworks display. We had teachers just grabbing kids, trying to get them out the door and out through the windows." Ryan was situated very close to the point of ignition. "When the bomb went off, I saw a big ball of flame in the middle of the room, and the next thing I know, I was blown out the door and I was running down the hall. I remember getting a blanket shoved over me, because my hair was on fire."

Amy remembers, "I had been thrown over a table, hitting part of a chalkboard in front of me. I headed out through the door, flames coming off my back. My teacher slapped the fire out, picked me up, and shoved me down the hallway to safety. That's when Glenna Walker saw me and just grabbed me and took me to the ambulance. They took my clothes off and were spraying me with water and putting blankets around me, and that's when my mom came.

"I will never forget the feeling I felt when I saw my mother, after not knowing if I'd ever see her again. Hearing her call my name, turning me around, and giving me a hug. That's when I heard the principal and a whole bunch of other people yelling 'We're all here. We counted and we're all here.' And then everybody in the town just started yelling that everybody was there. That was a great moment. Kids were burned, kids were hurt, but we were all alive."

Miraculously, the only two people who died that day were David and Doris Young. Glenna found her three children amid the chaos and ran to Katie, who was sitting on the grass rocking back and forth. Glenna says, "I embraced Katie and at that point she just stood up and said, 'Mommy, the angels saved us.' In the chaos and everything that was happening, I didn't take her literally."

But Katie wasn't the only child who told her parents that angels had been in the classroom that day. "Several weeks later, I went for counseling at the trauma center that had been set up," Glenna explains, "and one of the other mothers started talking about their child expressing that they had seen something, and then another said someone had helped their child, and it was just like a wave came over me. I realized that Katie had a story to tell, and I had overlooked what she was telling me.

"I went home that night and asked her to tell me the story. It was a very moving and special time for our family. We questioned Katie about the woman she had seen and took out several family photographs. She looked at them and said she couldn't find the lady in any of them. My mother had died when I was fifteen years old, and I had very few pictures of her. I went to my room and got a locket and took it to Katie. As soon as I opened the locket, she became excited."

Glenna starts crying when she remembers Katie's words. " 'That's the woman that helped me,' she said. She described my mother down to her hair, everything about this woman, as if she had known her all her life." Katie had never seen the picture in the locket before. Her maternal grandmother had died five years before Katie was even born. "When I saw the photo and they told me that she'd died," Katie says, "I came to the realization that she had been sent to help me. She is my guardian angel."

Parents and trauma counselors heard strikingly similar stories from many children who had seen their own guardian angels. It was an amazing coincidence, but even officials at the scene had to admit that some unseen force must have been at work on the day of the blast. Bomb technician Richard Haskell explains, "Had this bomb functioned the way it was designed to function, there should have been 153 people dead. Everything on the south side of the building should have been gone. There is no reason for what happened. The bomb should have functioned. The only way I can explain it is that there's a power greater than what I know."

Ryan explains it this way: "There was an angel for everybody that day, watching over them. I think it was family up in Heaven that protected us and made sure that we will live as long as God needs us to."

Christine Cook says, "I think so often in life we look at things and say, 'It was just the circumstances that did it,' and yes, there were a lot of things that played a part that day, but to me the whole thing boils down to a total miracle. There's no way you could put that many people in one room and have a bomb not kill one of us."

In the years since the blast, Cokeville has become an even closer, more tightly knit community, bound by the miraculous events that spared their precious children. No one moved away. No one put their children in a different school. "I think we were blessed," Christine says. "To know there was divine intervention made a big difference in why we all came back. Every one of us came back to the school. By the way, the teacher that came for her interview that day, she took the job. She helped us get the children out of the building, and then she took the job."

According to a *Time* magazine survey, 69 percent of Americans believe in angels, 46 percent believe there's at least one guardian angel for everybody, and 32 percent say they've felt an angelic presence in their own lives.

A Mother's Love

In 1956, when she was just three years old, something strange started happening to Jenny Cockell. Playing in the yard of her home in Northamptonshire, England, Jenny was flooded with memories of a life that wasn't hers. She had visions of a past life in which she was fully grown, a mother of eight children, the wife of a stern husband in a small Irish seaside town. Her name was Mary. It was Jenny's first glimpse of what would become a lifetime of memories of a life she believed she had once led in a different body, in a different time.

"Most of the memories were in much the same way you might remember your own childhood," Jenny recalls today. "It was just a remembering of the past, and what I was remembering were all kinds of day-to-day events about a village, a family, and a little cottage." The memories were so exact, so vivid, that from the very beginning Jenny felt they must be real. "I remember I lived in a little lane in the first cottage on the left. There was only one door, and when you entered the cottage, there was a wooden partition immediately in front. To the right, you entered a bedroom, to the left, a living room and a kitchen. There was a large fireplace that dominated the living area."

As a very young girl, Jenny, a Catholic, knew nothing of the concept of reincarnation. "I thought these memories were normal. I thought everybody had to cope with their memories of previous lives." She incorporated the visions into her play. They were a fulfilling and comforting part of her life. But then, in addition to the waking memories, Jenny began to have a recurring nightmare of the turning point in her supposed past life. Over and over, she dreamed of her own death.

In her dream, Jenny was in a Dublin, Ireland, hospital, dying from complications during the birth of her ninth child. "It was always the same dream. I had a high fever, difficulty breathing. There was considerable pain to start off with, and then at the point of death that seemed to vanish altogether," Jenny explains. "I'd wake up very upset, knowing that I'd left children behind, worrying what had happened to them, worrying how on earth I was going to find out where they were and if they were all right."

When Jenny began attending Sunday school, she thought she would find the answers to the disturbing questions raised by her memories and dreams. She says, "For the first time, I was in a place where people were talking about life and death and what happens after death. But they didn't mention previous lives. I was extremely shocked, because I had assumed that it was normal and that everybody remembered. I found it very difficult to cope. Why can I remember? I thought. I felt different, I didn't fit in. After that, I learned to speak only to people I could trust."

Only her mother and an uncle would ever know the vivid second life that existed inside Jenny. She shared with them the visions of the cottage, the children, and a wind-swept jetty; Mary's life and death. Her family didn't know what to make of it. This is a common thread among young children who experience past-life memories, says Dr. Brian Weiss, a noted psychiatrist and author of the best-selling book *Many Lives, Many Masters*, who has made an in-depth study of the phenomenon. Dr. Weiss explains, "If you dream of yourself in another time in a different body, that may not be a Freudian distortion or symbol, but an actual past-life memory fragment emerging."

In his research, Dr. Weiss has interviewed hundreds of people like Jenny Cockell: "I've had people know their way around

Europe, and they had never been there before. They know the streets, where the old church was, this kind of thing. These are spontaneous memories of past lifetimes." In Jenny's case, her spontaneous memories were so detailed, she could actually draw pictures of her home and her church. Throughout childhood, she continually drew maps of the town in her visions.

"I remember drawing the maps, refining them and drawing them better as I got older. I didn't want to forget, because I was determined to be able to go there one day. I just always knew it was Ireland and roughly what years I had been there. As Mary, I had been born around 1895, and I died in 1932. Other things, like the mode of dress, gave me clues, but it wasn't actually that. It was just a sense of awareness of the time period and the place," Jenny says.

When she was twelve, Jenny was given an atlas. She immediately turned to the map of Ireland, a place she had been only in her dreams. She remembers, "I thought if I looked at the atlas, I would know where Mary's village was. I spent a lot of time just looking at it and thinking, and the whole time I was drawn back to the same place. Again and again, I was drawn back to Malahide."

Malahide is a small seaside town on the northern coast of Ireland, three hundred miles from Jenny's childhood home. She felt she had to go there, but Jenny's family didn't have the money to spend chasing a dream. Jenny tried to stop the memories and put Malahide behind her, but her feelings for the place and the nagging sensation that she had a task to accomplish there were overwhelming. "The emotional content was difficult at times. It made it hard to carry on and live this life properly," Jenny says.

Jenny grew up, got married, and had two children. As her family in this life began to grow, Jenny's yearnings for her other past-life family also increased. "After my children were born," Jenny explains, "I felt I had to do something to try to be certain that these memories were real. I was approaching my mid-thirties, the same age that I remembered dying as Mary."

Coincidentally, at this same time, a new travel bookshop opened in Jenny's town. She went in and ordered a street map of Malahide. When the map arrived, she returned to the store with the street map she had drawn as a child. "I took my little drawing in and laid it out on a table. The shopkeeper laid out the map and we looked at the two of them side-by-side. We both just looked at each other, because there was no doubt about it. They were the same place," Jenny recalls. "I got north in the right direction. I got the length of the streets. The angles of the streets were the same. [See Photo 79.] I knew where in Ireland I wanted to go."

After years of wondering, Jenny finally traveled to Malahide in search of her past life. Would she find the jetty, the church, and the cottage that had haunted her memories for half a lifetime? Jenny remembers that first fateful trip. "Although I had gone to Malahide expecting to find things that I had remembered, the accuracy quite shook me. I mean, I was walking around without any problem, without a map, and I knew my way around.

"I started out looking for the jetty. I found it quickly, and there was a tremendous sense of having been there before. But it wasn't really enough, so I walked up to the church, and there I stopped in my tracks. I had not really taken in how detailed the drawing of the church I had made really was. The pitch of the roof, the piers that were on either side of the facade, were identical to my drawing. I felt elated. I knew this was Mary's village," Jenny explains.

But when Jenny followed her instinct to the place where she believed the cottage would be, she became disoriented. She says, "I had difficulty approaching the lane. It had changed a lot. There was a petrol station and considerably more houses than there had been in the 1920s." And where Jenny thought the cottage should be, she found only an empty field choked with weeds and brambles: "I didn't feel that I was in the wrong place, but I was so immersed in the memory of what the cottage had looked like, how it had been, that the amount of change took me by surprise. I think it's probably the same for anybody who goes back to the place where they used to live. It's never the same."

Jenny walked the old country lanes, searching for the missing link in the chain of her past-life memory. "I found somebody who had lived in the area for a long time," Jenny explains. "And he remembered a family of eight children and a mother named Mary. He had actually been to school with the children." Jenny had found the son of the man who had built the family's cottage. With an eerie sense of déjà vu, Jenny was led back to the very same empty field where she had felt so disoriented. There, she began to pull back the weeds and thorny vines.

"I found part of a wall that seemed to ring bells. It was totally overgrown, completely hidden from the road, but it was still there." Further in the field, she saw a stone wall, an oval-topped window, the ruins of a fireplace. Jenny felt that she was home. She recalls of that emotional discovery, "The first thing I wanted to do was burst into tears. It was the first, real tangible proof of something that had existed in the past that I had remembered. It was the first thing I could touch."

But as Jenny explored the remnants of what she was sure was a past life, she was flooded with visions of the children that Mary had left behind. She recalled Mary's death and realized what she was now meant to do. "The sensation that I was left with at that time was, what had happened to the children?" Jenny recalls.

If she had found Mary's town, her church, and her home, could Jenny find her children? The man who had led her to the ruins of the cottage gave her a vital piece of the puzzle. He confirmed that the mother's first name was Mary and that her last name was Sutton. Armed with a surname, Jenny was able to track down Mary Sutton's marriage license, dated 1917, and her death certificate, dated—as Jenny's memories had already told her—1932. Then, with the help of a priest, Jenny obtained baptism records for six of the eight Sutton children.

"I had a sense of responsibility to the children. It was almost an obsessive need to find out what happened to them, find out how they were. I had this tremendous feeling of maternalism toward these people. But I knew my presence and my story might upset them. It was a terrible dilemma, but I needed to find them," Jenny explains.

Jenny sought out Mary's oldest child, Sonny Sutton, now living in England. Sonny was thirteen when his mother died. Now he was seventy-three. Jenny made that first phone call with great trepidation. She recalls, "I knew from my memories that he had been a very direct, straightforward child, so I knew I'd have to be fairly direct in my explanation. I wanted to make it as simple as possible, so I said to him, 'This is going to sound strange, I'm afraid, but I remember your family through dreams.' As we talked he said, 'Describe the cottage.' And I said it was the first on the left along the lane. There was a family of eight children, and the mother died in 1932. And he said, 'Yes, that's right. That's my family.' Then, he sort of went quiet." Cautiously, Jenny revealed many details of her past-life memory as Sonny listened, speechless.

Sonny remembers his reaction at the conclusion of the phone call that had stirred up distant memories of childhood. "I said to myself, 'How in heaven's name can a person that was born twenty-one years after me mother died ring that telephone and tell me everything about me and about me family?' I put the phone down, and my wife said, 'What's wrong with you?' She says, 'You look like you've just seen a ghost.' So I said, 'I think I *have* seen a ghost. If not, then I've been speaking to me mother.' "

For her part, Jenny was as wary of her first contact with one of Mary's children as Sonny had been. "I didn't immediately think, Great, this is the right family. I needed more information," Jenny says. "I had to be absolutely sure that everything I remembered was documented, so that I would know that I had found the right children. I didn't want to let go of all this emotion on the wrong people. I had to be certain."

Jenny sought help from an intermediary who had had experience dealing with claims of past-life memory. "I had an independent researcher intervene. She told me not to meet Sonny, not to make any more phone calls until she had taken separate statements from us," Jenny explains. "The statements were very, very useful, because when we finally did meet, there were nine pages of minute detail that Sonny had also remembered. Everything matched."

When Jenny and her seventy-three-year-old "son" met, Sonny Sutton recalls, "The look in her eyes was the same as me mother, the same loving look." (See Photo 80.) It was a strained reunion, but as Jenny remembers, "The more we went on to discuss, the more Sonny realized that my memories were things that nobody but his family could have known."

Unlike the memories stereotypically associated with reincarnation, Jenny wasn't recalling a past life as Cleopatra or Marie Antoinette. Jenny shared with Sonny simple memories of a simple Irish family. She told him about the day Mary tried to shove an overstuffed mattress through the front door; pictures that hung on the wall of Mary's brother, who had died in World War I; Mary's father, who had worked the line as a steam engine conductor; Mary's death in childbirth.

Then she described a seemingly forgettable incident, in which the children had gathered in the front yard around a rabbit who had been trapped in a homemade snare. "And Sonny just sat there and looked quite blankly at me for a few minutes," Jenny recalls. "How could you possibly have known that?" Sonny asked. "It was something no one in the family would have ever admitted. Poaching was a serious crime at that time."

Sonny came to believe that Jenny was the reincarnation of his mother, and he confirmed the fears that had dogged Jenny's life. After Mary's death, her husband could not cope with eight children. Sonny and his brothers and sisters were separated, sent to different orphanages, and adopted out. With Sonny's help, Jenny searched dog-eared records all over England and Ireland and found all four of Mary's other surviving children: Christy, seventy-two; Phyllis, seventy-one; Frank, seventy; and Betty, sixty-two, who had grown up believing she was an only child.

"I told Jenny that I had always looked for my sister Betty," Sonny says. "I had reared Betty, even though I was only thirteen years old. I fed that baby. I changed her nappies, and then she was adopted. I never saw her after that, until Jenny found her. From the time that she was adopted to the time I met her in the B & I terminal in Dublin was sixty years."

It was an unforgettable reunion. Sonny remembers, "All of a sudden, in the far end of the terminal, I seen this woman walking slowly up the center. And would you believe, I recognized her, and now she's a married lady with sons and grandchildren." Betty was overcome with emotion as she clung to her long-lost brother on the railway platform. "I never even knew I was adopted. I didn't know I had brothers and sisters," Betty says today.

Because of Jenny Cockell's perseverance, all the surviving Sutton children finally met face-to-face at the site of their childhood cottage. (See Photo 81.) Standing in the bramble-choked ruins, long-buried memories were rekindled, memories that Jenny had envisioned in her own childhood. Betty recalls, "It was really wonderful. There was Sonny, who had nursed me when I was a baby and had missed me for sixty years. And it was the same as if we had never been apart. That was the way I felt about them all. Phyllis, Frank, Christy—I felt as though I'd always known them."

Memories came out in a flood. Phyllis began to cry as Jenny recalled a detail of her "daughter's" childhood. "Jenny said she used to come down to the railing at school at lunch hour with a billycan of soup," Phyllis says. "And I remembered me mommy did come down there with the billycans in her shawl to keep the soup warm. She did come down there every day."

At the jetty, Sonny helped Jenny realize the significance of the last unexplained detail in her past-life remembrances. Jenny says, "The jetty was one of the clearest of the memories. I remember walking out on the jetty and looking out for a boat. I remember wearing a shawl and drawing it around me, because it was dusk and quite chilly. When I had this vision, I could never figure out who I was waiting for. It seemed to be something I did quite often, but it was just a snippet of memory I wasn't able to work out."

Sonny revealed that as a boy, he had worked as a caddie. The golf course was on a little island, just offshore. His mother used to wait for him every evening when Sonny and the other boys rowed home. "I knew then that she was telling me something that nobody else could know. I'm the one that come in the rowboat. I'm the one who came up the jetty. And my mother was the one who came down to meet me."

It's an incredible story of elderly brothers and sisters reunited by a young woman's otherworldly memories. It's a case that Dr. Brian Weiss considers compelling evidence of reincarnation. He explains, "Jenny Cockell happens to be one of the most interesting cases of all, because there's such good documentation. The Irish children of Mary Sutton, who are now in their late sixties and seventies, are very believable people. They know that Jenny is coming up with knowledge of their childhood, things that were not published anywhere. They were not a famous family."

Betty explains Jenny's uncanny memories in terms of a supernatural energy. "Mummy died too young. She had left so much behind her, so many young children. She knew Daddy wasn't the type of man to cope with a family. She realized on her deathbed that the children would be separated, and I think that's the energy that Jenny has picked up from Mother." Sonny has a simpler explanation. "I know it's very hard for people to understand, but to me our mother came back to us."

For Jenny, finding the Sutton children has finally brought an end to the prophetic visions and dreams she has had since childhood. She explains, "There's a sense of freedom, which is strange. I don't feel the same responsibility toward them. I've been allowed to accept that they've grown up. I don't feel tied to the past in quite the same way that I felt for half a lifetime. I'm able to look at things from a different perspective now."

Before Jenny Cockell entered their lives, Sonny, Frank,

Christy, Phyllis, and Betty didn't share holidays, exchange family photos, or even write to one another. Whether or not Jenny is the reincarnated spirit of their dead mother, no one denies that she has brought the family back together as only a mother's love could.